# Woodworker's Jackpot:

## *49 Step-by-Step Projects*

*To my brother, Dr. James A. Nelson*

# Woodworker's Jackpot:

## 49 Step-by-Step Projects

John A. Nelson

**TAB BOOKS**

Blue Ridge Summit, PA

FIRST EDITION
THIRD PRINTING

Printed in the United States of America

Library of Congress Cataloging in Publication Data

Nelson, John A., 1935-
Woodworker's jackpot.

Includes index.
1. Woodwork.  I.  Title.
TT180.N45   1989      684′.08      88-35931
ISBN 0-8306-9154-5
ISBN 0-8306-3154-2 (pbk.)

TAB BOOKS offers software for sale. For information and a catalog, please
contact TAB Software Department, Blue Ridge Summit, PA 17294-0850.

Questions regarding the content of this book should be addressed to:

Reader Inquiry Branch
TAB BOOKS
Blue Ridge Summit, PA 17294-0214

Acquisitions Editor: Kimberly Tabor
Technical Editor: Joanne M. Slike
Production: Katherine Brown

Cover photograph by Deborah Porter, Peterborough, New Hampshire.

# Contents

# Acknowledgments

I would like to thank my very good friends, Bill Bigelow of Surry, New Hampshire, and Jerry Ernce of Broken Arrow, Oklahoma, for allowing me to use six projects we developed together for various magazine publications: Bill Bigelow for his Bird Mobile, Twig Settee, Book Shelf, Country Wall Shelf, and Ladderback Rocker, and Jerry Ernce for his Wood Jaw Clamp.

Many thanks to Nancy Van Campen of Dublin, New Hampshire for her help in painting the seven Projects with a Heart. She added a little warmth to these seven projects. Thanks also to Deborah Porter, who provided the excellent photographs of the projects.

A special thanks to Jim Jennings, original editor of *The American Woodworker* and David Camp, editor of *Popular Woodworking*, for all their help and guidance over the last few years. Without their help and input, this book could not have been written.

Thanks also to the new editor of *The American Woodworker*, David Sloan, for giving us permission to republish the Kitchen Helper, Small Shelf, Fire Extinguisher Holder, Towel and Tissue Rack, Wooden Wastepaper Basket, Wooden Basket, and Book Shelf.

# Introduction

If you like to do things yourself—if you thrive on that certain feeling of accomplishment, if you take pride in your work—then I think you will like this book. There is something for everyone, no matter what level of ability. There is a mixture of small and large, simple to somewhat complex, contemporary and traditional, indoor–outdoor, and a few toys for the kids.

In an effort to develop a book of interest to everyone, this book covers six completely different areas of projects: *kitchen projects* for use in and around the kitchen, *folk art projects* that are so popular these days, *toys for the kids* that might just get them interested in woodworking, *projects with a heart* that have that ''down-home'' charm, *weekend projects* for those who love woodworking but can't spare too much time, and of course, my favorite, *copies of antiques* for those who like things from the past.

Working with wood can be very rewarding. Taking a plain board and turning it into a useful object to be enjoyed by others for years to come is a wonderful feeling and gives one a sense of accomplishment. In addition, the home craftsperson can realize great savings by making woodworking projects rather than simply purchasing them. The woodworker can choose top-quality materials and still save a lot of money.

By starting with the simple projects the beginner will gain confidence, and hopefully, be stimulated into making the more advanced projects. To further help those making these projects each project has a one-, two-, or three-view fully dimensioned drawing of the finished project; an exploded view showing exactly how the projects are put together; and a parts list, listing each and every part, its size, and how many of each is required. Full written instructions and construction tips are given to further aid in making each project.

Some of the projects in this book are projects I have developed for the magazines *The American Woodworker* and *Popular Woodworking* over the last two years. The rest have been developed exclusively for this book. If you like these projects, you may wish to subscribe to these magazines for many more similar projects from which to choose.

Before starting each project, read through the instructions at least twice in order to get a good overall idea of exactly what you will be doing. Study the drawings as you read and mentally assemble the project in your mind. A thorough, in-depth understanding of the project saves you frustration and helps your work proceed steadily and smoothly.

All efforts have been made to check and recheck all drawings and dimensions for accuracy. To my knowledge, all drawings are correct, but it is still a good idea to recheck all dimensions and cuts as you make them. Furthermore, all projects in this book can be varied or changed slightly when and where necessary to suit a special need or personal taste. In doing this, you will be creating a one-of-a-kind piece that is truly YOURS. Please note: comments, good or bad, about this book or any projects are welcome. Many happy hours of woodworking.

# I

# *Kitchen Projects*

# Cutting Boards

Cutting boards are a very useful addition to any kitchen. If your home has Early American decor, you might want to consider making one of the early-style cutting boards. Most cutting boards are made from hardwood. Softwood *could* be used, if necessary, but it will probably not last as long.

## Antique-Style Cutting Board

Try to get knot-free, straight-grained wood that is as thick as possible. Maple or cherry make very nice cutting boards. As the basic design of this cutting board is completely laid out with a compass, the pattern can be drawn directly on a piece of wood, ¾ to 1 inch thick, about 15 inches wide, and 18 inches long. If you are going to make more than one cutting board, make up a cardboard pattern, as illustrated, using the ½-inch grid.

If it is necessary to glue up material to obtain the 15-inch width, you can glue up three, four, or more pieces. Be sure to use a waterproof glue, as cutting boards are subjected to water now and then.

## Instructions

Draw a light layout line across the center of the board. Set your compass at 7 inches and swing the main radius of the cutting board. Any size diameter will do to fit your particular need. Locate the center of the ⅜-inch-diameter hole 1½ inch from the opposite end, and swing a 1½-inch radius as shown.

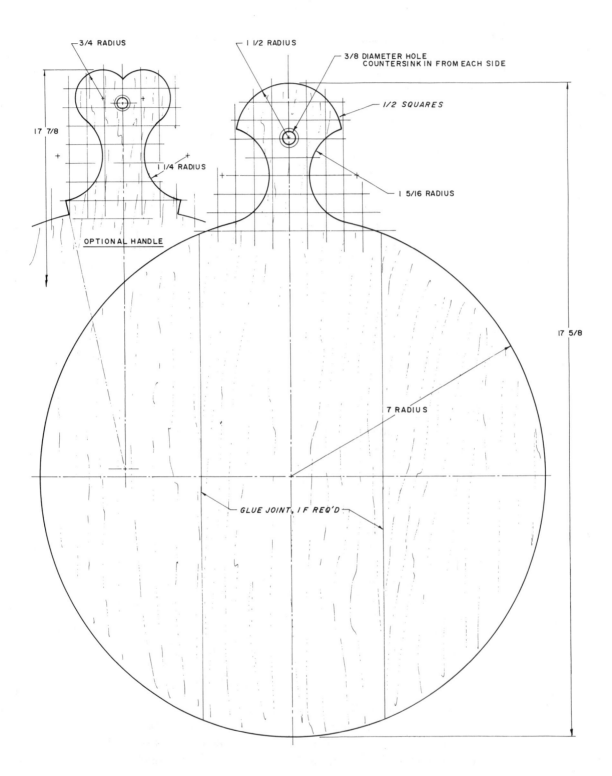

3/4 RADIUS

1 1/2 RADIUS

3/8 DIAMETER HOLE
COUNTERSINK IN FROM EACH SIDE

17 7/8

1 1/4 RADIUS

1/2 SQUARES

1 5/16 RADIUS

OPTIONAL HANDLE

17 5/8

7 RADIUS

GLUE JOINT, IF REQ'D

4

Adjust the compass to 1 5/16 inches and swing the other two arcs tangent (touching) to the 15-inch diameter.

(If you choose to make the optional handle, use the same procedure as outlined above.)

Cut the board just over the layout lines and sand down to the line. A 2½-inch-diameter drum sander is a great help in sanding the edges. Try to keep all edges square and sharp. Next, locate and drill the ⅜-inch-diameter hole, and countersink in from each side as shown. Then sand all over, using different grades of sandpaper, from medium down to very fine. You may wish to finish up with number 0000 steel wool.

## Finishing

Use any nontoxic finish of your choice. Salad bowl finishes are good to use. Be sure to coat *both* sides.

For a finishing touch, add a ⅛-×-⅛-inch leather strap or shoelace. Simply loop it through the hole and tie the ends. Your cutting board is now ready for many years of service and will add a lot of charm to the Early American kitchen in which it is hung.

# Modern-Style Cutting Board

The Pig Cutting Board should be made from a hard wood that is knot-free and straight-grained. It would be best to use a single, 10-inch-wide board, if at all possible. If you have a planer, you might want to consider gluing up your 1 to 2-inch-wide scrap pieces to obtain the 10-inch-wide piece. If you glue up material, be sure to use a waterproof glue and plane the surfaces. Then sand all over.

## Instructions

On a sheet of cardboard or heavy paper 10×17 inches, draw a ½-inch grid. Transfer the pig's shape, point-by-point, to the paper. Transfer the shape to your piece of wood and cut out. Cut just outside the line and later sand down *to* the line. Sand all over, starting with medium paper and ending with extra fine paper. Keep all edges rather sharp, then finish up with number 0000 steel wool.

## Finishing

Use a salad bowl finish on your board. Be sure *not* to use a toxic finish on your board. Your cutting board is now ready for use.

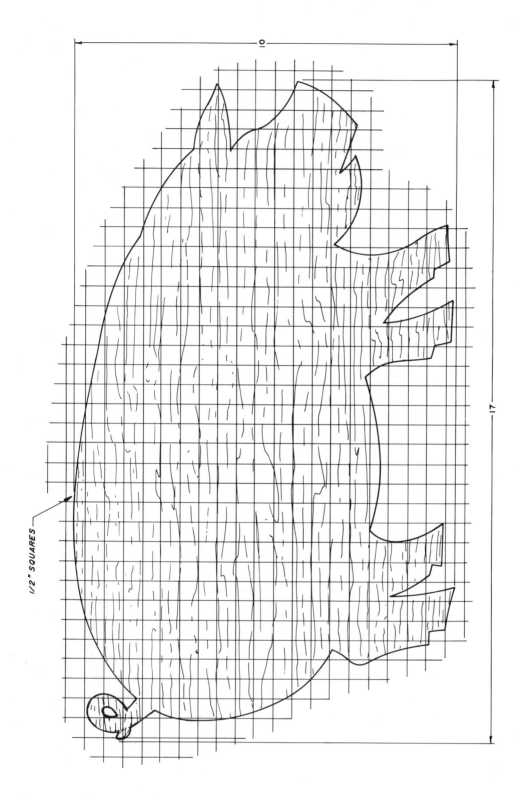

1/2" SQUARES

# Kitchen Helper

A T FIRST GLANCE YOU ARE PROBABLY THINKING I HAVE GONE MAD. WHAT *IS* this thing? Don't give up on me, this is actually a very useful kitchen tool. In fact, it is a combination of a few kitchen tools.

If you enjoy cooking pasta you will find this kitchen helper invaluable. It makes a great pasta server—a tool that can measure out the exact amount of spaghetti needed for one, two, three, four, or five people. Just fill the respective hole with spaghetti, and you will always get the same amount each time you cook. No more waste.

And the other end? It is an ingenious tool used as a ''push-pull'' device for your hot oven rack. It's a three-in-one kitchen helper that you will love. You probably will wonder how you ever got along without it!

## Instructions

First, obtain a piece of hardwood, ⅜ inch thick, 3 inches wide, and 16 inches long. Sand all over, using fine paper.

On a piece of thin paper, lay out a ¼-inch grid at each end as illustrated. Transfer the shape of the kitchen helper point-by-point. Take care to locate the *centers* of all holes, including the two ⅜-inch-diameter holes used at the ''push-pull'' end. Glue this paper to your piece of wood using rubber cement. Drill the ten ¼-inch-diameter holes, making sure not to split through the back side of the wood.

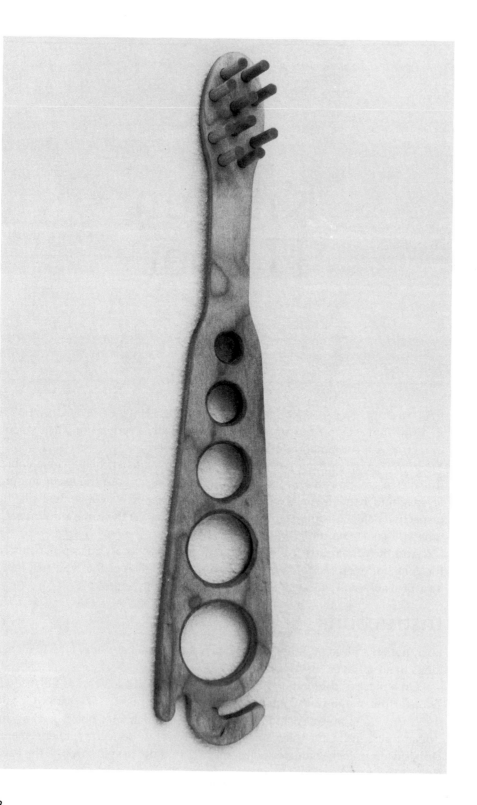

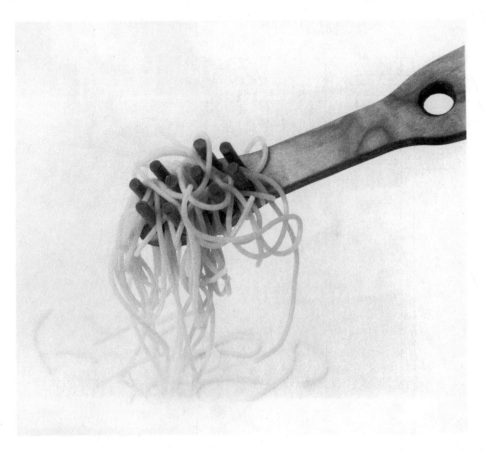

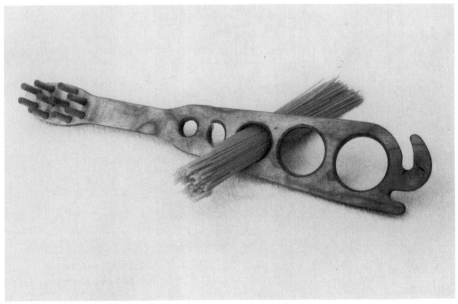

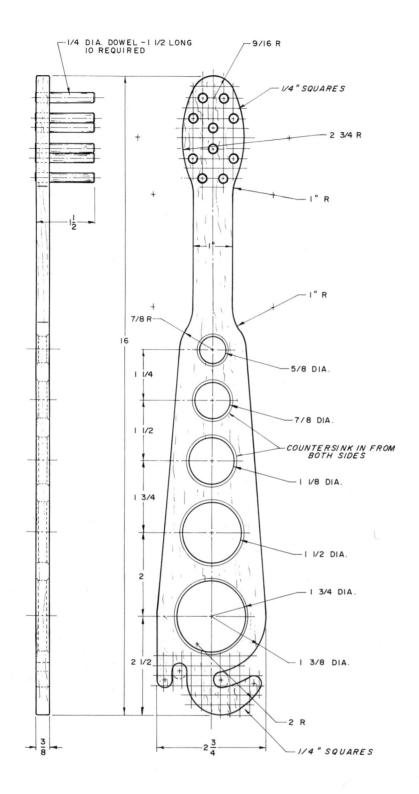

- 1/4 DIA. DOWEL – 1 1/2 LONG
  10 REQUIRED
- 9/16 R
- 1/4" SQUARES
- 2 3/4 R
- 1" R
- 1"
- 1" R
- 7/8 R
- 5/8 DIA.
- 7/8 DIA.
- COUNTERSINK IN FROM BOTH SIDES
- 1 1/8 DIA.
- 1 1/2 DIA.
- 1 3/4 DIA.
- 1 3/8 DIA.
- 2 R
- 1/4" SQUARES

1 1/2

16

1 1/4

1 1/2

1 3/4

2

2 1/2

2 3/4

3/8

Next, drill the ⅝-, ⅞-, 1⅛-, 1½- and 1¾-inch-diameter holes—again taking care not to break through the back side. It is a good idea to drill through from one side until the drill tip just cuts through the back side, then turn the board over and complete the drilling process from the back side, so as to prevent any tearing on the the back side. Round off the edges of the rims of these holes on *both* sides.

Drill the two ⅜-inch-diameter holes in the "push-pull" end. This will save you the problem of trying to cut these two tight radii with a saw. Cut the outside edges along the line.

Again sand all over using fine sandpaper. This sanding process should remove all the thin paper pattern that was glued in place. Sand all edges, slightly rounding the outside edges.

Cut ten ¼-inch-diameter dowels, 1½ inches long, using a stop fence so all dowels are *exactly* the same length. Chamfer one end very slightly.

Then, using waterproof glue, glue these dowels in place, flat end into the body of the helper. After the glue has set, sand the back side.

# Finishing

Apply a nontoxic salad bowl finish all over. Finally, hang this "whatever" in your kitchen and watch the response of your family and friends. No matter *what* they say, it *is* a handy tool!

# Salad Tongs

SUMMERTIME IS FOR OUTDOOR COOKING, EATING, AND, OF COURSE, SALADS! For those avid woodworkers that detest the chrome-plated or plastic utensils of today, this wooden salad tong is just what the doctor ordered. This salad tong is spring-loaded, as most tongs are, but this one has a *wooden spring* to reopen its jaws. Note on the illustration, as the tong jaws are closed, the two outer fingers of part B exert pressure against the sides of part A, thus giving a spring-action to the tongs.

This project takes very little wood, is simple to make, and can be made in 2 hours or so. Its length can be varied from about 12 inches to 16 inches long, in order to meet almost any particular need.(The 16-inch length is shown in the photo.) Any scraps of hardwood around the shop can be used, but I found mahogany worked best with the 6½-inch-long cutout and saw kerfs as illustrated.

## Instructions

Begin by cutting two pieces of wood to size: ⅜ inch thick, 1 inch high, and from 12 to 16 inches long, as shown. Sand all over, using fine-grit paper and keeping all corners sharp and square.

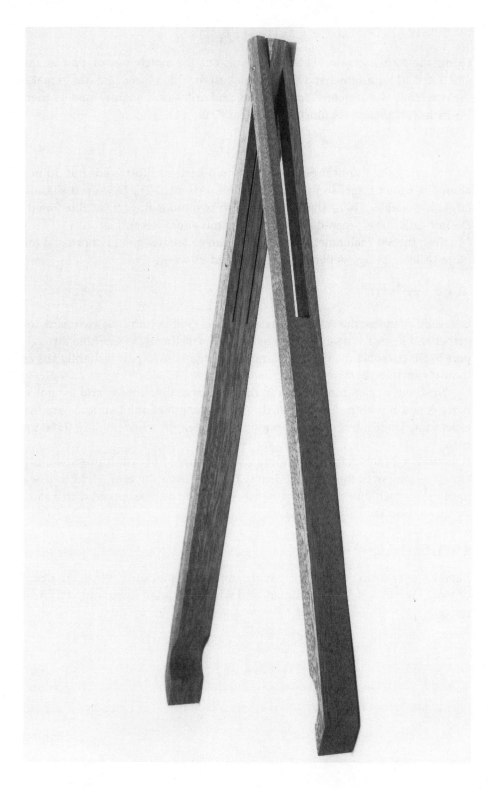

# Part A

Using the thinnest saw blade you have, cut the notch out of part A, as illustrated. (I found my band saw works best for this.) Take care not to make the notch any wider than ⅜ inch. Locate and drill a hole slightly smaller than ¹⁄₁₆-inch in diameter, as illustrated. Resand all over.

# Part B

Again, using the thinnest blade, cut the two kerfs as illustrated, but do not allow the center finger to be any larger than ⁵⁄₁₆ inch. Try to keep it slightly larger if possible. Then, slightly round the two outer fingers, as illustrated. Do not drill the ¹⁄₁₆-inch-diameter hole at this time. Resand all over.

*Note:* the 6½-inch notch and saw kerf can be lengthened or shortened for more or less spring, depending on the kind of wood used.

# Assembly

Carefully assemble the two parts as illustrated. Still holding the two parts together and using the hole in part A as a guide, drill the undersize hole through part B. Disassemble the two parts and redrill the hole in part B slightly larger than ¹⁄₁₆ inch in diameter.

Next, cut a brass pin ¹⁄₁₆ inch in diameter and 1 inch long, and assemble parts A and B with it. Check that the overall length of the two arms are the exact same length. If not, simply sand them to length while holding them together.

Using a 2-inch-diameter sanding drum mounted in a drill press, simply close the tong over the rotating drum, 1¼ inch from the end. Hold in place until the ³⁄₁₆-inch dimension is achieved. This could also be cut out with a saw, if you do not have a drill press.

# Finishing

Sand all over, using a fine-grit paper, and remove all dust. Wipe on a coat or two of nontoxic salad bowl finish, and whip up a salad to test out your new tongs!

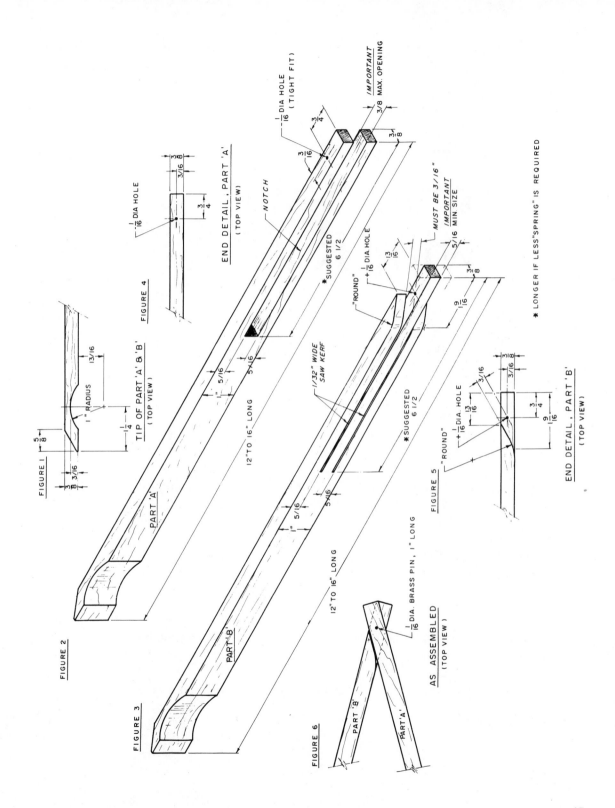

FIGURE 1

$\frac{5}{8}$

$\frac{3}{8}$ $\frac{3}{16}$

$\frac{1}{4}$

1" RADIUS

13/16

TIP OF PART 'A' & 'B'
( TOP VIEW )

FIGURE 2

PART 'A'

FIGURE 3

PART 'B'

12" TO 16" LONG

END DETAIL, PART 'A'
( TOP VIEW )

$\frac{1}{16}$ DIA HOLE
( TIGHT FIT )

$\frac{3}{4}$

$\frac{3}{16}$

$\frac{3}{16}$

$\frac{3}{8}$

3/8 MAX. OPENING    IMPORTANT

MUST BE 3/16"
IMPORTANT MIN SIZE

$\frac{13}{16}$

$+\frac{1}{16}$ DIA HOLE

5/16

$\frac{3}{8}$

$\frac{9}{16}$

"ROUND"

* LONGER IF LESS "SPRING" IS REQUIRED

NOTCH

* SUGGESTED
6 1/2

5/16

1"    5/16

12" TO 16" LONG

1/32" WIDE
SAW KERF

* SUGGESTED
6 1/2

FIGURE 4

$\frac{1}{16}$ DIA HOLE

$\frac{3}{8}$
3/16

$\frac{3}{4}$

END DETAIL, PART 'B'
( TOP VIEW )

$\frac{3}{8}$
3/16

$+\frac{1}{16}$ DIA HOLE

$\frac{13}{16}$

$\frac{3}{4}$

$\frac{9}{16}$

"ROUND"

FIGURE 5

1"    5/16

5/16

12" TO 16" LONG

$\frac{1}{16}$ DIA. BRASS PIN, 1" LONG

AS ASSEMBLED
( TOP VIEW )

PART 'B'

PART 'A'

FIGURE 6

# Small Shelf
# with Rack

THIS VERY SIMPLE BATHROOM SHELF WOULD MAKE AN EXCELLENT PROJECT FOR your son, daughter, or grandchild to make with you. A project such as this one could possibly get them started in woodworking. Today there are so many useless activities in which teenagers are involved, perhaps doing something constructive with their hands, such as woodworking, would be a practical skill they can develop throughout their lives.

This simple bathroom shelf also makes an excellent craft show item, as it can be made in an evening with very little materials.

As with any project, thoroughly study the drawings before you begin, so you understand how it all goes together.

## Instructions

Cut all pieces to size per the Materials List. Sand all parts on all sides and edges.

Next, lay out and cut the back (part 1), the shelf (part 2), and the two side pieces (part 3), per the illustration on p. 18. It is a good idea to cut out and sand the two sides while they are tacked together. In addition, to further ensure accuracy, locate and drill the two ½-inch-diameter holes for the rods (part 5), with the sides still together.

| Part No. | Name | Size | Req'd. |
|----------|------|------|--------|
| 1 | Back | ⅜ × 4½ – 20 Long | 1 |
| 2 | Shelf | ⅜ × 4¼ – 20 Long | 1 |
| 3 | Side | ⅜ × 4½ – 7¼ Long | 2 |
| 4 | Brace | ⅛ × ¾ – 10½ Long | 2 |
| 5 | Rod | ½ dia. × 17⅝ Long | 2 |

# Assembly

Assemble the back (part 1) to the shelf (part 2), and attach the two sides (part 3), keeping everything square. Center the two braces (part 4) with the sides, and leave a ¼-inch overhang on the sides and bottom as shown. Add the two rods (part 5) and the shelf is complete!

# Finishing

A simple clear finish is all that is needed to complete the shelf.

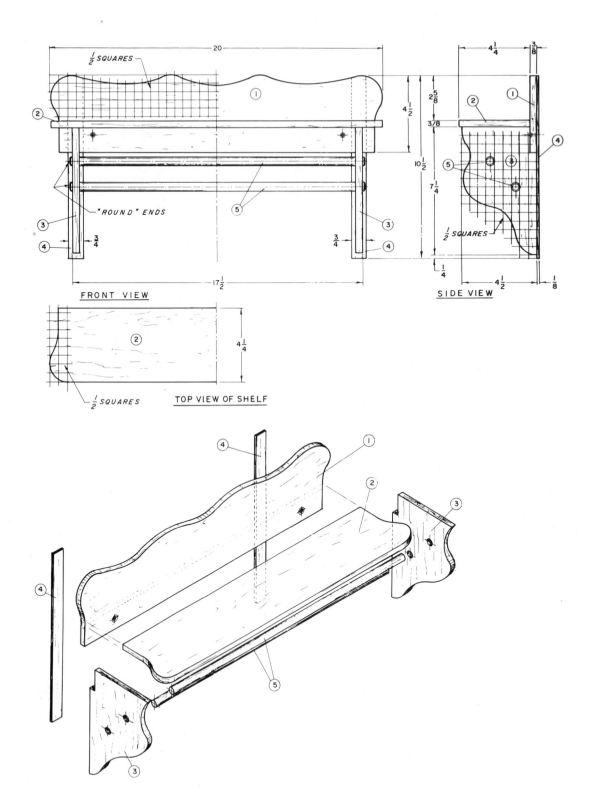

½ SQUARES

20

4½

2⅝

3/8

10½

7¼

4¼

¼

4¼

3/8

½ SQUARES

"ROUND" ENDS

¾

¾

17½

FRONT VIEW

¼

4½

⅛

SIDE VIEW

4¼

2

½ SQUARES

TOP VIEW OF SHELF

# Telephone Center

HAVE YOU EVER PICKED UP THE PHONE AND HAD AN IMPORTANT MESSAGE TO write down, only to find you didn't have a pencil or something to write on within reaching distance? Well, hopefully, this weekend project will solve that problem for you. Not only does this telephone center provide a convenient place to store pencils and paper, it dresses up a wall phone so that it will blend in with the room decor.

This project can be made of most any kind of wood and can be either stained or painted. For my project, I chose paint that goes with the color scheme of the room the telephone is in.

## Instructions

As with any project, even simple ones like this one, always begin by studying the plans so you know exactly how this project is constructed.

Carefully draw out a ½-inch grid on a piece of cardboard, or, if you intend to make several, a piece of thin plywood for a full-size pattern. Transfer the shape, square-for-square, as illustrated on the plans. As this is a somewhat simple shape, you should not have any difficulty.

Next, cut all ½-inch-thick wood to the exact sizes given on the Materials List. Keep everything exactly square as you proceed. Where duplicate sizes are required, cut all parts with a saw set at the exact size, so the parts will match.

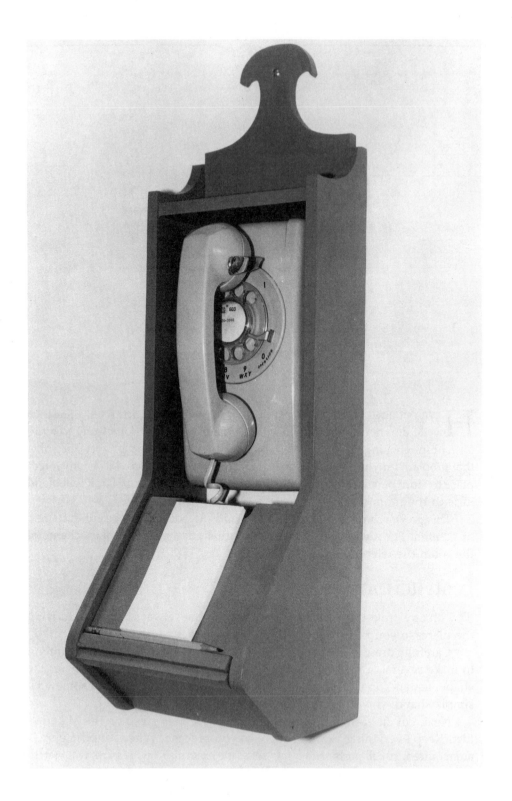

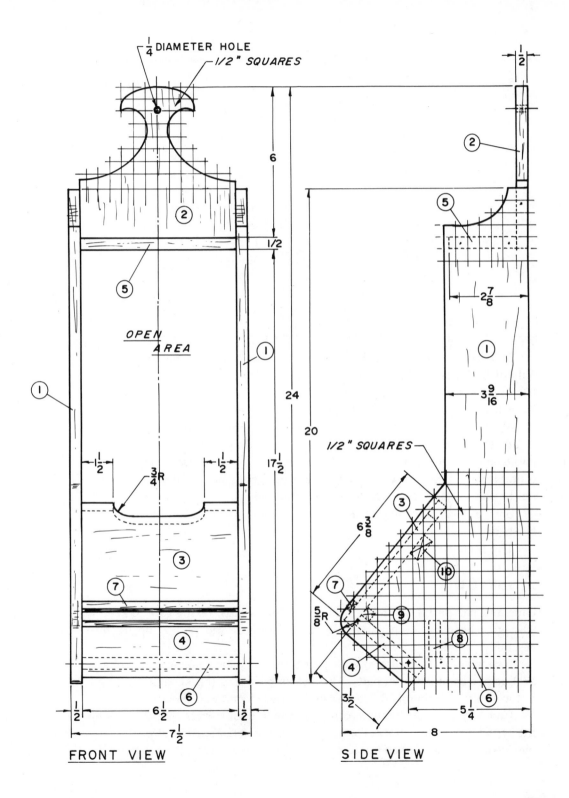

FRONT VIEW      SIDE VIEW

21

| Part No. | Name | Size | Req'd. |
|---|---|---|---|
| 1 | Side | ½ × 8 – 20 Long | 2 |
| 2 | Backboard | ½ × 6½ – 6½ Long | 1 |
| 3 | Platform | ½ × 6½ – 6⅜ Long | 1 |
| 4 | Front Board | ½ × 6½ – 3½ Long | 1 |
| 5 | Top Shelf | ½ × 6½ – 2⅞ Long | 1 |
| 6 | Bottom | ½ × 6½ – 4¼ Long | 1 |
| 7 | Lip | ¼ × ½ – 6½ Long | 1 |
| 8 | Fence | ½ × 6½ – 1½ Long | 1 |
| 9 | Brace | ½ × ½ – 6½ Long | 1 |
| 10 | Stop | ¼ × ½ – 1" Long | 2 |
| 11 | Screw Round Head | No. 6 – 1" Long | 2 |
| 12 | Nail – Finish | 4d | 10 |

Transfer the patterns to the wood that has been cut to overall size. The only difficult part of this project is cutting out the shape of parts 1, 2, and 3. If you have a band saw, jigsaw or a saber saw, this really is not very hard. After these parts have been cut out, sand all edges, keeping them sharp.

*Note:* simple butt joints have been used throughout this project. If you are an advanced woodworker, you might wish to dado part 1 to part 5, part 6 to part 8, and part 3 to part 4. I really do not think this is necessary, as the phone center is very rugged. If you do dado, don't forget to add enough extra material to parts 4, 5, 6, and 8 to reach into the dadoes.

Sand all surfaces of all parts at this time, taking care not to round any edges. Next, dry-fit *all* pieces to check for good tight fits at all joints.

The project is now ready for final assembly.

# Assembly

Glue and nail part 3 (platform) to part 4 (front board), taking care to keep a 90-degree bend between parts. Add part 9 (brace) and part 7 (lip) to this assembly. Put aside to set.

Assemble part 6 (bottom) with part 8 (fence), again taking care to have a 90-degree bend between parts. Then assemble part 2 (backboard) with part 5 (top shelf), keeping a 90-degree bend between parts as shown.

Carefully mark the locations on one of the interior surfaces of part 1, using the actual parts as a pattern. Place the opposite *interior* surface of part 1 side-by-side against the marked up side, and transfer the exact locations to this side.

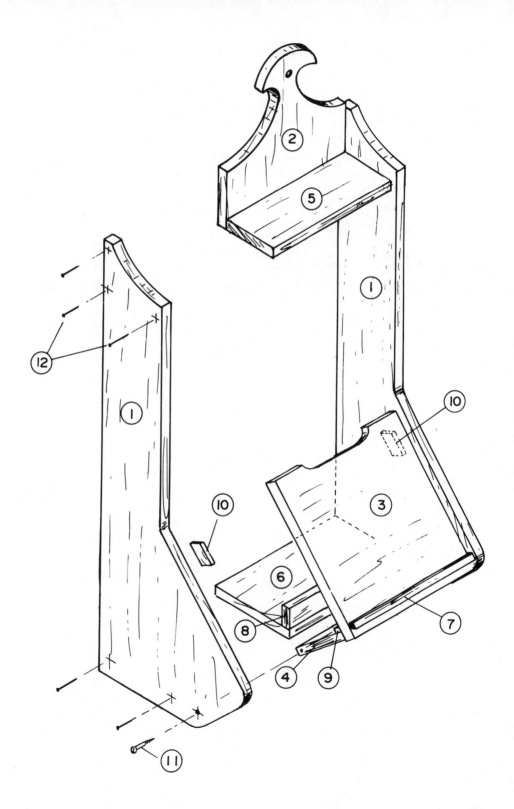

23

Take care that both sides are exactly the same, and make sure that you have marked both interior surfaces.

Assemble parts 2, 5, 6, and 8 to the sides (part 1), taking care to keep everything square. Allow time for the glue to set.

Locate the hole for the two screws (part 11), and drill through the sides as shown. Take extra care that the platform assembly (parts 3, 4, 7, and 9) swings freely. Turn the assembly over, locate and glue the two stops (part 10) as shown. I added magnetic door catches (not shown) next to the stops, to ensure that the platform stays securely closed.

Sand all over but do not round edges, except to remove the very sharp edge. The telephone center is now ready for finishing.

# Finishing

Finish this project in either a stain of your choice or a semigloss color to match your room trim.

Now you do not have an excuse for forgetting to write down that very important phone message.

# Fire
# Extinguisher
# Holder

EVERY KITCHEN SHOULD HAVE A FIRE EXTINGUISHER CLOSE AT HAND JUST IN case, but a red fire extinguisher hanging over a kitchen stove in sight just is a little tacky. Yet if you keep it hidden away someplace, you might not be able to find it in an emergency. This project provides an excellent place to store and hide your small, auto-type fire extinguisher without detracting from your room decor. It can also be used as a small wall shelf to store odds and ends. Just add two or more shelves to suit.

Simple butt joints have been used throughout this project. If you are an advanced woodworker, you might wish to incorporate dado joints.

In the event you do not wish to make the letters yourself, most wood suppliers sell 1-inch-high letters. However, the letters are rather simple and quick to make, and the wood will match better.

## Instructions

Carefully study the drawings before starting so you know exactly how it is put together.

Next, cut all parts to size per the given Materials List.

Lay out a ½-inch grid on a piece of paper or cardboard and draw out the top portion of the back (part 1). At this time, carefully locate the centers of the six holes in the three hearts.

## MATERIALS LIST

| Part No. | Name | Size | Req'd. |
|---|---|---|---|
| 1 | Back | $\frac{1}{2} \times 5\frac{3}{4}$ - 19 Long | 1 |
| 2 | Side | $\frac{1}{2} \times 4\frac{1}{2}$ - $14\frac{1}{2}$ Long | 2 |
| 3 | Bottom/Top | $\frac{1}{2} \times 4\frac{11}{16}$ - $5\frac{3}{4}$ Long | 2 |
| 4 | Door Stop (Shelf) | $\frac{1}{4} \times 3\frac{1}{2}$ - $4\frac{3}{8}$ Long | 2 |
| 5 | Door | $\frac{1}{2} \times 4\frac{3}{8}$ - $14\frac{1}{2}$ Long | 1 |
| 6 | Hinge - Brass | $1 \times \frac{3}{4}$ size | 2 |
| 7 | Knob - Brass | $\frac{1}{2}$ Diameter | 1 |
| 8 | Letters | $\frac{1}{4} \times 1\frac{1}{16}$ - 13 Long | 1 |

Part No. 4—Shelf is Optional—Add 2 if required.

Transfer this pattern, along with the six centers, to the wood.

Locate and drill the six holes first, then cut out the three hearts. Cut the outside shape per your layout, then add the notches for the sides (part 2).

*Note:* the bottom portion of the back (part 1) should be $4\frac{3}{8}$ inches as dimensioned.

Except for the $\frac{1}{2}$-×-$4\frac{3}{8}$-inch notch in the top (part 3), all parts are simple rectangular pieces with 90-degree cuts.

To cut out the $\frac{3}{16}$-inch recess for the letters in the door (part 5), make up a simple rectangular router guide and clamp it in place over the door. The required recess size, as dimensioned, is $1\frac{3}{8} \times 3\frac{7}{8}$ inches, and $\frac{3}{16}$ of an inch deep.

The interior size of the guide is determined by the diameter of the router bit you are using and the diameter, *at the base*, of your router. To calculate the required length of the guide opening, *subtract* the router bit diameter from the required recess length and add the router diameter. To calculate the height of the guide opening, *subtract* the router bit diameter from the required recess height of the guide opening and *subtract* the router diameter.
Example:

(Using the given dimensions, a $\frac{7}{16}$-inch-diameter router bit size and a 6-inch-diameter router base.)

Guide-opening *length*:

| | | |
|---|---|---|
| | $3\frac{7}{8}$ inches | Required recess length |
| − | $\frac{7}{16}$ inch | Router bit diameter |
| | $3\frac{7}{16}$ inches | |
| + | 6 inches | Router base diameter |
| | $9\frac{7}{16}$ inches | Guide opening length |

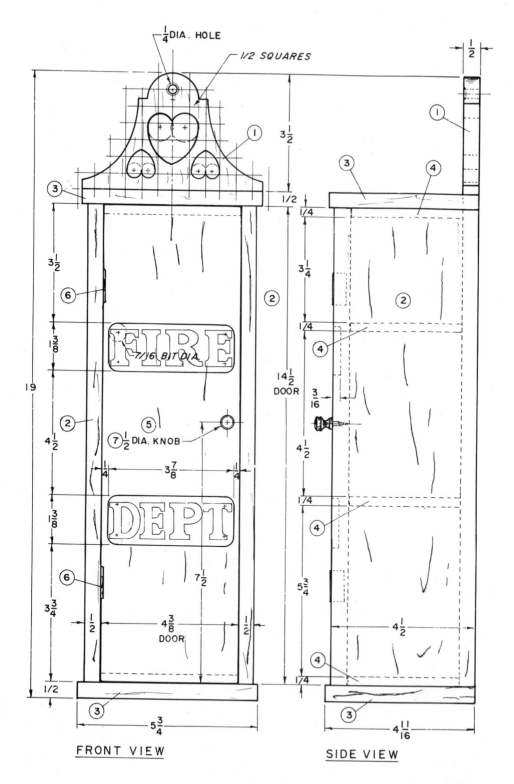

FRONT VIEW

SIDE VIEW

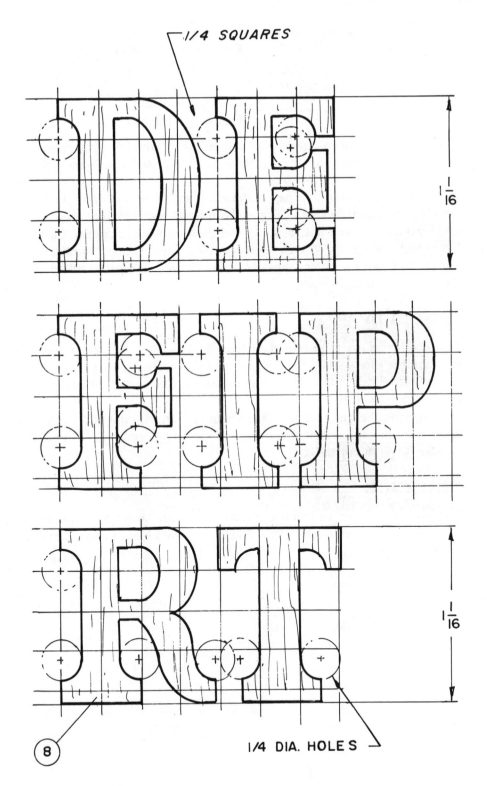

1/4 SQUARES

$1\frac{1}{16}$

$1\frac{1}{16}$

8

1/4 DIA. HOLES

Guide-opening *height*:

|   | 1 ⅜ inch | Required recess height |
|---|---|---|
| − | 7/16 inch | Router bit diameter |
|   | 15/16 inch | |
| + | 6 inches | Router base width |
|   | 6 15/16 inches | Guide opening height |

Thus, the inside dimensions of your router guide should be 9⁷/₁₆ inches long and 6¹⁵/₁₆ inches high. Set the router bit to a depth of ³/₁₆ inch and rout out the recess in the two given areas.

Next, on a sheet of thin paper, draw a ¼-inch grid and draw the letters per the illustration. Be sure to locate all centers of the ¼-inch-diameter holes and lay out *two* letter E's. Glue this paper to ¼-inch-thick material. Carefully locate and drill out the ¼-inch-diameter holes. Cut all *interior* surfaces first, and then cut out the outer shapes of the letters with the paper still glued to the wood. Sand all over.

# Assembly

Glue the letters (part 8) to the door (part 5). The letters will extend out ¹/₁₆ inch. Let the letters set and then sand them down, flush with the face of the door. Notch the door for the two hinges (part 6). Locate and drill a pilot hole for the knob (part 7).

Assemble the case, keeping everything square. You might want to glue and clamp the case assembly together with the door temporarily in place to be sure it will fit correctly.

# Finishing

This project can be either painted or stained. Because I was going to use mine in the kitchen, I painted mine red. Finally, attached hinges (part 6) and the brass knob (part 7).

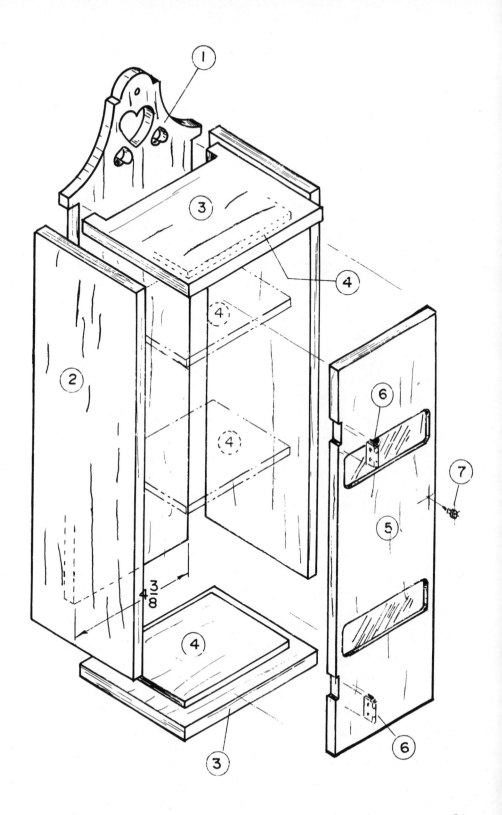

# Towel and
# Tissue Rack

THIS HANDY KITCHEN OR BATHROOM RACK PROVIDES A CONVENIENT PLACE TO store a large paper towel roll, a medium-size tissue box, and a cloth towel. This project can be made of most any kind of wood, from soft pine to hard oak. The one in the photo is made of white oak.

## Instructions

Rough-cut all parts per the Materials List and sand all over. On a sheet of paper or cardboard, draw out a 1-inch grid and, point-for-point, transfer the shape of the side (part 1) to the sheet. Locate the center of the two 1-inch-diameter holes for the two bars. On the sheet, carefully lay out the location for the support (part 3).

Temporarily tack the two sides (part 1) together with small finishing nails, and transfer the shape of the side from the paper to the wood. Locate and drill two small, $1/32$-inch-diameter holes through the two parts to exactly locate the two 1-inch-diameter holes that will be added later. Cut out the sides (part 1), and sand all edges *before* separating the two sides.

On the *inside* surface of the sides and from the *center* of the two $1/32$-inch-diameter holes, drill the two 1-inch-diameter holes $1/4$ inch deep. *Be sure you have a matching pair and take care not to drill through the sides.*

On the inside surfaces of the sides, carefully locate and mark the exact location where the support (part 3) will be located.

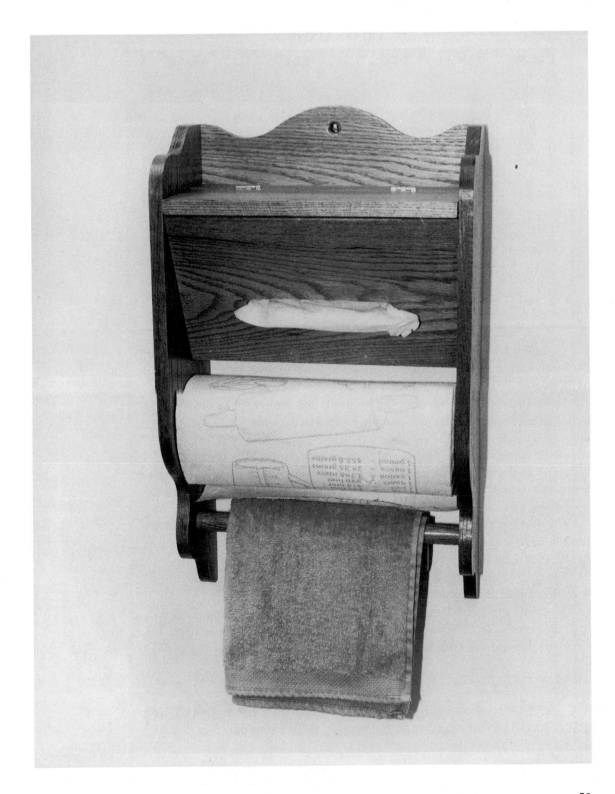

| Part No. | Name | Size | Req'd. |
|---|---|---|---|
| 1 | Side | ½ × 6½ – 21½ Long | 2 |
| 2 | Top - Back | ½ × 7⅝ – 11¼ Long | 1 |
| 3 | Support | ½ × 5⅜ – 5⁹⁄₁₆ Long | 2 |
| 4 | Bottom | ½ × 3⅝ – 11¼ | 1 |
| 5 | Face Board | ½ × 7 – 11¼ Long | 1 |
| 6 | Top Board | ½ × 1⅞ – 11¼ Long | 1 |
| 7 | Lid | ½ × 4¼ – 1³⁄₁₆ | 1 |
| 8 | Bar | 1" Dia. – 11¾ Long | 1 |
| 9 | Bar – Part 1 | 1" Dia. – 8 Long | 1 |
| 10 | Bar – Part 2 | 1" Dia. – 5⅜ Long | 1 |
| 11 | Spring (1⅜ Long) | ⁹⁄₁₆ Inside Dia. | 1 |
| 12 | Hinge – Brass | ¾ × 1 | 2 |
| 13 | Nail – Finish | 4d | 20 |

Carefully lay out and transfer the shape of the *top* of the top board (part 2), per the illustration, and cut out. Note that the bottom edge of part 2 is cut at 25 degrees.

Lay out and cut the two supports (part 3), and glue them in place on the sides. Be sure both are identical and are located in the exact same place in the sides. Put aside to let glue set.

Next, cut the bottom (part 4) and the face board (part 5) to the given size. Note the 25-degree angular cut. Locate and drill two ½-inch-diameter holes in the face board, 2¾ inches up from the bottom and 2¼ inches in from the two sides. Cut out the slot between the two ½-inch-diameter holes.

Cut the top board (part 6) and the lid (part 7). Notch the top board for the two hinges (part 12). Add hinges to the two parts to check for a correct fit. If everything is correct, remove the hinges at this time.

Cut the bottom bar (part 8) to length and chamfer the ends slightly. Now turn the end of the middle bar (part 9).

*Note:* this part has a ½-inch-diameter shoulder, 2⅝ inches long. Drill a ½-inch-diameter hole 3 inches deep into the matching middle bar (part 10). Chamfer the ends of both bars slightly.

# Assembly

Nail and glue the top-back (part 2) in place, using the support (part 3) as a guide. Attach the top board (part 6) in place, again using part 3 as a guide.

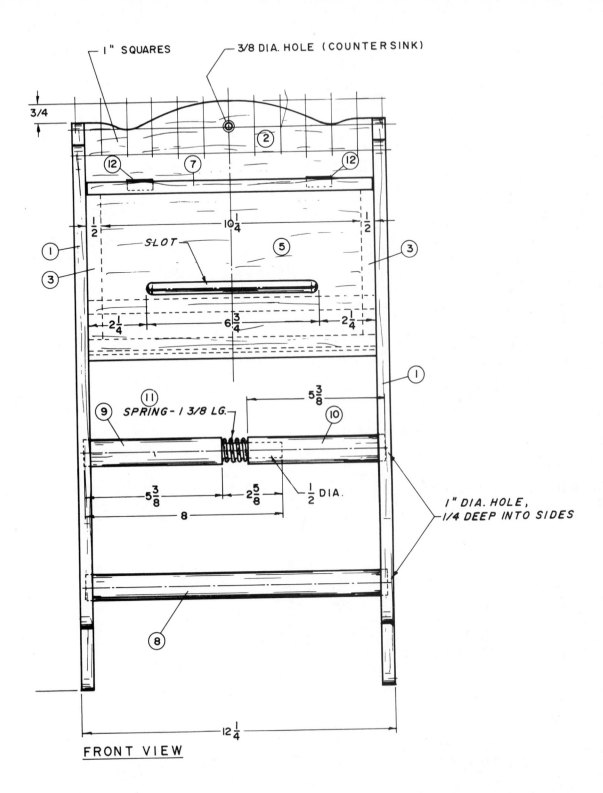

1" SQUARES

3/8 DIA. HOLE (COUNTERSINK)

3/4

⌀4

②

⑫  ⑦  ⑫

①
③

SLOT

⑤

③

10 1/4

1/2

1/2

2 1/4    6 3/4    2 1/4

①

⑪

SPRING - 1 3/8 LG.

5 3/8

⑨    ⑩

5 3/8    2 5/8    1/2 DIA.

8

1" DIA. HOLE,
1/4 DEEP INTO SIDES

⑧

12 1/4

FRONT VIEW

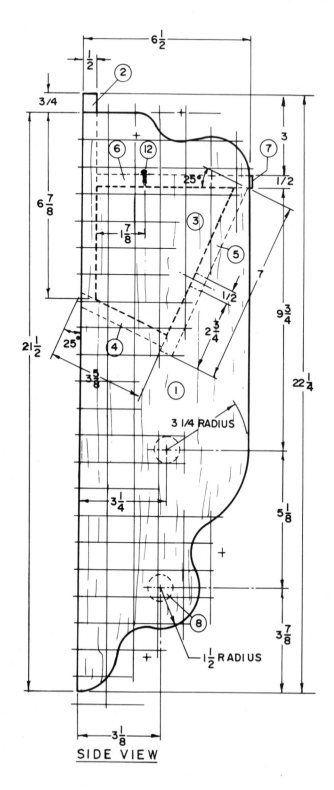

SIDE VIEW

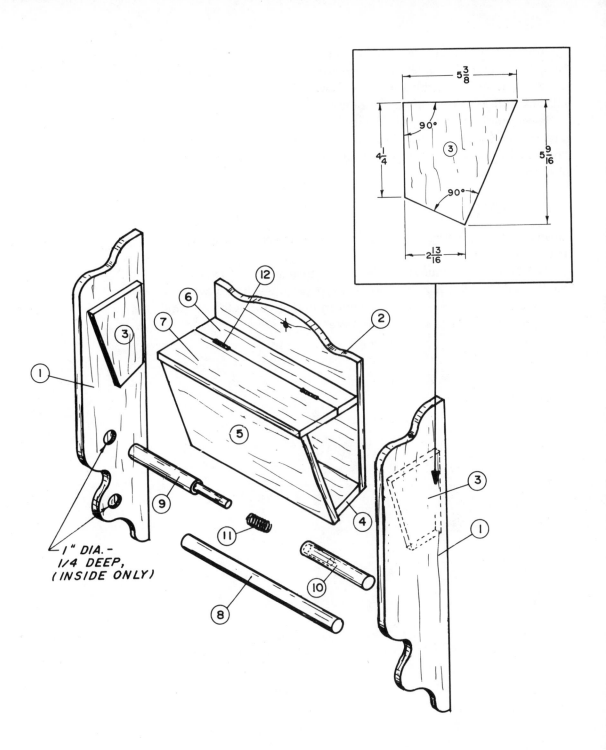

1" DIA. –
1/4 DEEP,
(INSIDE ONLY)

Add the face board (part 5) and bottom (part 4) to the assembly, once again using the support as a guide. Don't forget to add the bottom bar (part 8) before you glue and nail everything in place. Take care not to get any glue on any finished surfaces. Wipe off any extra glue.

Next, attach the lid (part 7) using the two hinges (part 12). Check for a good fit. Check the fit for the middle bar and spring (parts 9, 10, and 11). Adjust if necessary—you want a snug fit but not a tight fit. Sand all surfaces, keeping all edges sharp.

# Finishing

Finish this project as you would any project using your favorite stain and top coat.

This Towel and Tissue Rack will make a great addition to your workshop, too. It would be nice, just once, to have a paper towel handy whenever you need one in your shop. I know I never can find anything to wipe my hands on but my pants—just ask my wife Joyce!

# Wastepaper Basket

A WOODSHOP CAN NEVER HAVE ENOUGH WASTEPAPER BASKETS. AND WHAT could possibly make a better wastepaper basket than a wooden basket? This project will give you a chance to make use of all those wood scraps piling up in your shop. It takes a 26 gallon garbage bag—the heavy-duty type is best. If your shop looks like mine, you will *need* a heavy duty garbage bag—not a ''wimpy'' bag.

## Instructions

You will probably have to glue up material to make the 16-inch width. This is a good way to use up those various narrow pieces of wood you might never use otherwise. Glue up enough material for the two sides (part 2), the front (part 1), the back (part 1), the top (part 3), and the bottom (part 6).

Cut all parts to size per the Materials List, keeping everything square. Rabbet the front and the back (part 1), ¼ inch deep and ¾ inch wide, as shown. Glue and nail the front and back (part 1) to the sides (part 2). Then glue and nail the bottom (part 6) in place, 2 inches above the bottom. Check that everything is square in all directions. Sand all over, keeping all edges sharp.

Next, make a cardboard pattern of the feet per the ½-inch-square grid, and transfer the feet to the front, back, and sides. Cut out the feet and sand all edges.

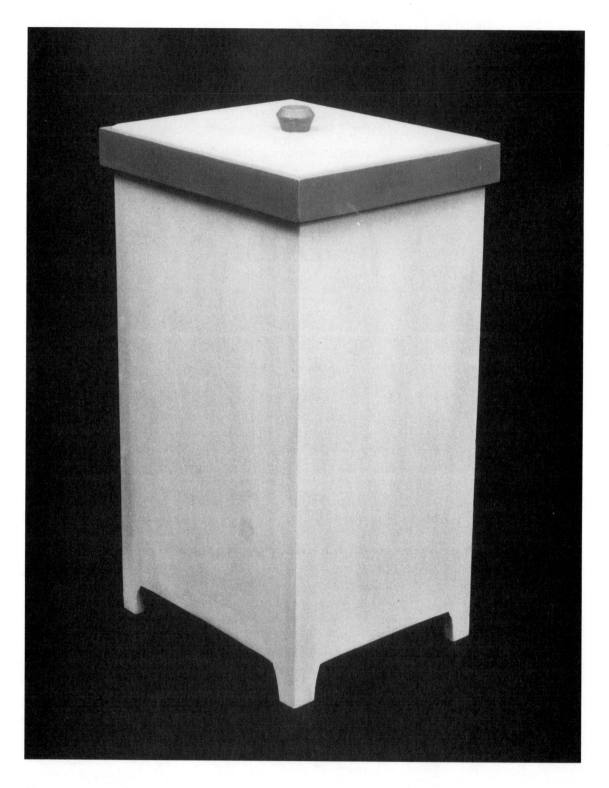

| Part No. | Name | Size | Req'd. |
|---|---|---|---|
| 1 | Front/Back | ¾ × 16 – 26 Long | 2 |
| 2 | Side | ¾ × 12 – 26 Long | 2 |
| 3 | Lid | ¾ × 13 – 16 Long | 1 |
| 4 | Lip – Front | ¾ × 2 – 17 Long | 2 |
| 5 | Lip – Side | ¾ × 2 – 14 Long | 2 |
| 6 | Bottom | ¾ × 11½ – 14½ Long | 1 |
| 7 | Handle | 2 Diameter | 1 |

Cut the lip front (part 4) and the lip side (part 5) to overall size. Rabbet the top ⅜ inch down and ⁵⁄₁₆ inch in. Then rabbet the bottom, ⅜ inch up and ⁵⁄₁₆ inch in, as illustrated. Carefully fit the lip to the basket keeping a snug, but not too tight, fit to allow room for the plastic garbage bag. It is the lip that actually holds the plastic garbage bag in place.

Cut the corners to 45 degrees, as if you were making a picture frame. The actual lid (part 3) is fitted into the top rabbet of the lip assembly. After fitting the lid, cut a 45-degree chamfer ¼ × ¼ inch on all four top edges of the lid, as shown. Check for correct fit, the top should not be too tight a fit. Cut a handle (part 7) for the lid (part 3), and screw it in place in the center of the lid.

# Finishing

This project can be either painted or stained. If you paint it, be sure to undercoat it before painting. Any knots should be varnished over so they will not bleed through later. Be sure to finish the *inside* surface as well as the outside surface of the basket.

This would make a great project to apply tole painting to if anyone in the family knows how.

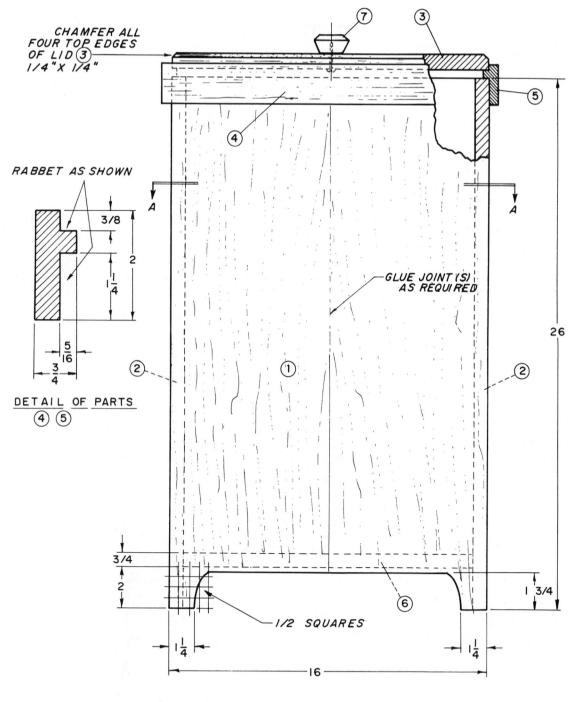

CHAMFER ALL
FOUR TOP EDGES
OF LID ③
1/4" X 1/4"

RABBET AS SHOWN

3/8

2

1 1/4

5/16

3/4

DETAIL OF PARTS
④ ⑤

A

A

GLUE JOINT (S)
AS REQUIRED

26

3/4

2

1/2 SQUARES

1 3/4

1 1/4

1 1/4

16

FRONT VIEW

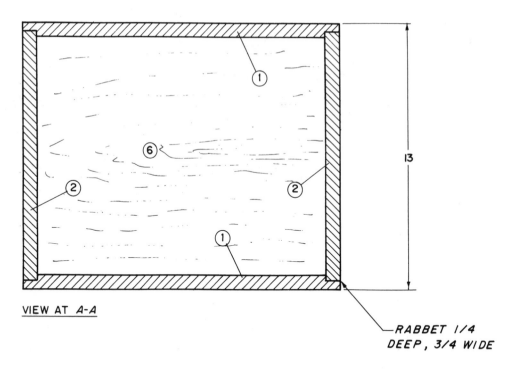

VIEW AT *A-A*

RABBET 1/4
DEEP, 3/4 WIDE

13

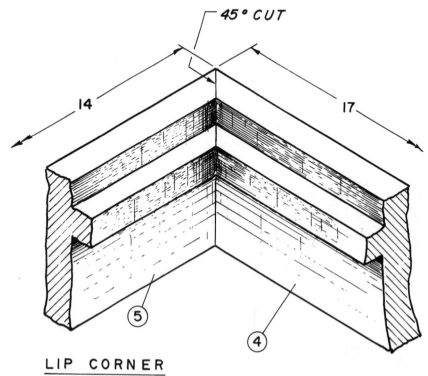

45° CUT

14

17

LIP CORNER

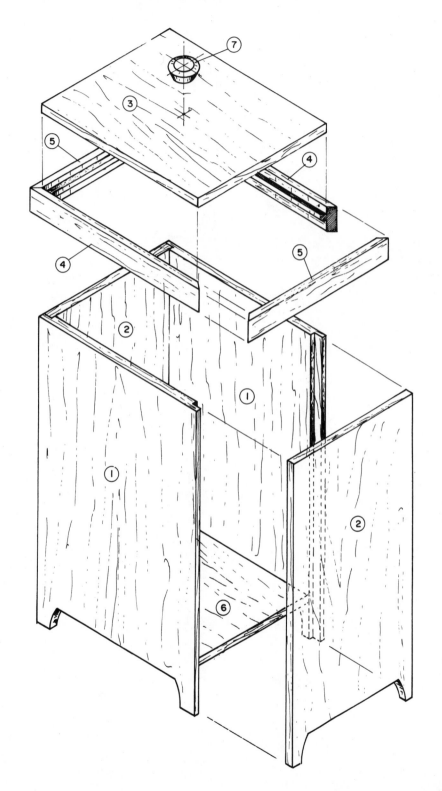

# II

## *Folk Art Projects*

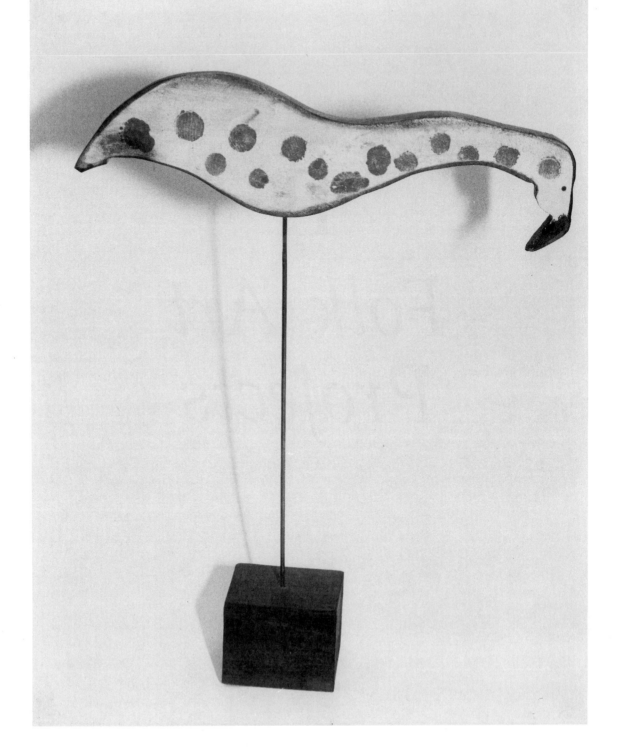

# Spotted Bird

AT FIRST GLANCE, MOST READERS ARE PROBABLY THINKING: "THE AUTHOR HAS gone out of his mind, this project is really dumb!" At first glance, *everyone's* reaction is exactly the same. I copied this "spotted bird" from an original one from Tennessee. It is an excellent example of folk art, which is becoming very popular these days and also getting increasingly expensive to purchase and collect. The dealer who had it claimed it was made in 1925, although I have no idea how he knew this for sure. If you want an interesting conversation piece—this is it!

For those of you who make things to sell at craft fairs, don't pass over trying this one. These dumb birds require almost no material and take very little time to make. My wife, Joyce, has made a stencil for the spots, so painting on the spots does not take much time either. And believe it or not, in southern New Hampshire, these sell very easily for $12 to $15 each. We have sold some at— don't laugh—$22 each. Some of our friends who have asked me to make them one, have them proudly displayed in their front window. Make one or two of these birds and see what reactions you get. See if you can top my $22 price. I think you will be surprised!

## Instructions

As you can see, the bird is very easy to make. On a 2½-×-9½-inch piece of cardboard (or thin plywood, if you plan to make lots of these), lay out a ½-inch grid. Transfer the bird's body, point-by-point, from the drawing to the cardboard. Don't worry if you're off a little; I doubt if anyone will notice.

Transfer the pattern to a ½-inch-thick piece of hardwood. Then, using a saber saw or band saw, cut it out. Sand the sides and edges, rounding the edges slightly. (When making them, I usually tack four pieces together and cut them all out, four at a time. My band saw can easily cut four bird bodies at a time. It is just as easy to make four as it is to make one. Everyone who sees this spotted bird will surely want one, so it is best to make more than one at a time.) Sand a slight taper on the sides of the beak so it looks somewhat natural and not too thick.

The base is cut from any hardwood you have around. The size can vary some but you will need the heft of hardwood—you wouldn't want your bird to fall over, would you? Stain the base with most any stain you want to use up.

# Finishing

Paint the body using a flat, off-white color. Let it dry and add the brick-red beak. Cut a simple stencil and stencil the blue spots on both sides, approximately as illustrated. Let dry for a day or two.

Using a fine sandpaper, sand the bird all over. Be sure to sand through the paint at the edges and sand some of the blue spots away to simulate years of wear. Then with a walnut stain, stain over the entire body and wipe off immediately. This will give your bird an antique-looking effect.

A welding rod makes an excellent post for your bird, a piece of rod 9 inches long is about right. Drill a ³⁄₃₂-inch-diameter hole ¾ inch deep into the body, at the angle illustrated. This is important so the bird will stand properly. Drill the same diameter hole, 1 inch deep into the center of the base.

Set your bird up in some prominent place of importance in your home and watch your friends' reactions.

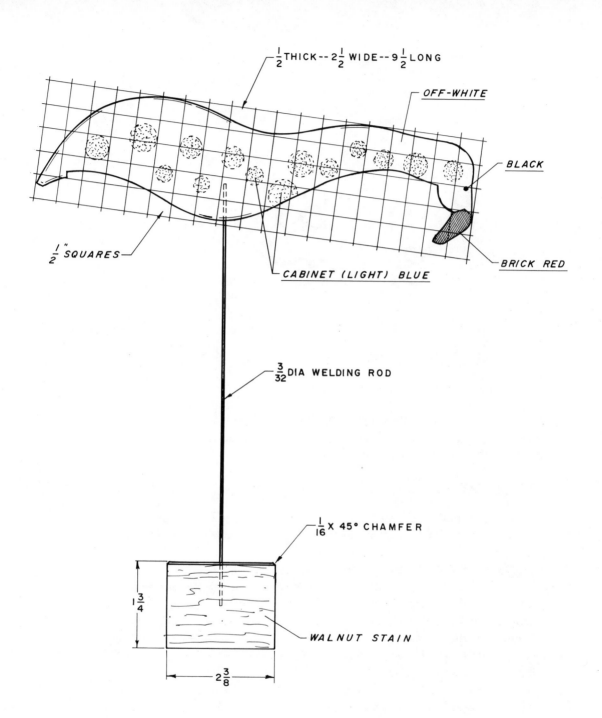

$\frac{1}{2}$ THICK -- 2$\frac{1}{2}$ WIDE -- 9$\frac{1}{2}$ LONG

OFF-WHITE

BLACK

BRICK RED

$\frac{1}{2}$" SQUARES

CABINET (LIGHT) BLUE

$\frac{3}{32}$ DIA WELDING ROD

$\frac{1}{16}$ X 45° CHAMFER

1$\frac{3}{4}$

WALNUT STAIN

2$\frac{3}{8}$

# Band Saw Basket

B ASKETS COME IN ALL SHAPES AND SIZES. THEY ARE MADE OF JUST ABOUT everything you can think of. This one is really unique; it folds flat for storing and makes an interesting conversation piece.

## Instructions

Choose a straight-grain, knot-free piece of hardwood, about ¾ inch thick, 7 or more inches wide and 13 or more inches long. Sand the top and bottom surfaces.

On a piece of thin paper, draw a straight line horizontally across the paper in the middle, and another line vertically, 90 degrees from the center of the first line. From the center (or where the two lines intersect), measure along the horizontal line 3 inches in both directions and make a small dash line. The *left* dash indicates the left swing point for the compass. From the *right* dash line, measure *down* exactly ⅛ inch. This is the right swing point for the compass.

Using a good compass, and starting from the left swing point, swing a 1¼-inch-radius arc. From the right swing point, swing a 1⅜-inch-radius arc. Keep swinging larger and larger arcs at ¼-inch spaces. Take your time as this must be as accurate as possible to ensure a good fitting basket.

The last arc, which is the handle is 5/16 inch wide, *not* ¼ inch as all other arcs are. Carefully draw connecting straight lines between the arcs on the right and left ends as shown. Shade in the ⁵⁄₁₆-inch-wide handle, so you will remember where the handle is.

From the center lines measure ⅜ inch at either side of the vertical center line. This indicates the location of the center foot. Your drawing should look exactly like the TOP VIEW of the basket illustrated.

Next, coat the back side of the paper with rubber glue and let the glue completely dry. Wipe the surface of the wood to remove all dust and attach the layout paper to the top surface of the board. Now, carefully transfer the two lines for the bottom foot to the bottom surface of the basket. Be sure to keep it directly below the two lines above.

Band saw the outer surface of the basket keeping just over the line. Sand down to the line keeping all edges square.

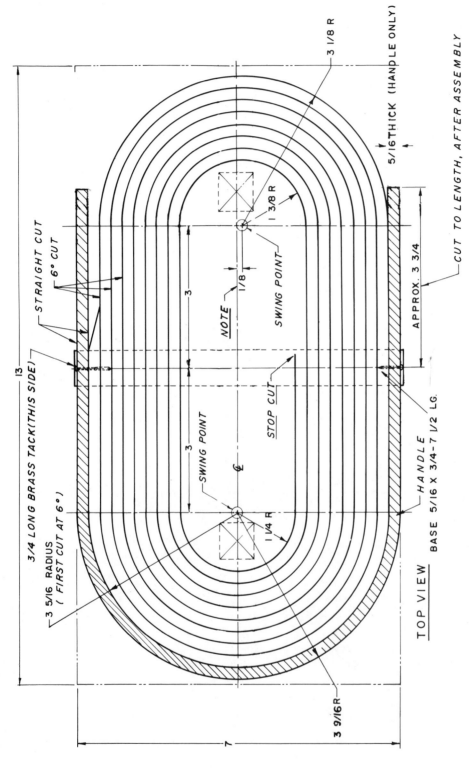

TOP VIEW

BASE 5/16 X 3/4 - 7 1/2 LG.

3 1/8 R

5/16 THICK (HANDLE ONLY)

CUT TO LENGTH, AFTER ASSEMBLY

1 3/8 R

SWING POINT

NOTE

1/8

APPROX. 3 3/4

STOP CUT

HANDLE

SWING POINT

3

3

SWING POINT

1 1/4 R

STRAIGHT CUT

6° CUT

3/4 LONG BRASS TACK (THIS SIDE)

3 5/16 RADIUS ( FIRST CUT AT 6°)

13

7

3 9/16 R

54

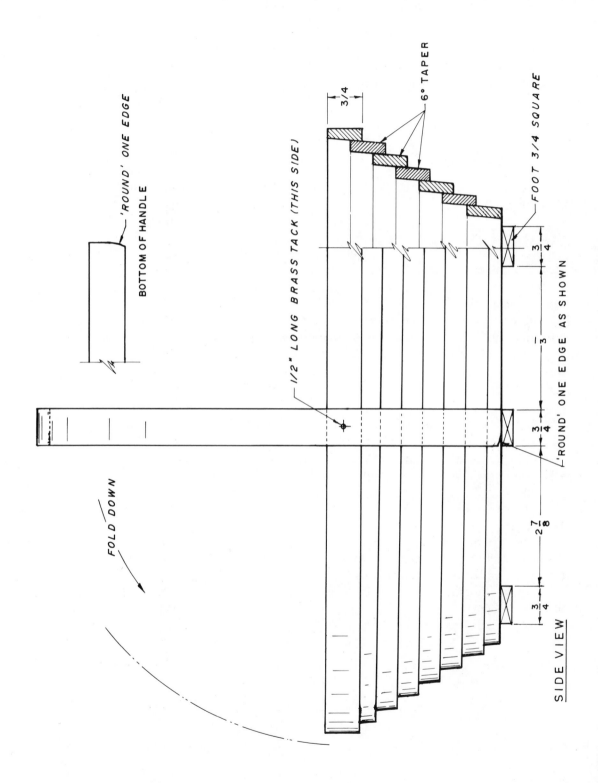

'ROUND' ONE EDGE

BOTTOM OF HANDLE

FOLD DOWN

1/2" LONG BRASS TACK (THIS SIDE)

6° TAPER

3/4

FOOT 3/4 SQUARE

'ROUND' ONE EDGE AS SHOWN

3/4

3

3/4

2 7/8

3/4

SIDE VIEW

55

Along the outer edge of the basket, locate and drill a $\frac{1}{16}$-inch-diameter hole in the center of the edge, $\frac{3}{4}$ inch deep where the $\frac{3}{4}$-inch-long tack will be located. Turn the basket over and locate and drill a $\frac{1}{16}$-inch-diameter hole in the center of the outer edge, $\frac{1}{2}$ inch deep where the $\frac{1}{2}$-inch-long tack will be.

Cut the inside surface of the handle so the handle is cut free—this time keep the center of the line. Sand the outer surface, again still keeping all edges square.

Adjust the band saw table to 6 degrees and, starting from the largest, outer arc, cut around the basket keeping on the line all the way around. Cut until you get to the area marked, "stop cut." Shut off the band saw and carefully back your way out.

# Assembly

Turn the basket over and glue the center foot in place. Take care to glue it exactly across the center as shown. Locate and glue the two other $\frac{3}{4}$-×-$\frac{3}{4}$-square feet in place.

Temporarily add the handle with two finishing nails. Pull the basket up into shape and check the length of the handle ends. The ends should be cut so the basket is extended to its highest possible position. This will lock the basket in the open or highest position. Mark the handle ends and cut off to suit. Round one corner of the handle so it will start to "lock" the handles in place easier (see illustration).

Check that the handle locks in place correctly and adjust if necessary. Sand all over, and the basket is ready to finish.

Add a tight-fitting $\frac{3}{4}$-inch-long brass tack to one side of the handle and a $\frac{1}{2}$-inch-long brass tack to the other side of the handle. Check for a good, tight fit.

# Finishing

Add a coat of stain to suit if you wish, or simply apply a coat of Watco oil, tung oil, Deft, or some similar finish product of your choice.

Now you can impress people by telling them the basket is cut from ONE piece of wood.

# Bird Mobile

THIS PROJECT FEATURES A BIRD MOBILE CONSTRUCTED OF FIVE DIFFERENT PARTS: body, wings, fishline, dowel, and counterweight. The mobile will actually "fly" for a few moments after the weight is gently pulled down and released. The wings and body realistically simulate the bird in flight. This mobile is an excellent project for craft sales, as well as an ideal gift for that person who seems to have everything.

## Instructions

Select material for the wings and body of the bird. Thin solid wood is not the best choice because of the likelihood of it splitting or warping. Plywood would be your best choice, as it will stay flat. The more plywood layers the better. Multiple layers of high-quality plywood are best for finishing, especially around the edges. The material used must be smooth as possible.

The mobiles can be stained, wood burned, wire brushed, or textured. These different techniques enable you to produce a great variety of mobiles using the same basic overall design.

Start by laying out a pattern for the body and wings on a sheet of thick paper. Transfer the patterns to the wood, and cut out the number of parts as required.

If you plan to make more than one mobile, the bird bodies and wings should be cut out in stacks, so they all will be exactly the same size and shape. Cut the wood to general overall size. The tabs are added in the event you plan to mass-produce the mobile. Simply attach the patterns to the top board and nail the stack together on the suggested tabs using finish nails. For only one bird mobile simply omit the tabs. If tabs are used, cut into side of the tab as shown to simplify cutting off later.

Edge-sand the parts using whatever tools you have. If you are making multiple parts, sand all edges *before* separating the stack of parts. The overall shape of the bird has been designed to aid in sanding the edges.

Locate and drill the 1/16-inch-diameter string holes before separating the stack, so they will all be exactly the same. After all edge-sanding and drilling has been done, separate the stack by completing the tab cut. Discard the tabs and sand the remaining edges where the tabs were.

# Finishing and Assembly

Whatever finishing process you choose, do before assembling. Shown is a white painted bird with a black beak. If you are mass-producing these birds, it probably would be best to spray-paint them.

The support dowels are cut to the 9½-inch length, and the 1/16-inch-diameter hole is drilled in the ends as shown. It would be best to use a V-block to drill the holes, so the holes will be in-line and through the center.

Use monofiliment fishline to attach the wings to the body and to hang the mobile. It is best to use small glass beads between the body and wings as shown. Attach the wings to the body *loosely*. Do not pull the line too tight, as the bird will not fly correctly. Use a drop of superglue from a glue pen *through* the glass beads to secure the lines together.

The four lines are then strung from the ½-inch-diameter top ring, through the dowel, then down to the four holes in the wings as shown. A lead sinker is hung 16 inches or so below the bird's body as a counterweight. Experiment until you get the correct weight to balance the bird and allow it to "fly" uniform and correctly.

Now, sit back and watch everyone pull the string when they first see the bird. It is amazing how no one can resist pulling the string.

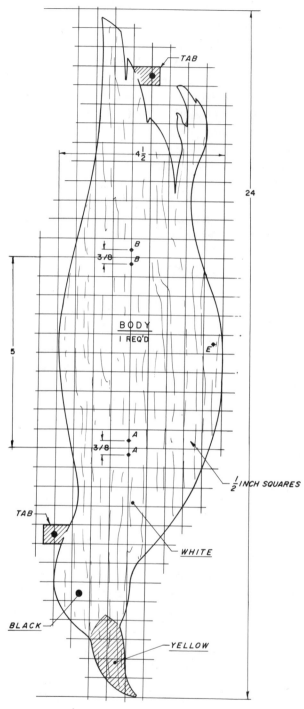

TAB

$4\frac{1}{2}$

24

B
B
3/8

BODY
1 REQ'D

5

E

A
A
3/8

$\frac{1}{2}$ INCH SQUARES

TAB

WHITE

BLACK

YELLOW

3/16 X $4\frac{1}{2}$ -- 24 LONG -- 1 REQUIRED

60

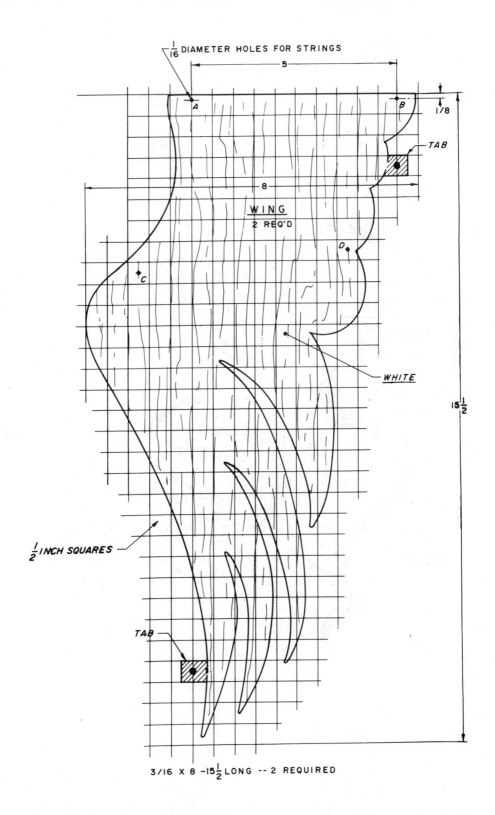

$\frac{1}{16}$ DIAMETER HOLES FOR STRINGS

5

A

B

1/8

TAB

8

WING
2 REQ'D

D

C

WHITE

15$\frac{1}{2}$

$\frac{1}{2}$ INCH SQUARES

TAB

3/16 X 8 –15$\frac{1}{2}$ LONG -- 2 REQUIRED

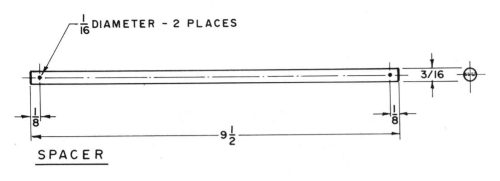

$\frac{1}{16}$ DIAMETER – 2 PLACES

3/16

$\frac{1}{8}$

$\frac{1}{8}$

$9\frac{1}{2}$

SPACER

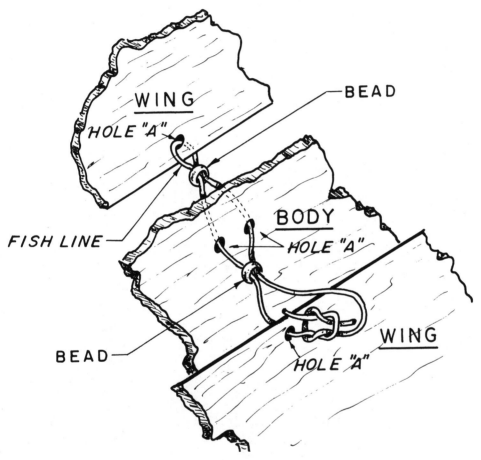

WING

HOLE "A"

BEAD

FISH LINE

BODY

HOLE "A"

BEAD

WING

HOLE "A"

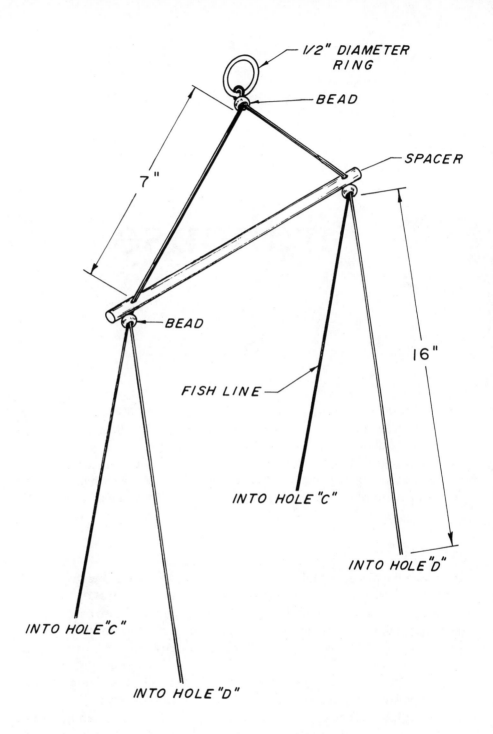

1/2" DIAMETER RING

BEAD

SPACER

7"

BEAD

FISH LINE

16"

INTO HOLE "C"

INTO HOLE "D"

INTO HOLE "C"

INTO HOLE "D"

# Birdhouse

AT ONE TIME OR ANOTHER *EVERY* WOODWORKER MAKES A BIRDHOUSE. IT SEEMS inevitable. You just can't get out of it. Well, here is still another version: a Victorian birdhouse. If you must build one, you might as well build one with style. This also makes an excellent, first project for your son, daughter, or grandchild that will help instill in them the value of working with their hands. The Victorian Birdhouse makes a great weekend project and will serve a good purpose.

## Instructions

Look over the plans carefully before starting. This project is straightforward and, except for a couple of 60-degree cuts, very simple to make.

Use a good grade of knot-free wood. You will have to purchase ¼-inch-thick material, resaw thicker material to size, or plane ½-inch-thick stock to size. This project does not take much wood so the cost will not be very much, even if you purchase it already ¼-inch thick.

Cut all parts to exact sizes as given in the Materials List, and number each so you know which part is which. Sand all parts on all surfaces. Draw a center line through the middle of the front and back pieces (part 1). Carefully lay out the 3½-inch bottom dimension and locate the widest point 3½ inches up and 5⅜ inches across as shown. Draw straight lines between all points and cut both the front and the back parts together so you will have an exact pair.

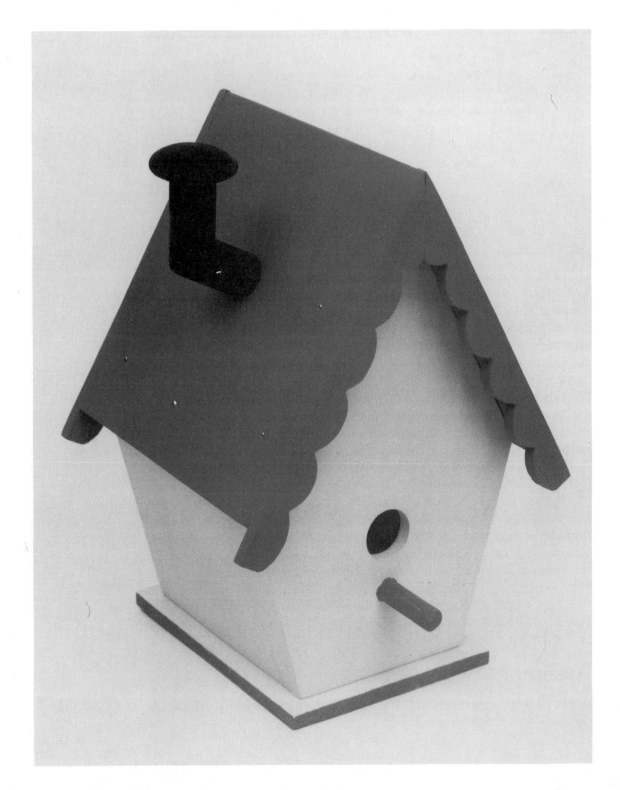

| Part No. | Name | Size | Req'd. |
|---|---|---|---|
| 1 | Front/Back | ¼ × 5⅜ – 8¼ Long | 2 |
| 2 | Side | ¼ × 4 – 4¼ Long | 2 |
| 3 | Bottom | ¼ × 4 – 5¼ Long | 1 |
| 4 | Roof | ¼ × 6½ – 5½ Long | 2 |
| 5 | Trim | ⅛ × ⅝ – 6½ Long | 4 |
| 6 | Support | ¼ Dia. – 6 Long | 1 |
| 7 | Pin | ⅛ Dia. – ⅝ Long | 1 |
| 8 | Chimney Base | ¾ Dia. – 1¼ Long | 1 |
| 9 | Chimney | ¾ Dia. – 1¾ Long | 1 |
| 10 | Chimney Cap | 1¼ Dia. – ¼ Long | 1 |

Cut the two rabbets in the edges ⅛ inch deep and ¼ inch wide along the two sides, so as to support both sides (part 2). Locate and drill the ¼-inch-diameter holes as shown in both the front and back. Separate and drill the 1-inch-diameter hole in the *front* piece only. (You may wish to drill a larger hole depending on what kind of a bird you wish to attract.)

Set the saw blade at 15 degrees and cut the bottom edge of the sides (part 2). Reset the blade to 45 degrees and cut the top edge. Be sure to maintain the 4-inch dimension.

Reset the saw blade at 30 degrees and, clamping the roof (part 4) to a vertical scrap piece of wood, run it through the saw *vertically*, using your fence as a guide. This should give you the required 60-degree angle (90 degrees minus 30 degrees). Locate and drill a ⅛-inch-diameter hole in *one* roof for the pin (part 7). This pin locates and holds the chimney in place.

The four pieces of trim (part 5) are only ⅛ inch thick, so the ¼-inch-thick material will have to be resawed to obtain the ⅛-inch thickness. Tack or tape the four pieces of trim together, and draw the scallop design on the top piece. This does not have to be exact. Cut them all out together and while they are still attached together, sand all edges. Separate the parts and sand the side surfaces.

Cut a ¾-inch-diameter dowel as shown for the chimney (part 8 and 9). The chimney hood is cut from any scrap about 1¼-inch-diameter and about ¼ inch thick.

# Assembly

Dry-fit all parts to ensure correct and tight fits between all joints. Adjust any part now that is not exact.

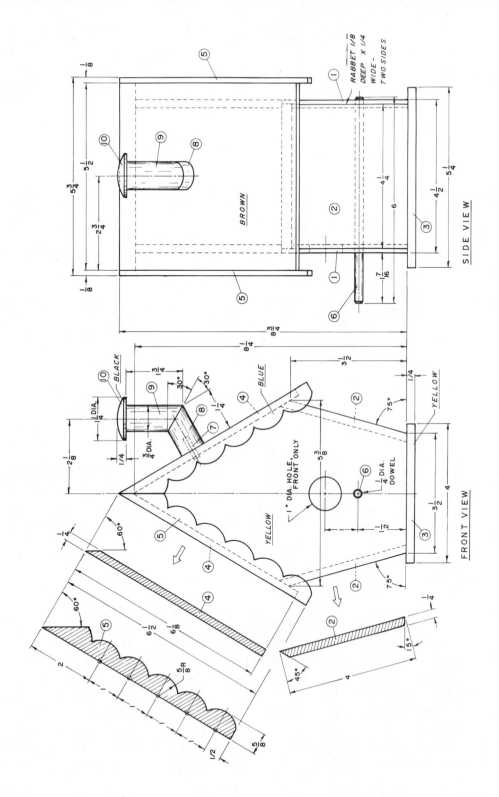

SIDE VIEW

FRONT VIEW

RABBET 1/8
DEEP X 1/4
WIDE—
TWO SIDES

BROWN

BLACK

BLUE

YELLOW

YELLOW

1" DIA. HOLE,
FRONT ONLY

1/4 DIA.
DOWEL

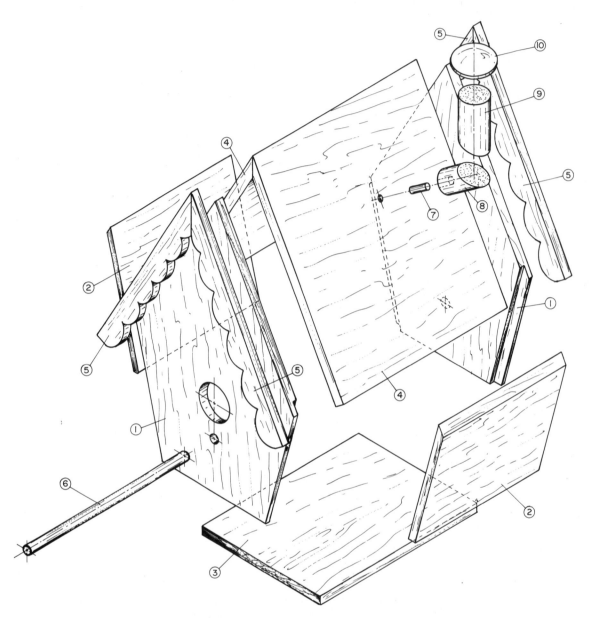

Glue or tack the front and back (part 1) to the sides (part 2). I chose to tack this one together with short brass brads, but glue would work just as well. Sand all surfaces, but keep the corners sharp. You may wish to paint the house at this time, as it is easier to do while still in pieces.

Next, attach the support (part 6) to the house, and glue in place. Then glue or tack the two roofs (part 4) together at the peak and let set. After the glue sets, sand the roof at the peak and along the edges. You may wish to paint the roof before assembling with the house walls. Glue or tack the roof to the house walls. Be sure to center the roof on the house.

Glue the chimney parts, 8, 9, and 10 together as shown and let it set. Afterwards, drill a ⅛-inch-diameter hole in the base of the chimney (part 8) for the pin (part 7). Paint the chimney assembly at this time.

The bottom (part 3) should be held in place by screws so it can be removed to clean out the birdhouse at a later date. Paint the bottom (part 3) and center it under the walls of the house. Use six small brass screws to hold it in place. You may want to predrill the six holes so the wood will not split.

Attach the four trim pieces (part 5). Try to get a good, tight fit at the peak.

The chimney is now ready to be installed. Simply glue it in place, but be sure it is pointed straight up when the glue sets.

## Finishing

Because this is a Victorian house, let your imagination run wild. Paint various trim here and there for authenticity. Now, hang the birdhouse with two eyelets and a wire and your birdhouse is ready for occupancy.

# Wooden Basket
# with Handle

THE POPULARITY OF BASKETS HERE IN NEW ENGLAND IS AMAZING. EVERY ANtique shop, every crafts show, every flea market, and most yard sales have baskets for sale. Adult evening classes and most colleges offer classes on basket-weaving. Here, in the small New Hampshire town of 5,500 people where I live, are two large basket manufacturing companies.

Baskets come in all shapes and sizes and are made of all kinds of materials. This basket is still *another* style, made entirely of wood. It can be made of most any kind of wood and perhaps would be a good way for you to use up some of your scrap wood. This particular basket can be extended longer than the 16-inch size if desired. The largest pieces are the ends (part 1) and the bottom (part 2). Both are really not very large, so this project really does not require much material. This basket can be made in an evening or so.

## Instructions

As with any project, look over the plans carefully before you begin so you fully understand how it all goes together and are sure you have enough materials.

Start by cutting the two end pieces (part 1) to overall size, and temporarily tack the two ends together with two small finishing nails. Lightly draw a vertical center line across the top board, as illustrated on the detail drawing of part 1. Carefully locate the centers of the four ¼-inch-diameter holes on both sides of the center line. Measure over from the center line and up from the center line, using the given dimensions. Drill the ¼-inch-diameter holes down through

---

**MATERIALS LIST**

---

| Part No. | Name | Size | Req'd. |
|:---:|:---|:---|:---:|
| 1 | End | $3/4 \times 6\,3/4$ – 12 Long | 2 |
| 2 | Bottom | $3/4 \times 8$ – $16\,1/4$ Long | 1 |
| 3 | Handle | $3/4 \times 1\,1/4$ – $6\,5/8$ Long | 2 |
| 4 | Side – Wide | $1/4 \times 1\,1/2$ – $16\,1/4$ Long | 4 |
| 5 | Side – Narrow | $1/4 \times 1\,5/16$ – $16\,1/4$ Long | 4 |
| 6 | Bar | $5/8$ Dia. 18 Long | 1 |
| 7 | Foot – Plug | $1/2$ Dia. | 4 |
| 8 | Screw – Roundhead | No. 8 – $1\,1/4$ Long | 2 |

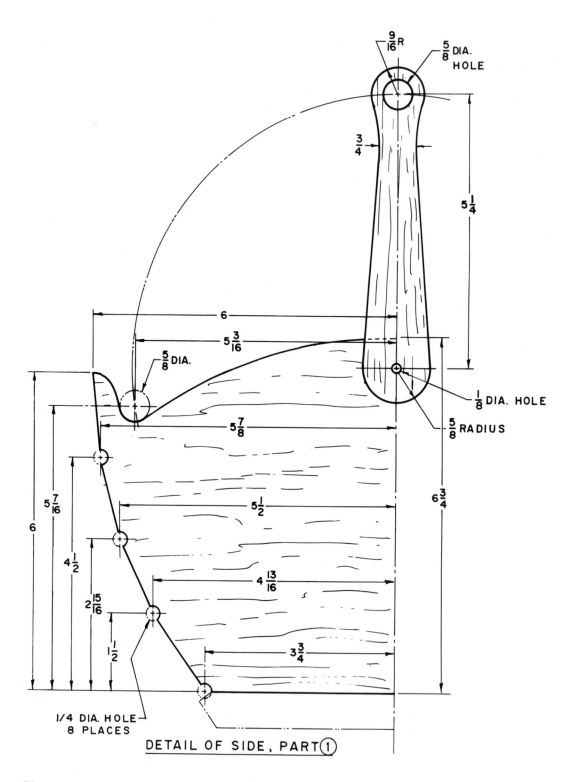

$\frac{9}{16}$R

$\frac{5}{8}$ DIA. HOLE

$\frac{3}{4}$

$5\frac{1}{4}$

6

$5\frac{3}{16}$

$\frac{5}{8}$ DIA.

$\frac{1}{8}$ DIA. HOLE

$\frac{5}{8}$ RADIUS

$5\frac{7}{8}$

$6\frac{3}{4}$

$5\frac{7}{16}$

$5\frac{1}{2}$

6

$4\frac{1}{2}$

$4\frac{13}{16}$

$2\frac{15}{16}$

$1\frac{1}{2}$

$3\frac{3}{4}$

1/4 DIA. HOLE
8 PLACES

DETAIL OF SIDE, PART ①

*both* pieces of wood. Locate and draw the ⅝-inch-diameter holes on both sides of the center line as noted.

Next, locate and drill a 1/16-inch-diameter hole for the screw that holds the handle assembly in place. It is located on the center line and down from the top 9/16 inch, as illustrated. Drilling the holes with the two parts tacked together ensures that both parts will be identical.

Draw *straight* lines from the centers of the ¼-inch-diameter holes to form the sides of the basket. Sketch the top surface of the basket, starting from the top center and curving down to the ⅝-inch-diameter holes on both sides as illustrated. Cut the ends (part 1) with the two parts still tacked together. Sand all edges of the two ends, then separate the ends and sand the four surfaces.

Cut the bottom board (part 2) to size per the given dimensions. Trim the two edges with the saw set at 40 degrees as illustrated.

In making the handle (part 3), rough-cut the two pieces and, as was done with the ends, tack them together. Locate and drill the ⅝-inch-diameter hole through both parts and locate and drill a ⅛-inch-diameter hole through both parts for the handle assembly. Lay out the outer shape of the handle and cut out. Sand the edges of the two handles with the two parts still tacked together. Keep all edges sharp.

The rest of the basket is very simple: cut all remaining parts to size as noted on the Materials List and sand all over. Again, keep all edges sharp.

## Assembly

Glue and nail the sides (part 1) to the bottom (part 2), leaving a ⅛-inch overhang on both ends. Take care to keep everything square. Glue and nail the side parts (parts 4 and 5). Line up the sides with the ¼-inch drilled holes as a guide. Be careful when nailing the two TOP side parts in place at the ends, as part 1 is a little weak up near the ⅝-inch-diameter holes.

Attach the handles (part 3) to the bar (part 6), keeping everything square. It is a good idea to temporarily screw the handle assembly to the ends before the glue sets to ensure a good, tight fit.

After the glue sets, remove the handle assembly. Drill four ½-inch-diameter holes, ¼ inch deep into the bottom board as illustrated, to accept the four feet, or plugs (part 7). Glue the four feet in place. Sand all over to remove any rough edges.

## Finishing

Either stain or paint your new basket with your favorite brand. Follow the instructions given on the can.

Now your basket can be set along all the other baskets. In years to come perhaps *your* basket will be a collectors item.

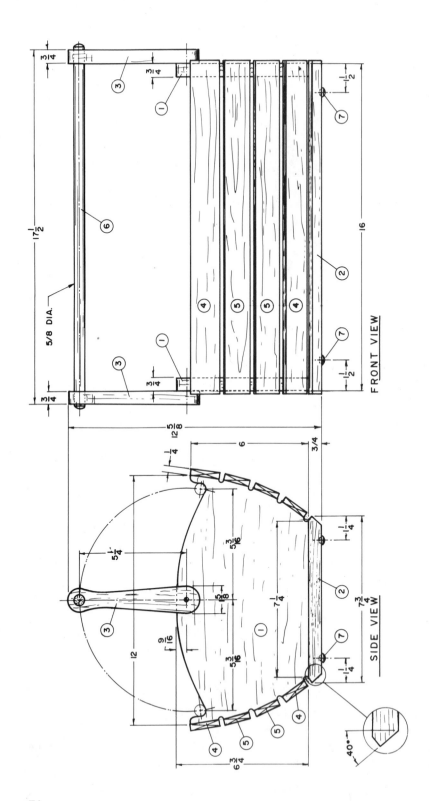

FRONT VIEW

SIDE VIEW

$17\frac{1}{2}$

$12\frac{5}{8}$

5/8 DIA.

16

$\frac{3}{4}$

$\frac{3}{4}$

$\frac{3}{4}$

$\frac{3}{4}$

$\frac{1}{2}$

$\frac{1}{2}$

$5\frac{1}{4}$

$5\frac{3}{16}$

$5\frac{3}{16}$

$7\frac{1}{4}$

$7\frac{3}{4}$

$\frac{5}{8}$

$\frac{9}{16}$

12

6

3/4

$1\frac{1}{4}$

$1\frac{1}{4}$

$\frac{1}{4}$

$6\frac{3}{4}$

40°

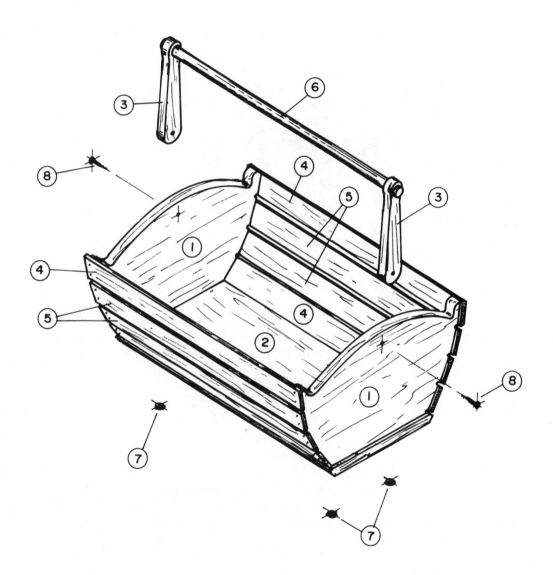

# New Hampshire Doormat

THIS IS A SIMPLE PROJECT THAT WILL GIVE YOU A CHANCE TO USE UP ALL THOSE scrap pieces of wood that usually fill up a shop. You know, all that stuff that is too good to throw out, but not really good enough to use. It can be made in an afternoon and will be a very useful product—especially if you have kids around.

## Instructions

From your best scraps, cut the four border strips (parts 1 and 2). From your second-best scraps, cut the seven baseboards (part 3).

The rest is cut into strips $3/4 \times 3/4$ inch $\times$ whatever lengths you have available. The cutting chart lists the minimum material you will need to complete one doormat assembly. I simply cut up scrap until I thought I had enough strips. It is better to cut more strips than you actually need, so you can eliminate material with any knots or imperfections.

## Assembly

Tack the seven baseboards (part 7) to two "real" pieces of scrap, taking care to keep the baseboards parallel and exactly 2 inches apart (see Step 1). Take care also to keep all the ends all even.

**━━━━━━━━━━━━━━━━━━━━━MATERIALS LIST━━━━━━━━━━━━━━━━━━━━━**

| Part No. | Name | Size | Req'd. |
|---|---|---|---|
| 1 | Border – Long | ¾ × 1½ – 35¾ Long | 2 |
| 2 | Border – Short | ¾ × 1½ – 17¼ Long | 2 |
| 3 | Baseboard | ¾ × ¾ – 34¼ Long | 7 |
| * 4 | Floor | ¾ × ¾ – 36 Long | 5 |
| * 5 | Floor | ¾ × ¾ – 28 Long | 8 |
| * 6 | Floor | ¾ × ¾ – 18 Long | 4 |
| * 7 | Floor | ¾ × ¾ – 11 Long | 6 |
| 8 | Nail – Finish | 6d | 100 |

\* About 48 Feet Total.

Turn the assembly over and, starting with a longer floor piece (part 5, the shaded floorboard on drawing), nail the first board in place (see step 2). Use a finishing nail, no longer than 1¼ inch long, for this. Refer to the TOP VIEW of the drawing. Place it in, on the baseboard (part 7), 4⅜ inches from the top-left side as shown. Then line up the other with the bottom-right corner. This should give you the required 30-degree angle. As the spaces between all flooring is exactly ¾ inch, use an extra floor piece for a spacer. Working either direction, nail all floor pieces (parts 4, 5, 6, and 7), in place. Allow them all to overlap the baseboards on all sides and ends as shown in step 2.

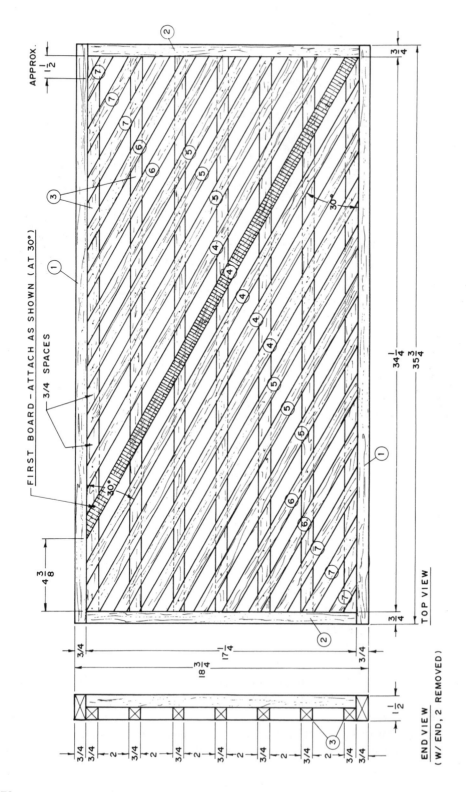

FIRST BOARD—ATTACH AS SHOWN ( AT 30°)

3/4 SPACES

APPROX. 1½

30°

30°

4⅜

34¼
35¾

3/4

3/4

3/4

17¼

18¾

TOP VIEW

1½
1½

3/4
3/4
2
3/4
2
3/4
2
3/4
2
3/4
2
3/4
2
3/4
3/4

END VIEW
( W/ END, 2 REMOVED )

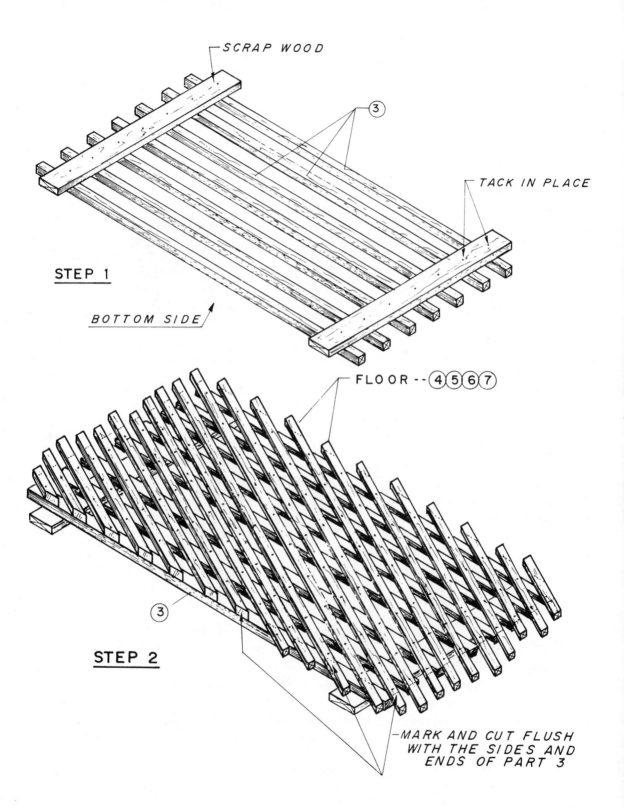

SCRAP WOOD

③

TACK IN PLACE

STEP 1

BOTTOM SIDE

FLOOR -- ④⑤⑥⑦

③

STEP 2

MARK AND CUT FLUSH
WITH THE SIDES AND
ENDS OF PART 3

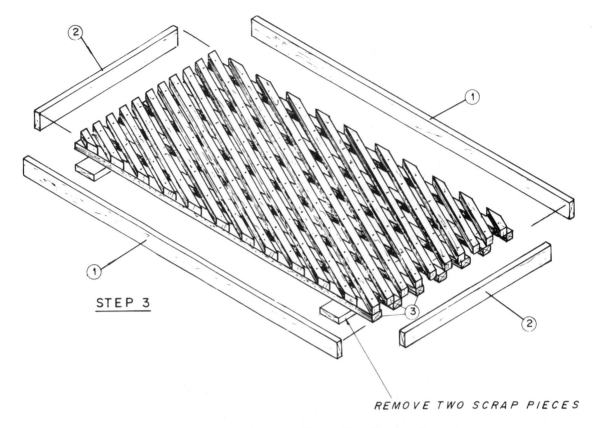

STEP 3

*REMOVE TWO SCRAP PIECES*

Very carefully, draw two horizontal cutting lines, directly over the outer baseboards (part no. 3), onto the floorboards. Up from the *ends* of the baseboards (part 3), draw two vertical cutting lines on the floorboards.

Turn the assembly over and remove the two pieces of scrap wood. Add the two short border boards (part 2) to the assembly. Be sure the ends line up correctly. Add the final two long border boards (part 1). This completes the assembly of the doormat.

# Finishing

Set all nails slightly, fill with putty if you wish, and sand all over. You can finish this doormat any way you wish, using any finish you think will be appropriate for your house and its style. For a contemporary house, a painted finish would be good. For a traditional house, just leave it unfinished and let it weather.

Now go out and find three or four kids with the dirtiest shoes imaginable and try out your new, authentic, New Hampshire doormat.

# Lawn Chair

L AWN CHAIRS COME IN ALL SHAPES AND SIZES. THIS ONE IS ADJUSTABLE AND IS stored within itself. It takes up an area of only 5 inches deep, 18 inches wide, and 39 inches long. It can be made of most any kind of hardwood and really look nice in most any lawn setting. Because they fold up into such small sizes they are also portable, and can be used at that Little League baseball game or wherever you wish.

## Instructions

On a piece of heavy paper, 5×40 inches, draw a 1-inch grid. Carefully lay out the outer rail shape (part 1) on the paper as shown.

To make the two outer rails, temporarily tack or tape together two pieces of straight-grained hardwood, 5 inches wide and 40 inches long.

Transfer the pattern to the top piece of wood, and cut out the two pieces at the same time. Keep just *outside* of the layout lines. While the parts are still attached, sand down to the line on the edges, all the way around.

Separate the parts and sand the surfaces, keeping all edges sharp. Be sure to mark the bottom ends. This completes the two outer rails.

To make the two inner rails (part 2), temporarily tack or tape two more pieces of straight-grained hardwood together and, using one of the outer rails as a pattern, transfer the shape to the top piece of wood. The inner rails must be $\frac{1}{16}$ inch smaller *all the way around*, so very carefully cut out the two inner

rails keeping just *on* the line. After the two inner rails have been cut out, scribe a new line about $\frac{1}{32}$ inch all around and, while the parts are still attached, sand down to this new line. This should put you about $\frac{1}{16}$ inch smaller, all the way around, than the outer rail.

Separate the part and sand the surfaces, keeping all edges sharp at this time. Mark the bottom ends. This completes the two inner rails.

Next, cut the long and short slats (parts 3 and 4) to size and sand all over, keeping all edges square at this time. Drill and countersink the holes in the

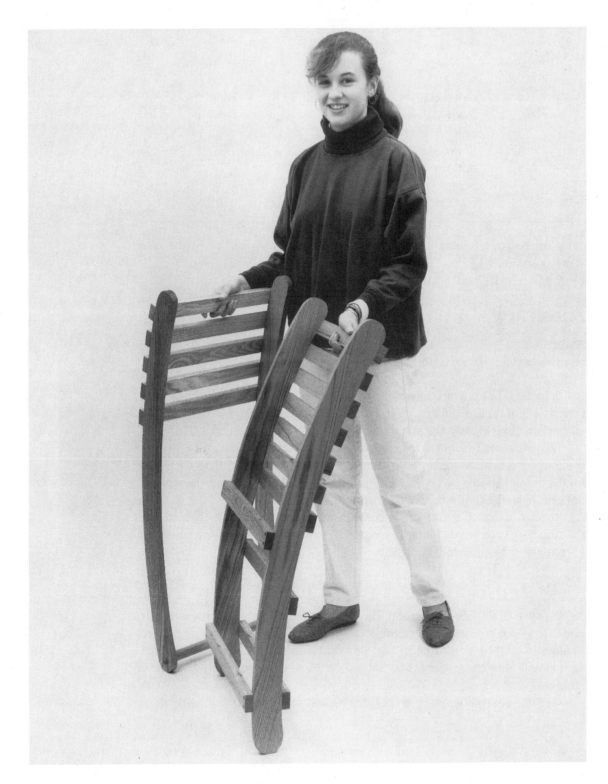

| Part No. | Name | Size | Req'd. |
|----------|------|------|--------|
| 1 | Outer Rail | ¾ × 6 – 40 Long | 2 |
| 2 | Inner Rail | ¾ × 6 – 40 Long | 2 |
| 3 | Long Slat | ¾ × 1⅝ – 18 Long | 11 |
| 4 | Short Slat | ¾ × 1⅝ – 16¼ Long | 5 |
| 5 | Bottom Brace | 1″ Dia. – 16¼ Long | 1 |
| 6 | Screw – Flathead | No. 8 – 2″ Long | 64 |

ends as shown. Use a drilling jig if possible so all holes will be in the *exact* same positions.

Cut a 1-inch-diameter dowel 16¼ inches long, to make up part 5.

# Assembly

Assemble the two inner rails (part 2) with the bottom brace (part 5) and the short slats (part 4). Space the short slats approximately as dimensioned, 1⅛ inch apart.

*Important:* Keep everything square as you go. if you plan to make more than 4 or 5 of these lawn chairs, it may pay to make up an assembling jig so all parts will be exactly the same and *square.*

Assemble the two outer rails (part 1) with the longer slats (part 3). Space the longer slats approximately as dimensioned, 1 inch apart. The *center* slat on the bottom should be positioned to suit after final assembly so this slat can later be moved slightly one way or the other.

Be sure to use brass or plated screws, so the screws will not rust and ruin the finish of your lawn chairs. If you wish, you could countersink and plug all screws to hide them completely.

# Finishing

As this lawn chair slides inside of itself, it would be best if this project is stained and oiled—not painted. Natural or any light stain would be nice and it will mellow in time to a nice hue. If you do want a color, use a color stain coat, as this will not show wear marks caused by moving the chair in and out of storage.

Get out your sunglasses, a cool drink, and enjoy your new lawn chair.

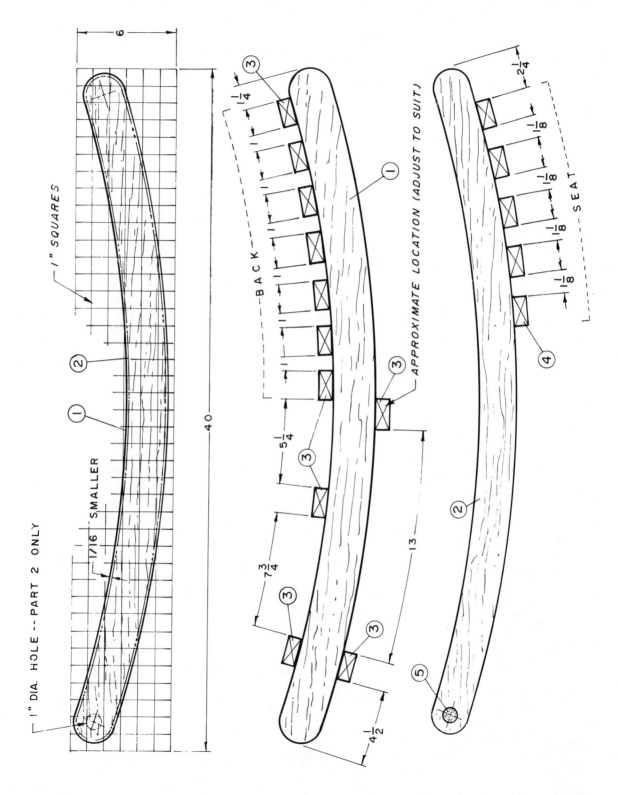

1" SQUARES

1" DIA. HOLE -- PART 2 ONLY

1/16 SMALLER

6

40

BACK

SEAT

APPROXIMATE LOCATION (ADJUST TO SUIT)

$2\frac{1}{4}$

$1\frac{1}{8}$

$1\frac{1}{8}$

$1\frac{1}{8}$

$1\frac{1}{8}$

$5\frac{1}{4}$

$7\frac{3}{4}$

$1\frac{1}{4}$

13

$4\frac{1}{2}$

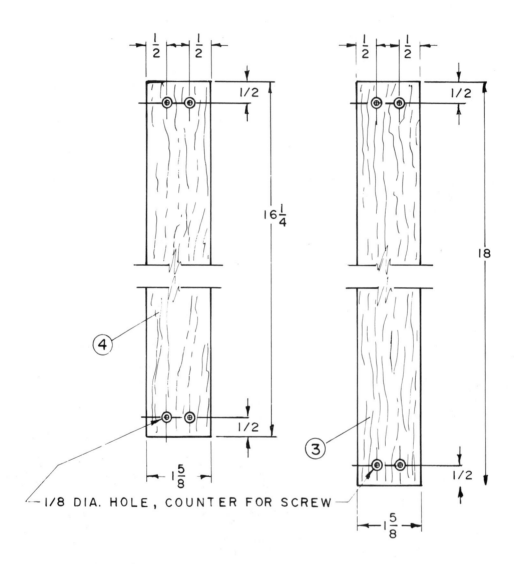

$\frac{1}{2}$ | $\frac{1}{2}$

$\frac{1}{2}$

$16\frac{1}{4}$

④

$1\frac{5}{8}$

$\frac{1}{2}$

─1/8 DIA. HOLE, COUNTER FOR SCREW─

$\frac{1}{2}$ | $\frac{1}{2}$

$\frac{1}{2}$

18

③

$\frac{1}{2}$

$1\frac{5}{8}$

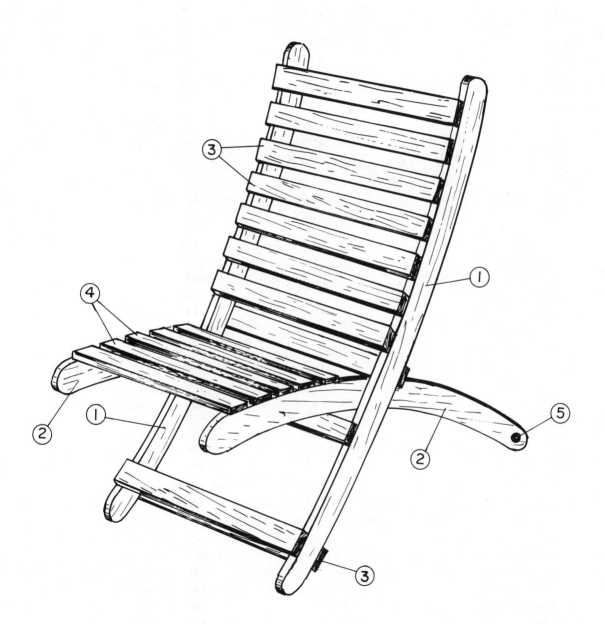

# Twig Settee

TWIG FURNITURE IS EXPERIENCING A COMEBACK IN POPULARITY. THE SETTEE design illustrated in this book was made in Appalachia back in the 1930s. The chair plans presented here differ from the original only in the curved brace under the chair frame. The originals had straight braces cut at a 45-degree angle. I felt the curved brace would be more graceful and, as an added benefit, easier to cut.

## Instructions

Choose wood that is limber and bendable. Although wood choice may be more a matter of availability than the ideal, several characteristics are important. If the twigs are to be peeled for the best appearance, experiment with different species first. Choose a wood that will not be gummy and or resinous to clothes. Try to get a light and strong wood that will not split with nails.

Cut a quantity of wood no thicker than your wrist, tapering down to the size of the little finger. The back and bent seat will require branches up to 6 feet long, and as straight as can be found.

I found cutting the parts to length with a bow saw safe and easy. The branches were extended over the edge of the porch and cut in a kneeling position. If you are using common shop equipment, you should observe several safety practices. Cutting stock that is round and irregular is not a safe practice on the table saw. The stock may shift and roll and nasty kickbacks are possible.

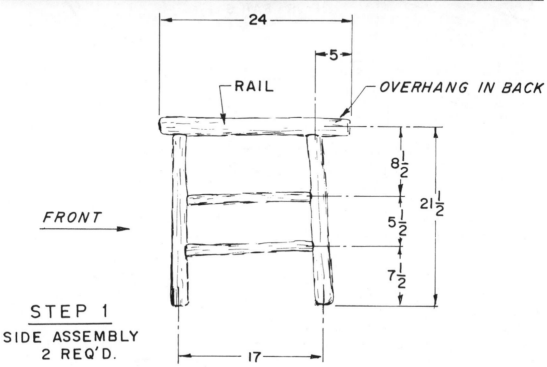

RAIL

24

5

OVERHANG IN BACK

$8\frac{1}{2}$

$5\frac{1}{2}$

$7\frac{1}{2}$

$21\frac{1}{2}$

FRONT →

## STEP 1
### SIDE ASSEMBLY
### 2 REQ'D.

17

If the branches are trimmed on the band saw, a V block should be used to keep the wood from rolling and breaking the blade.

# Assembly

The chair parts are cut and assembled in five steps illustrated.

**Step One**. Nail two end frames together. Be certain the wood used is no thicker than your wrist; otherwise, the furniture may appear too klunky when finished.

**Step Two**. The end frames are nailed together to form the basic frame. Note the chair is six inches narrower in the back than the front.

**Step Three**. Nail on three supports (A,B,C) for the back and seat parts. Part C on the armrest must be nailed slightly behind the rear legs to provide lean to the back of the chair. Let parts B and C hang out six inches from the chair frame on either end. They will be trimmed to size after step four.

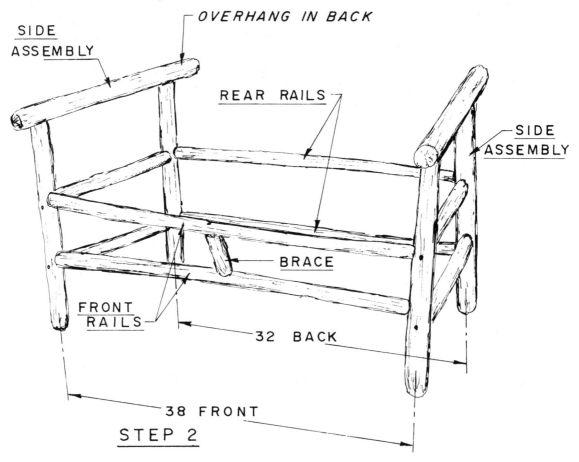

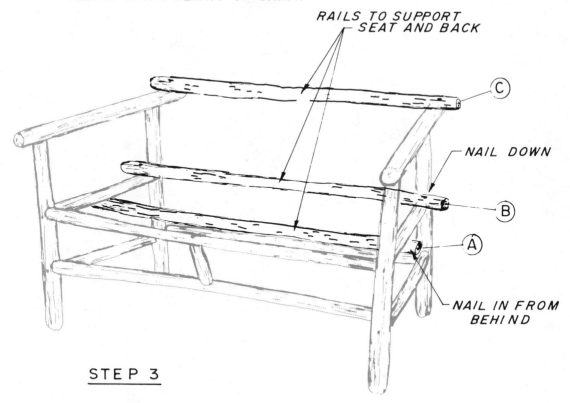

NOTE: POSITION C, BACK OF LEG TO
ALLOW BACK SLANT OF CHAIR

RAILS TO SUPPORT
SEAT AND BACK

C

NAIL DOWN

B

A

NAIL IN FROM
BEHIND

## STEP 3

**Step Four**. The back bows (3) and a brace is added under the chair. Choose the back bow parts carefully. They must be straight and limber. If the butt of each piece has a slight crook, they secure to the chair easier. Nail the butt end first and bend the small end down to be secured. Reverse direction on the next bow. The back bow parts nail *behind* part B and in *front* of part A. Then trim off the excess from part A and B that hangs out beyond the back bow parts. Finally a brace is bent and nailed under the front frame of the chair to add rigidity to the frame.

**Step Five**. Nail part D in place. Locate part D so that the seat branches will butt into part D and then be bent down and nailed to the frame and eventually to the back bow. The seat branches are next nailed in place. The seat branches should be selected to be as close to the same thickness as possible. Note that the seat twigs are close together on part B. They spread apart slightly over the length of part A and fan out gracefully over the back bows. Space the seat parts close enough for comfort and nail first in part B, then spread to cover the longer part A. Finally nail the seat parts to the back bows.

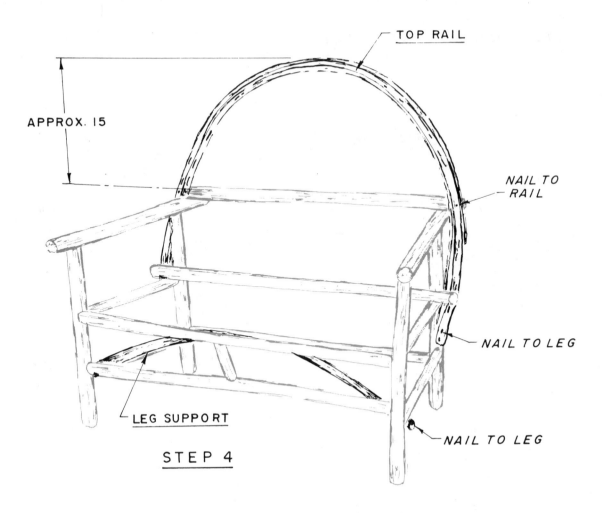

TOP RAIL

APPROX. 15

NAIL TO RAIL

NAIL TO LEG

NAIL TO LEG

LEG SUPPORT

STEP 4

Nail two boards under the chair to the legs. This will keep the side frames from spreading apart over the years.

For the final fitting sit in the chair with a pocket knife and whittle off knots and protrusions that feel uncomfortable. Whittle chamfers on the armrests and parts that show. Finally, perhaps to settle future arguments, whittle your name and the date the chair was made!

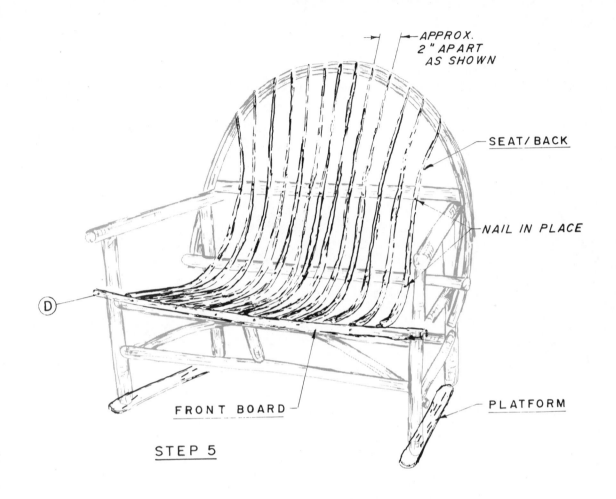

APPROX.
2" APART
AS SHOWN

SEAT/BACK

NAIL IN PLACE

D

FRONT BOARD

PLATFORM

STEP 5

93

# III

# *Toy Projects*

# Child's Hutch

THIS TOY HUTCH WAS FOUND ON THE TOP OF A HEAP OF TRASH IN A DUMP IN northern Vermont. Except for broken glass and two cracked door panels, it was complete and in excellent condition. It seemed a shame to let it rot there and, having a 6-year-old daughter, I brought it home. I thought she would like it the moment I saw it. I was right, and now, even after 8 years she still makes good use of it. In years to come, I'll bet my daughter will give this toy hutch to her daughter.

As the small 1-×-2¼-inch celluloid name tab on the back of the top trim indicates, the hutch was commercially manufactured. The tab reads:

Manufactured for:
*F.A.O. Schwarz*
*TOYS*
Fifth Avenue and Thirty First Street
New York

Because of the preplastic celluloid tab, I would estimate the hutch to have been made between 1920 and 1930. Perhaps a reader could shed some light on this.

## Instructions

The hutch is built of two complete assemblies held together by two flathead wood screws. Construction of the top assembly and the bottom assembly

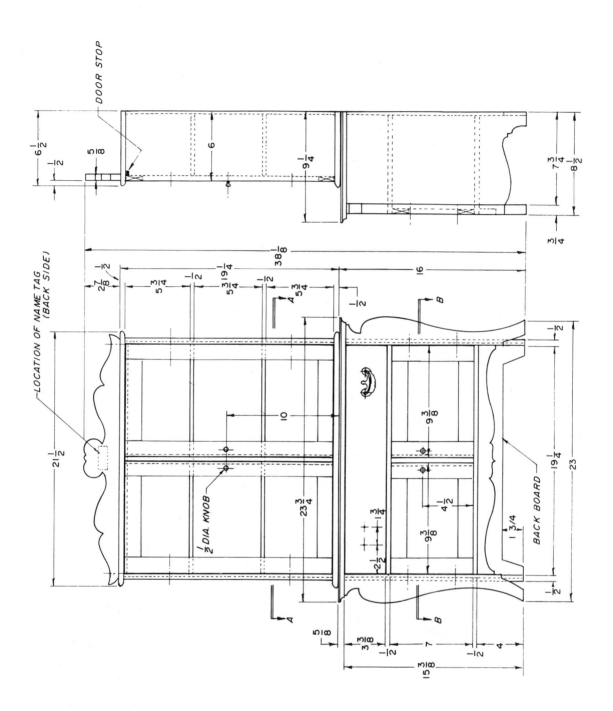

DOOR STOP

LOCATION OF NAME TAG
(BACK SIDE)

$\frac{1}{2}$ DIA. KNOB

BACK BOARD

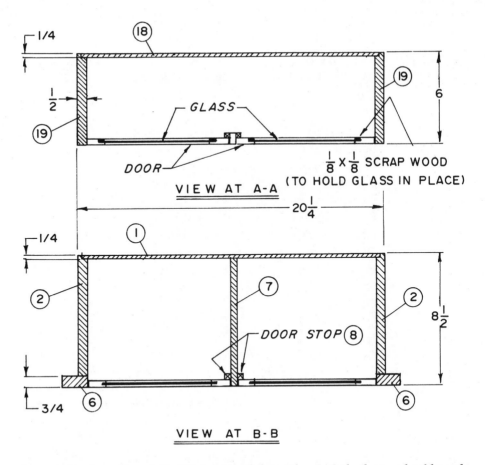

VIEW AT A-A

GLASS

DOOR

$\frac{1}{8} \times \frac{1}{8}$ SCRAP WOOD
(TO HOLD GLASS IN PLACE)

DOOR STOP ⑧

VIEW AT B-B

is very simple, with only butt joints used throughout. Only the two backboards were rabbeted into the side panels. All joints were glued and nailed together with small finishing nails.

As with any project, carefully cut all boards to size per the Materials List. Some boards will have to be glued up to size and others will have to be planned to correct thickness. All size dimensions have been carefully checked and rechecked, but it is a good idea to dry-fit all parts, to recheck correctness of fit before final assembly.

## Assembly and Finishing

After putting the two assemblies together, sand all over and seal before applying the finish coat of paint. The hutch can be painted any color, but the original was painted a satin white. Because this will be used by a child, it would be a good idea to paint it with a nontoxic paint. For safety sake, in place of the glass, it is recommended that two pieces of plexiglass be used. This will not be noticed after assembly.

## MATERIALS LIST/BOTTOM ASSEMBLY

| Part No. | Name | Size | Req'd. |
|---|---|---|---|
| 1 | Back | ¼ × 19¾ – 15⅜ Long | 1 |
| 2 | Side | ½ × 7¾ – 15⅜ Long | 2 |
| 3 | Shelf | ½ × 8¼ – 19¼ Long | 2 |
| 4 | Top | ⅝ × 9¼ – 23¾ Long | 1 |
| 5 | Bottom Trim | ½ × 1½ – 19¼ Long | 1 |
| 6 | Leg | ½ × 2½ – 15⅜ Long | 2 |
| 7 | Divider | ½ × 7 – 8¼ Long | 1 |
| 8 | Door Stop | ⅜ × ⅜ – 7 Long | 2 |
| 9 | Drawer Front | ⅝ × 3⅜ – 19¼ Long | 1 |
| 10 | Drawer Back | ⅜ × 3¹⁄₁₆ – 18½ Long | 1 |
| 11 | Drawer Side | ⅜ × 3⅜ – 8 Long | 2 |
| 12 | Drawer Bottom | ⅛ × 8 – 19 Long | 1 |
| 13 | Drawer Side | ⅜ × 1¼ – 7 Long | 4 |
| 14 | Door T/B | ⅜ × 1¼ – 7⅜ Long | 4 |
| 15 | Door Panel | ⅛ × 5 – 7⅜ Long | 2 |
| * 16 | Hinge | | 4 |
| * 17 | Drawer Pull | 1¾ Hole | 2 |

## MATERIALS LIST/TOP ASSEMBLY

| Part No. | Name | Size | Req'd. |
|---|---|---|---|
| 18 | Back | ¼ × 19¾ – 18¼ Long | 1 |
| 19 | Side | ½ × 6 – 18¼ Long | 2 |
| 20 | Shelf | ½ × 5⅜ – 19¼ Long | 2 |
| 21 | Top/Bottom | ½ × 6½ – 21½ Long | 2 |
| 22 | Top Trim | ⅝ × 3 – 20 Long | 1 |
| 23 | Door Spacer | ½ × ¾ – 18¼ Long | 1 |
| 24 | Door Stop | ⅜ × ¾ – 19¼ Long | 1 |
| 25 | Door Side | ⅜ × 1¼ – 18¼ Long | 4 |
| 26 | Door T/B | ⅜ × 1¼ – 7⅞ Long | 4 |
| 27 | Glass | ³⁄₃₂ Tk. 7⅜ × 16 Long | 2 |
| * 28 | Hinge | | 4 |
| * 29 | Knob – Brass | ½ Dia. | 4 |
| 30 | Screw – Flathead | No. 8 – 1" Long | 4 |

* *The Woodworkers' Store*: No. D3018 Hinge, No. D3038 Knob, No. E8200 Drawer Pull, No. D3601 Bullet Catches.

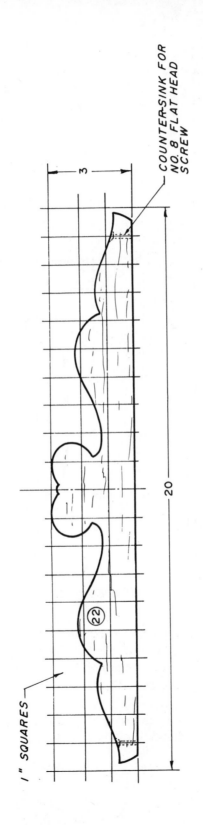

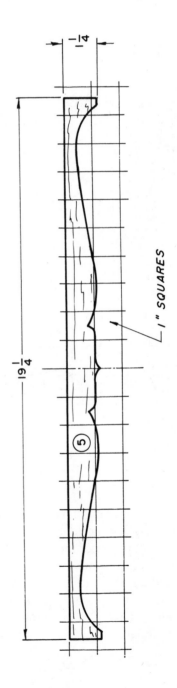

COUNTER-SINK FOR
NO. 8 FLAT HEAD
SCREW

3

20

22

1" SQUARES

$1\frac{1}{4}$

$19\frac{1}{4}$

5

1" SQUARES

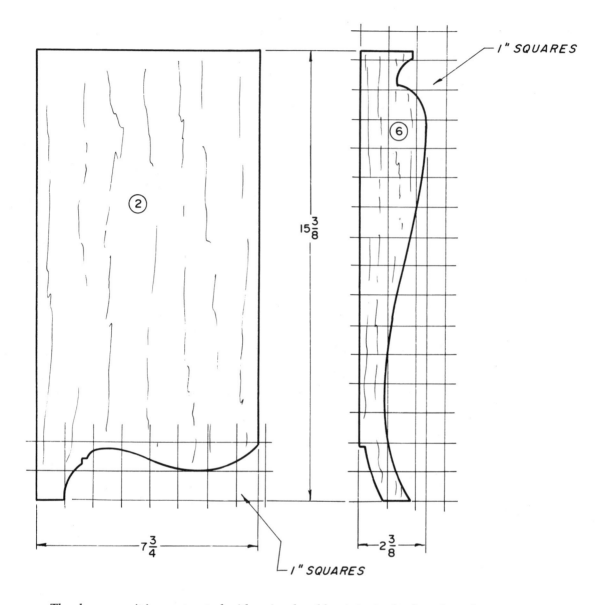

1" SQUARES

6

2

$15\frac{3}{8}$

$7\frac{3}{4}$

$2\frac{3}{8}$

1" SQUARES

The drawer unit is constructed with a simple rabbet joint in the front board and a simple ⅛-inch dado along the sides for the bottom board. The front board was the only part of the drawer assembly that was painted. Very inexpensive drawer pulls were used; in fact, very inexpensive hardware was used throughout the hutch.

Door stops were simply large-headed brass tacks left high enough to cause friction and hold the doors closed. Small bullet-type catches would work a little better today.

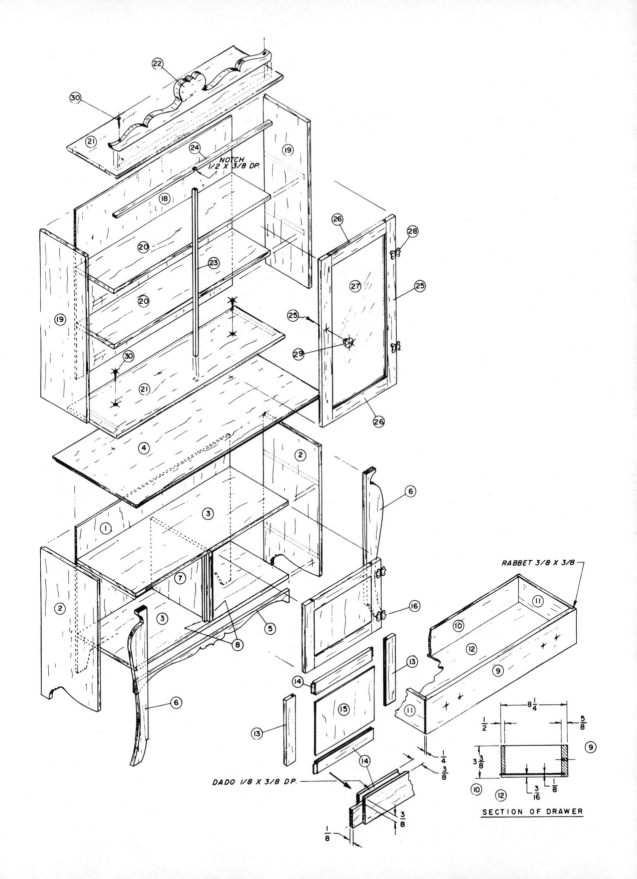

NOTCH 1/2 X 3/8 DP.

RABBET 3/8 X 3/8

DADO 1/8 X 3/8 DP.

SECTION OF DRAWER

When the two assemblies are finished and painted, line up the two back surfaces and center the top assembly upon the bottom assembly and screw the parts together with two, 1-inch-long flathead screws.

You now have a piece of furniture that may become an heirloom to be passed down for many years to come.

# Toy Truck

IN A WORLD OF PLASTIC TOYS, THIS WOODEN TRUCK WILL BE A WELCOME CHANGE. This toy truck will give kids of today a chance to see and, more importantly, to get a *feel* for the toys of yesterday. I am 52 years old. I grew up in the "preplastic era" and can vividly remember caring parents or grandparents making toys like this one for their children. Toys like this came in all shapes and sizes and it was easy for a child to have a whole fleet of trucks, similar to this one.

## Instructions

Instructions for this project are very simple. As most of the parts are ¼ inch thick, I recommend that you either purchase your wood to correct thickness, or plane down to size yourself.

Cut all parts to the basic size per the Materials List provided.

Cut the 45-degree chamfer for the engine (part 2). Notch and cut the window and back pieces (parts 5 and 6). Cut to shape the cab sides (part 7) and the grill (part 10). Locate and drill the ⅜-and ⅛-inch-diameter holes as illustrated. Lay out and cut out the two fenders (part 3) as illustrated. Remember, you must make a *pair* of fenders—a right-hand and a left-hand set. The only difference is in the location of the two ³⁄₁₆-×-¼-inch notches.

Next, locate and drill the two ⅛-inch-diameter holes in the bumper (part 16) so they line up with the holes in the grill (part 10).

Cut or turn the four wheels (part 19). Be sure to locate the *exact* center of the wheels for the 5/16-inch-diameter holes. Be sure to drill them to a depth of 3/8 inch deep.

Sand parts all over, taking care not to round any edges at this time; keep all edges SHARP.

# Assembly

Dry-fit all parts to ensure all parts fit correctly before the final gluing.

Locate and glue the grill (part 10) to the base (part 1). Glue the two fenders (part 3) in place as shown. Be sure to place the 3/16-×-1/4-inch notches in against the base. Refer to the exploded view. Add the window (part 5), back (part 6), sides (part 7), seat (part 8), and top (part 9) to the above assembly.

Locate and glue the front axle (part 4), so the front wheels will be in the center of the fenders approximately 1⅜ inch in from the front end of the base. Locate and glue the rear axle (part 4), 1⅝-inch in from the back of the base.

Add the truckbed parts (11,12,13,14 and 15). The tailgate (part 18) must be rounded slightly on the bottom as shown, so it can clear the base (part 1), when in the dropped position.

| Part No. | Name | Size | Req'd. |
|---|---|---|---|
| 1 | Base | $\frac{3}{4} \times 2 - 9$ Long | 1 |
| 2 | Engine | $1\frac{7}{16} \times 2 - 2\frac{1}{2}$ Long | 1 |
| 3 | Fender* | $\frac{15}{16} \times 1\frac{1}{16} - 5\frac{1}{4}$ Long | 2 |
| 4 | Axle | $\frac{3}{4} \times \frac{3}{4} - 2$ Long | 2 |
| 5 | Window | $\frac{1}{4} \times 2\frac{3}{8} - 3\frac{3}{4}$ Long | 1 |
| 6 | Back | $\frac{1}{4} \times 2\frac{3}{8} - 3\frac{3}{4}$ Long | 1 |
| 7 | Cab Side | $\frac{1}{4} \times 2 - 3$ Long | 2 |
| 8 | Seat | $\frac{1}{4} \times \frac{15}{16} - 1\frac{1}{2}$ Long | 1 |
| 9 | Top | $\frac{1}{4} \times 2\frac{3}{8} - 2\frac{15}{16}$ Long | 1 |
| 10 | Grill | $\frac{1}{4} \times 2 - 2\frac{3}{8}$ Long | 1 |
| 11 | Bed Front | $\frac{1}{4} \times 1\frac{7}{16} - 3\frac{1}{8}$ Long | 1 |
| 12 | Bottom | $\frac{1}{4} \times 3\frac{1}{8} - 4\frac{9}{16}$ Long | 1 |
| 13 | Bed Side | $\frac{1}{4} \times 1\frac{7}{16} - 5\frac{1}{16}$ Long | 2 |
| 14 | Stop | $\frac{3}{32}$ Square $- 1\frac{3}{16}$ Long | 2 |
| 15 | Support | $\frac{1}{8}$ Dia. $- \frac{7}{16}$ Long | 2 |
| 16 | Bumper | $\frac{1}{4} \times \frac{1}{4} - 3\frac{5}{8}$ Long | 1 |
| 17 | Headlight | $\frac{3}{8}$ Dia. $- \frac{3}{16}$ Long | 2 |
| 18 | Tailgate | $\frac{1}{4} \times 1\frac{7}{16} - 3\frac{3}{32}$ | 1 |
| 19 | Wheel | 2 Dia. $- \frac{3}{4}$ Thick | 4 |
| 20 | Shaft | $\frac{5}{16}$ Dia. $- 2\frac{7}{8}$ Long | 2 |
| 21 | Lock "L" | $\frac{1}{8} \times \frac{5}{16} - \frac{1}{2}$ Long | 2 |

\* Left- and Right-Hand Pair

*Note*: this part must be nailed in place with two small finishing nails or brads and must work freely.

Cut and shape the two lock L's (part 21), and attach them to each side of the truckbed sides with a small finishing nail or brad—one for each side. Check that they turn correctly and let the tailgate (part 18) drop like a real truck tailgate would. If this truck is to be used by a very young child it would be best to *glue* the tailgate in place, thus eliminating the nails or brads that could become loose and be swallowed.

Glue the headlights (part 17) and the two supports and bumper (part 16) in place.

Slide the two shafts (part 20) into the two axles. Glue the wheels (part 19) to the shafts. Check that the wheels clear the base and turn correctly. There should be about $\frac{1}{16}$-inch clearance between the wheels and the base.

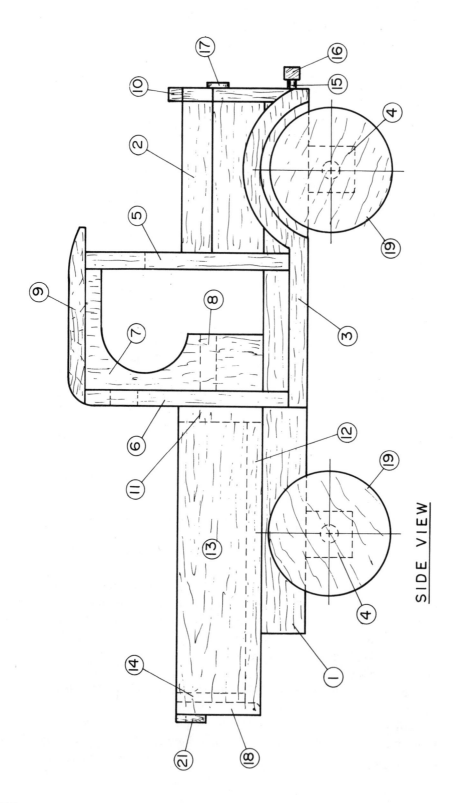

SIDE VIEW

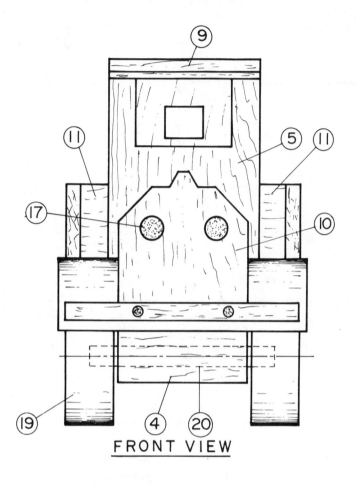

FRONT VIEW

## Finishing

Finish the truck with either a stain, as illustrated in the photo, or with a coat of nontoxic, *lead-free* paint. Sign and date your truck.

Your truck is now ready for heavy work and will be enjoyed for years to come.

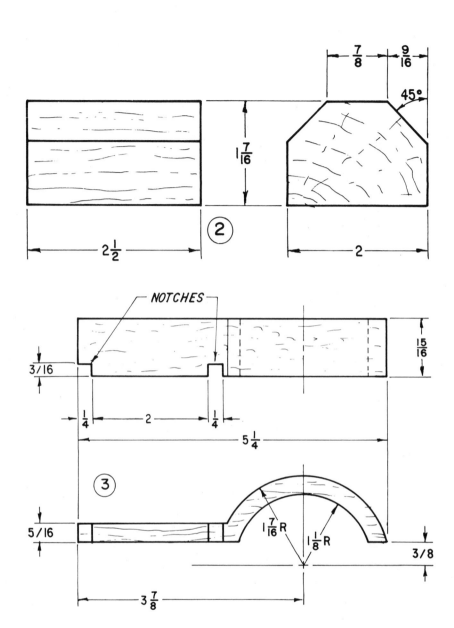

NOTCHES

②

③

110

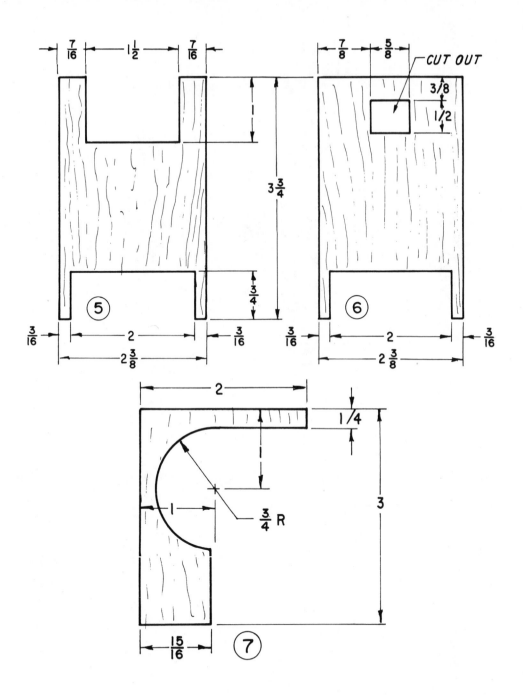

CUT OUT

⑤

⑥

⑦

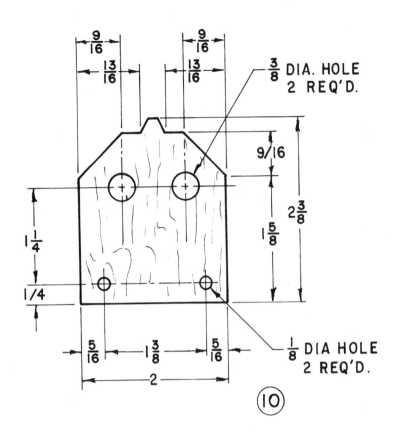

$\frac{3}{8}$ DIA. HOLE
2 REQ'D.

$\frac{1}{8}$ DIA HOLE
2 REQ'D.

⑩

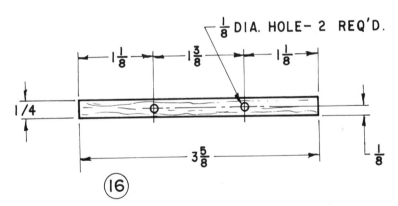

$\frac{1}{8}$ DIA. HOLE – 2 REQ'D.

⑯

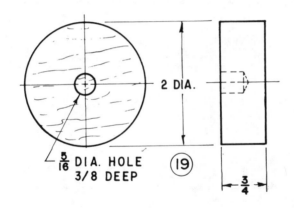

2 DIA.

$\frac{5}{16}$ DIA. HOLE 3/8 DEEP

19

$\frac{3}{4}$

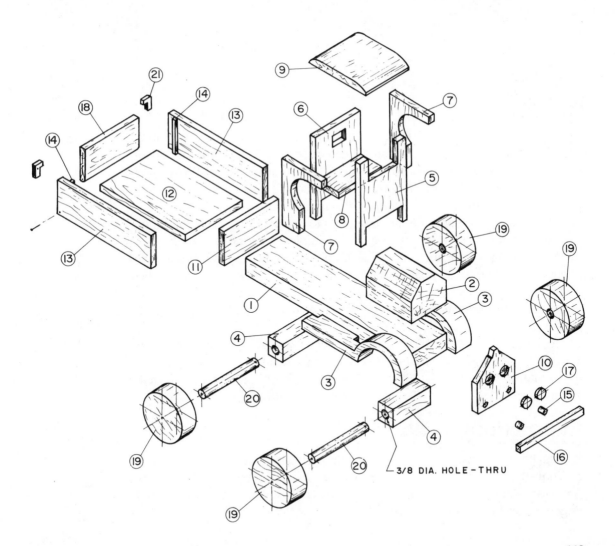

3/8 DIA. HOLE—THRU

113

# Toy Log Cabin

THIS IS A TOY THAT WILL DELIGHT MOST ANY CHILD. IT IS A TOY THAT WILL KEEP them playing for hours and instill constructive and creative thinking—something not found in most toys of today. Another feature of this project is that it can be made completely from scrap wood. If you work, as I do, you probably make a lot of mistakes that end up as scrap.

The materials List specifies enough parts to build one complete log cabin, as shown in the three-view drawing. The completed log house will be 14½ inches in length × 9 inches in depth, and about 12⅜ inches high. If you plan to make more than one, I suggest that you make two or three times the number of individual parts listed in the Materials List. This will not entail much extra work, as it is the setup of the saw that is so time-consuming. Cutting the parts goes relatively quickly.

A new carbide router bit (#LC-01-S), made especially to cut logs of this kind, is available from *Furnima Industrial*, Biernackle Road, P.O. Box 308, Barry's Bay, Ontario, Canada K0J-1B0. If you do not wish to invest in a router bit, simply cut the logs with a 45-degree chamfer on all four sides.

## Instructions

As usual, read all instructions before starting. This may save you a little time and effort. There are probably better ways to make the logs, but this is the way I made mine. Take extreme care when cutting the notches and keep your fingers away from the dado blade.

Use whatever soft, knot-free scrap wood you have around, and cut it into exactly ¾-inch-thick, ¾-inch-wide pieces. Cut twice as much material as you think you will need.

*Note*: the longer the pieces the better, as they are easier to hold and feed into the saw blade faster.

If you wish to use a new board, not scrap, a piece of knot-free wood, ¾-inch thick × 10 inches (9½″) wide × 10 feet long should be large enough for the complete project.

Using a router, carefully rout each side, feeding the wood into the router slowly. Use a feather board if you can so the wood does not wander. Adjust the router bit so the cut maintains the full ¾-inch width of the pieces after being routed. Be sure to note the small lip or step on each side and the flat spot on the top and bottom of each part. This is helpful to keep the log stable later, when you cut all the notches out.

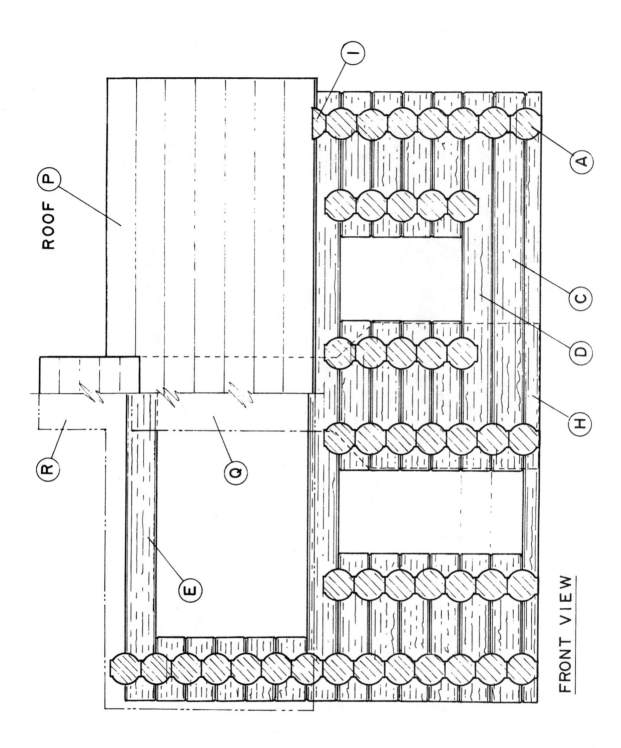

ROOF P

FRONT VIEW

116

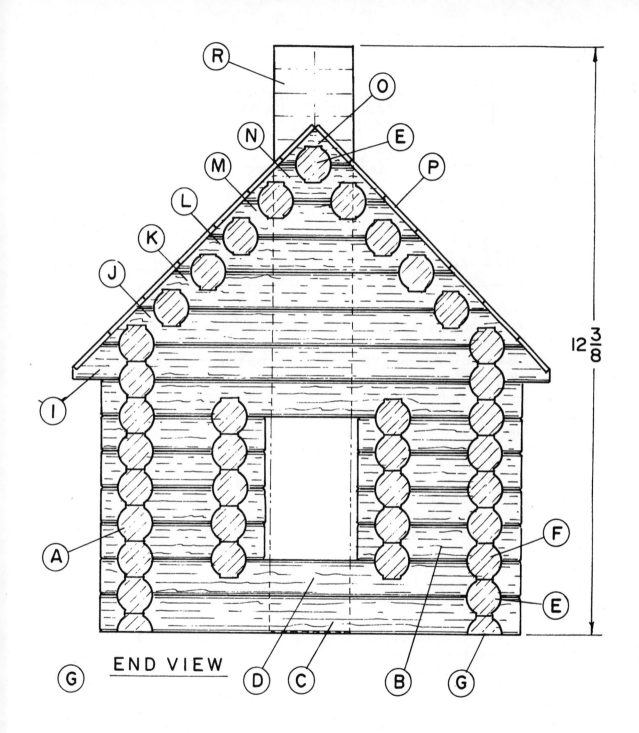

END VIEW

$12\frac{3}{8}$

117

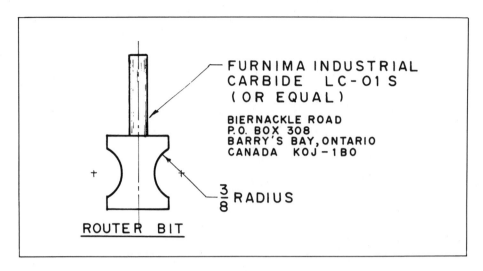

FURNIMA INDUSTRIAL
CARBIDE LC-01 S
(OR EQUAL)

BIERNACKLE ROAD
P.O. BOX 308
BARRY'S BAY, ONTARIO
CANADA KOJ-1B0

$\frac{3}{8}$ RADIUS

ROUTER BIT

Using a stop-fence on your saw, cut the required length of parts C,D,E,F,G, and H. Take care to be exact; all dimensions must be cut as accurately as possible so that the logs will go together easily. Parts A and B should be cut to length *after* notching, as it could be dangerous trying to hold short pieces in your hand while making the notches.

Attach a dado blade to your saw. Adjust the blade to make a 3/16-inch-deep × 3/4-inch-wide cut. Practice cutting a notch at the top and bottom of two or three pieces until the cut is perfect and the parts lock together easily *with a little extra space*, in the event everything is not exact. Again, using a stop-fence, adjust it so the notch is exactly 3/8 inch in from the end of the log. Cut the *end* notches, top and bottom, in parts C,D,E,F,G, and H using a stop-board. Do not cut the other notches at this time. *Take care as working with the dado blade on such small parts could be dangerous.*

To make part B requires a few extra steps. With the same setting as above, take a long piece of material that has already been routed and notch the top and bottom of one end only. Using another saw with a stop-fence, cut the piece to the required 3½-inch length. Carefully notch the other ends with the dado blade. Take care not to rush this cut and do not dado into a knot, which could be dangerous.

To make part A also takes a few extra steps. Again, take a long piece of material that has already been routed and notch the top and bottom of one end. Take it over to the other saw and cut it to the required 1½-inch length. Repeat these steps until you have cut all required pieces to size. Be sure to cut a few more parts than is called for in the Materials List.

Make part O using the same steps as used on part A, except cut only one notch as shown. Using a band saw, cut the 45-degree angles. There are only two of these so the extra time involved is minimal.

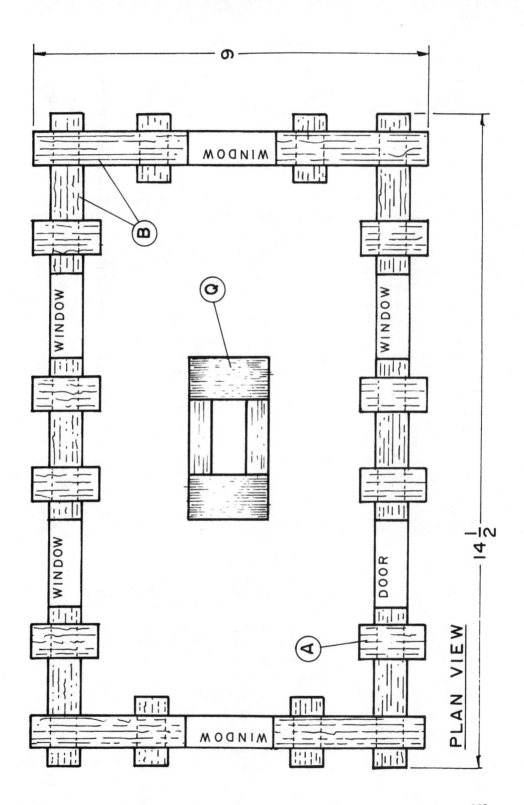

PLAN VIEW

119

Carefully adjust the stop-board to make the second notch in parts D,F, and H. Adjust it so that it is *exactly* 1¼ inch from the first notch as illustrated. Cut the second notch in all parts, top and bottom, except part letter H.

Again, carefully adjust the stop-board to make another notch, top and bottom, 2¾ inches from the last notch you made. If your measurements are correct, you should have exactly 1¼ inch left between the last two notches. This is important: double check before cutting too many parts. This finishes cutting the notches in parts A,B,C,D,E,F,G, and H.

Using the same techniques, cut to length parts I,J,K,L,M, and N. Use a stop-fence to cut the notches in from each end as shown. Start by cutting all the *bottom* notches ⅜ inch in from each end (except part letter I which is 1 inch in). Adjust the stop-fence 1⅛ inch from the end and cut the notches in the *top* of each part. Using a band saw, or any such saw, cut the 45-degree angles on the ends as shown.

The fireplace, part Q, is cut from a piece of scrap 1¾-×-3½-×-10½ inches. Cut the overall shape as shown. The chimney (part R) is cut from scrap 1¾-×-1¾-×-2½ inches. Cut the notch to agree with the roof line.

The roof can be made one of two ways, refer to part P for the first, and simplest, method. This is simply a board ⅛ inch thick × 1¹⁄₁₆ inch wide and 15 inches long. This creates a simple, flat, nonoverlapping roof with no trim board on the top of the roof.

Your log cabin will be more attractive, however, with overlapping roof boards, as shown in the photo. This method involves part P (optional), which is ⅛ inch thick × 1⅜ inch wide and 15¼ inches long. It has a small ⅛-×-⅛-inch piece glued to the bottom surface, ¼ inch in from the edge. This takes more time to make, but creates a more realistic roof line with a trim board on the top of the roof.

Before going further check to see that all parts go together correctly and that they do not stick. Adjust if necessary.

# Finishing

To finish my log cabin, I simply mixed together whatever leftover stains I've had around for years and thinned the mixture out slightly. I put the walnut-colored stain in a large container and submerged the logs into the stain. Then I rolled the logs around until they were stained all over. After removing the pieces from the stain, I wiped off each.

You can follow the same procedure with the roof boards using, perhaps, thinned green paint. (I am certain *all* log cabins had green roofs.) Be sure to wipe each part as you remove it from the paint. This creates a nice washed coat to the roof. The chimney is simply painted a brick-red color. I got a little carried away and made scribe lines to simulate bricks; this is optional.

Your log cabin is done. All you need now are cowboys and Indians.

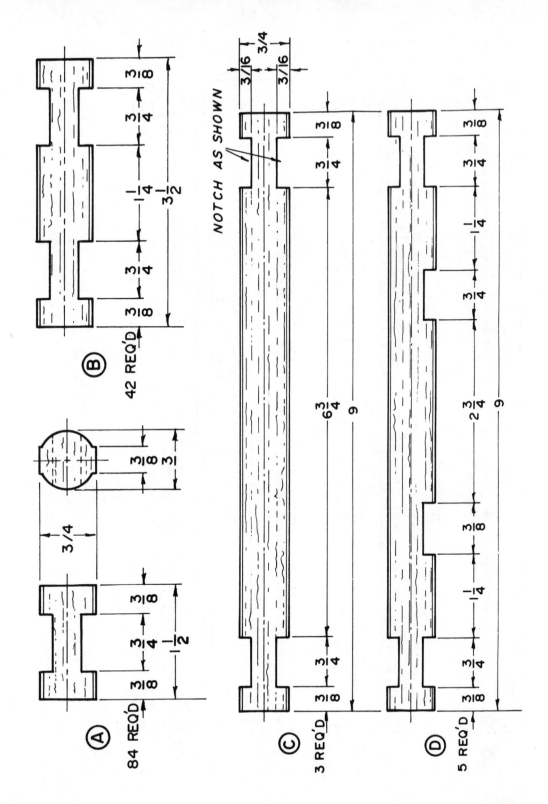

3/4

3/16 3/16

3/4

NOTCH AS SHOWN

Ⓐ
84 REQ'D

$\frac{3}{8}$  $\frac{3}{4}$  $\frac{3}{8}$

$1\frac{1}{2}$

$\frac{3}{8}$  $\frac{1}{3}$

Ⓑ
42 REQ'D

$\frac{3}{8}$  $\frac{3}{4}$  $1\frac{1}{4}$  $\frac{3}{4}$  $\frac{3}{8}$

$3\frac{1}{2}$

Ⓒ
3 REQ'D

$\frac{3}{8}$  $\frac{3}{4}$  $6\frac{3}{4}$  $\frac{3}{4}$  $\frac{3}{8}$

9

Ⓓ
5 REQ'D

$\frac{3}{8}$  $\frac{3}{4}$  $1\frac{1}{4}$  $\frac{3}{8}$  $2\frac{3}{4}$  $\frac{3}{4}$  $\frac{3}{8}$

9

121

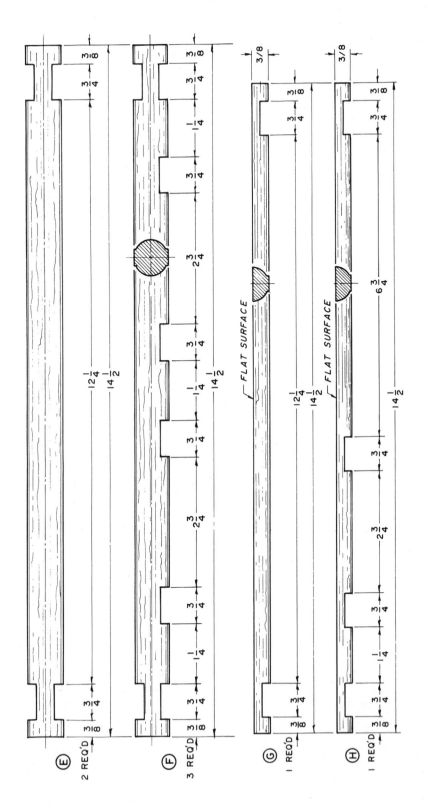

E
2 REQ'D

F
3 REQ'D

G
1 REQ'D

H
1 REQ'D

122

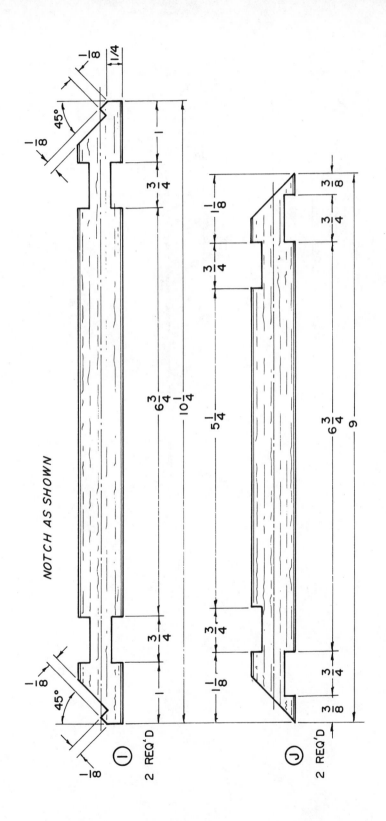

NOTCH AS SHOWN

$\frac{1}{8}$

45°

$\frac{1}{8}$

1/4

1

$3\frac{1}{4}$

$6\frac{3}{4}$

$10\frac{1}{4}$

$3\frac{1}{4}$

1

45°

$\frac{1}{8}$

$\frac{1}{8}$

I

2 REQ'D

$3\frac{1}{8}$

$3\frac{1}{4}$

$1\frac{1}{8}$

$3\frac{1}{4}$

$5\frac{1}{4}$

$6\frac{3}{4}$

9

$3\frac{1}{4}$

$1\frac{1}{8}$

$3\frac{1}{8}$

J

2 REQ'D

123

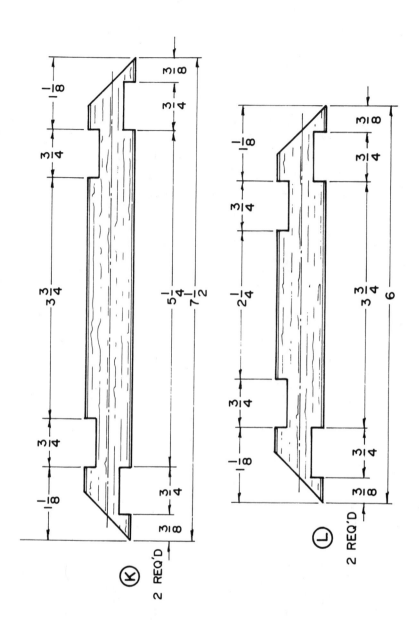

K
2 REQ'D

L
2 REQ'D

124

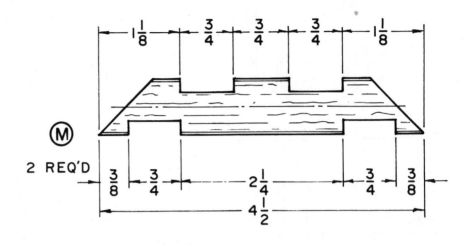

M 2 REQ'D

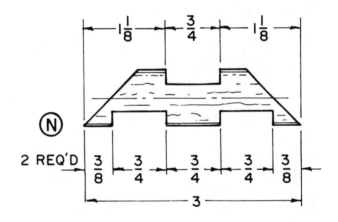

N 2 REQ'D

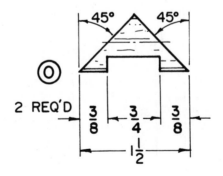

O 2 REQ'D

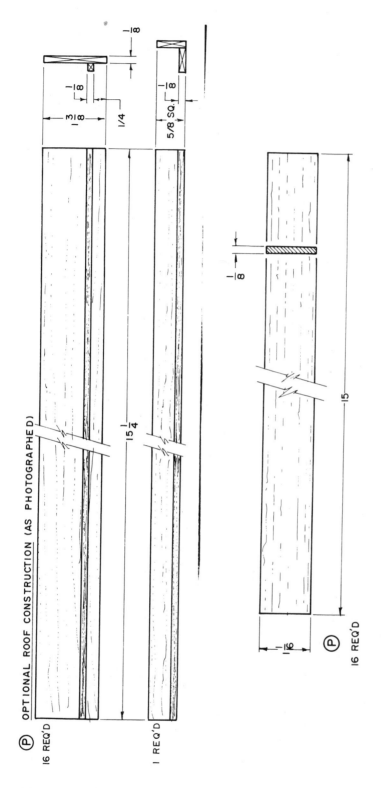

OPTIONAL ROOF CONSTRUCTION (AS PHOTOGRAPHED)

Ⓟ 16 REQ'D

1 REQ'D

Ⓟ 16 REQ'D

126

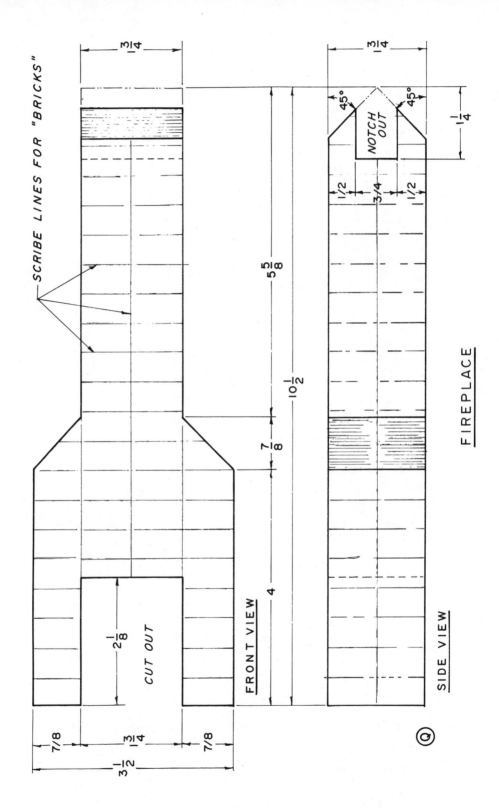

SCRIBE LINES FOR "BRICKS"

$3\frac{1}{4}$

$3\frac{1}{4}$

45°     45°

NOTCH OUT

$1\frac{1}{4}$

1/2   3/4   1/2

$5\frac{5}{8}$

$10\frac{1}{2}$

$\frac{7}{8}$

$2\frac{1}{8}$

CUT OUT

4

FRONT VIEW

SIDE VIEW

FIREPLACE

7/8

$3\frac{1}{4}$

7/8

$3\frac{1}{2}$

Ⓠ

127

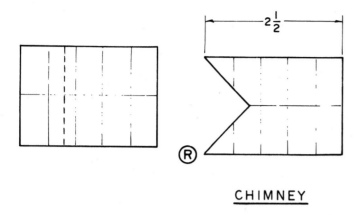

2 ½

CHIMNEY

# Toy
# Christmas Sleigh

WHAT WOULD CHRISTMAS BE WITHOUT SANTA AND WHAT WOULD SANTA BE without his sleigh? Here is the chance for you to build a sleigh that will be displayed every Christmas for years to come. This is a fun project which can be completed in a weekend or so. And you will need very little material. The entire project is made from one board, 3/16 inch thick, 8 inches wide, and 6 feet, 6 inches long; and a few dowels. Dowels required are: 1/8 inch in diameter × 4½ inches long, 3/16 inch in diameter × 12 inches long, 7/16 inch in diameter × 5 7/16 inches long, and 5/8 inch in diameter × 5/16 inch long.

A hardwood should be used as the bottom runners are a little fragile and would not last if made of softwood. A hardwood such as cherry, walnut, or maple is recommended, but any available hardwood would do.

## Instructions

Start with wood that is 3/16 inch thick and sanded smoothly on both sides. Roughly cut out each piece about ¼ inch larger than the given overall size and lightly number each piece of wood corresponding to the given number on the drawings. Be sure to cut out duplicate pieces, if a pair is required such as the two side panels or the two runners.

If you are going to make only one sleigh, make full-size paper patterns of each part. If you plan to make more than one sleigh, make a full-size cardboard pattern of each part, so you can use it over and over. To make the patterns, carefully draw a grid of the required square size and transfer the shape of the part to the grid. If you vary the shape slightly it will not matter, but the overall required size should be as accurate as possible in order to have the matching parts all go together correctly.

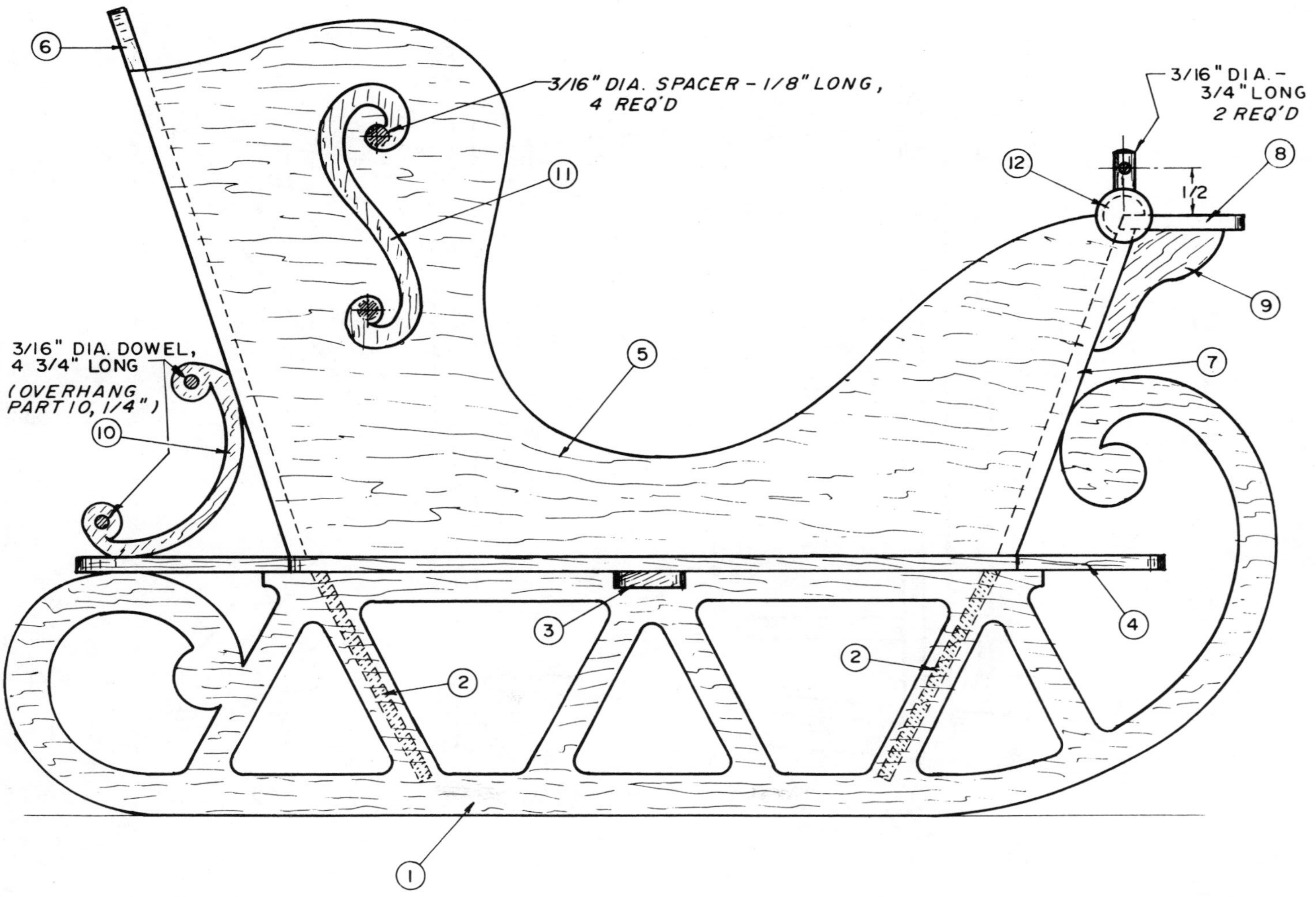

6
3/16" DIA. SPACER - 1/8" LONG, 4 REQ'D
11
3/16" DIA. - 3/4" LONG 2 REQ'D
12
8
1/2
9
5
7
3/16" DIA. DOWEL, 4 3/4" LONG
(OVERHANG PART 10, 1/4")
10
3
4
2
2
1


SIDE VIEW

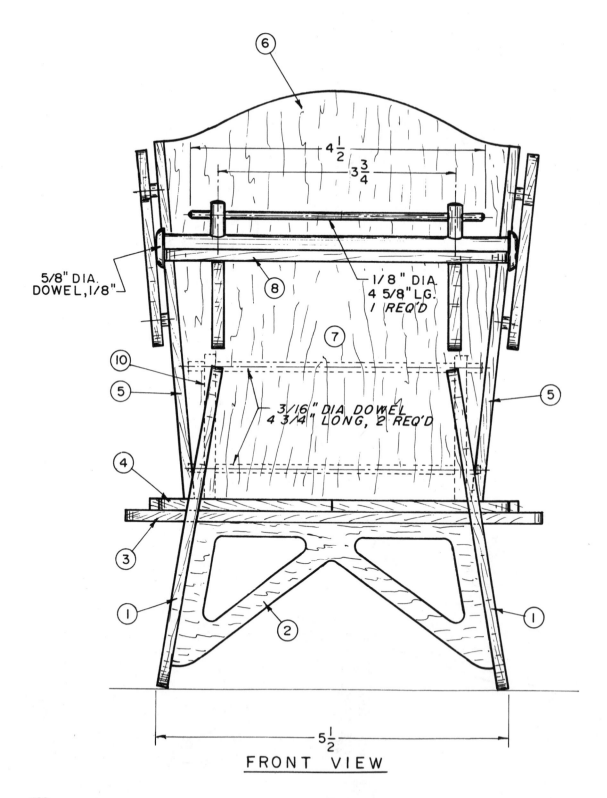

5/8" DIA.
DOWEL, 1/8"

4 $\frac{1}{2}$

3 $\frac{3}{4}$

1/8" DIA.
4 5/8" LG.
1 REQ'D

3/16" DIA DOWEL
4 3/4" LONG, 2 REQ'D

5 $\frac{1}{2}$

## FRONT VIEW

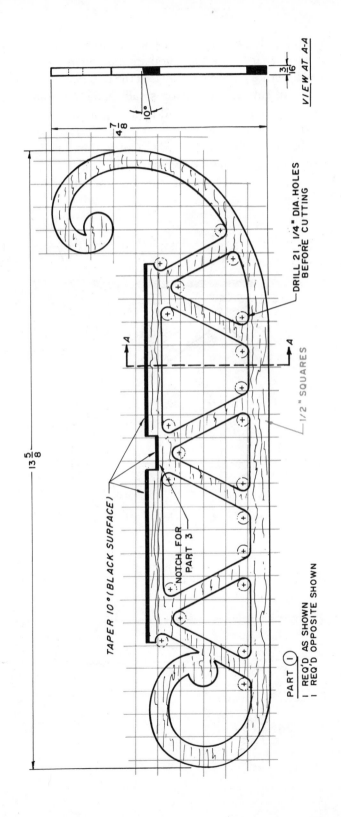

VIEW AT A-A

$\frac{3}{16}$

10°

$4\frac{7}{8}$

DRILL 21, 1/4" DIA. HOLES
BEFORE CUTTING

A

A

1/2" SQUARES

$13\frac{5}{8}$

TAPER 10° (BLACK SURFACE)

NOTCH FOR
PART 3

PART ①
1 REQ'D AS SHOWN
1 REQ'D OPPOSITE SHOWN

Using rubber cement, lightly glue the paper patterns to the cutout wood parts. (Trace around the cardboard patterns, if you are making more than one sleigh.) Where there are duplicate parts, carefully tack the two matching pieces of wood together in open or cutout areas using small brads. By doing this, the pairs can be cut out together, thus will end up being identical pairs.

Drill all the ¼-inch-diameter holes, as noted, on the two rails (part 1) and the two braces (part 2), before starting any cutting. Cut to the outside of the lines on the patterns, and later file or sand down to the lines. Cut out all parts and sand all over using fine-grit paper. Take care not to round any edges, keep everything square and sharp.

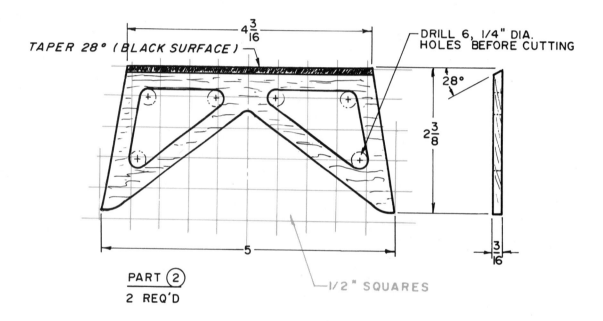

TAPER 28° ( BLACK SURFACE )

$4\frac{3}{16}$

DRILL 6, 1/4" DIA.
HOLES BEFORE CUTTING

28°

$2\frac{3}{8}$

5

$\frac{3}{16}$

PART ② 

2 REQ'D

1/2" SQUARES

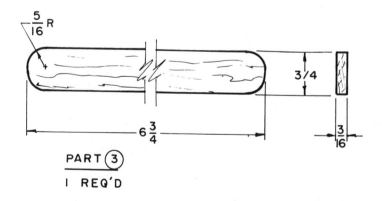

$\frac{5}{16}$ R

3/4

$6\frac{3}{4}$

$\frac{3}{16}$

PART ③

1 REQ'D

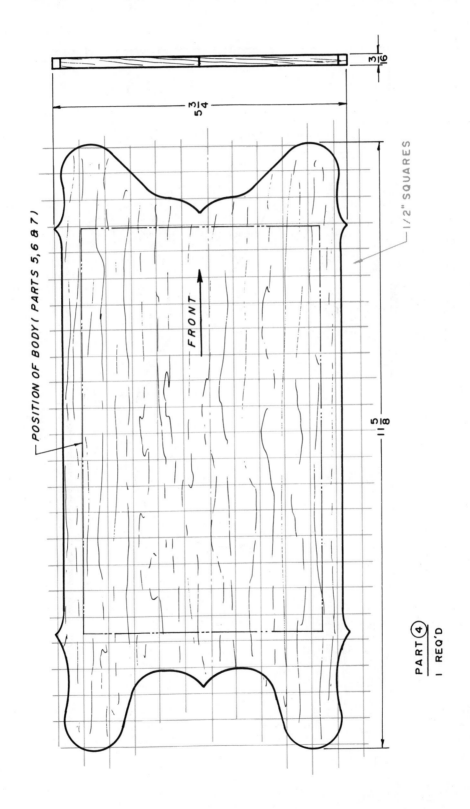

POSITION OF BODY ( PARTS 5, 6 & 7 )

FRONT

1/2" SQUARES

$5\frac{3}{4}$

$\frac{3}{16}$

$11\frac{5}{8}$

PART ④
I REQ'D

135

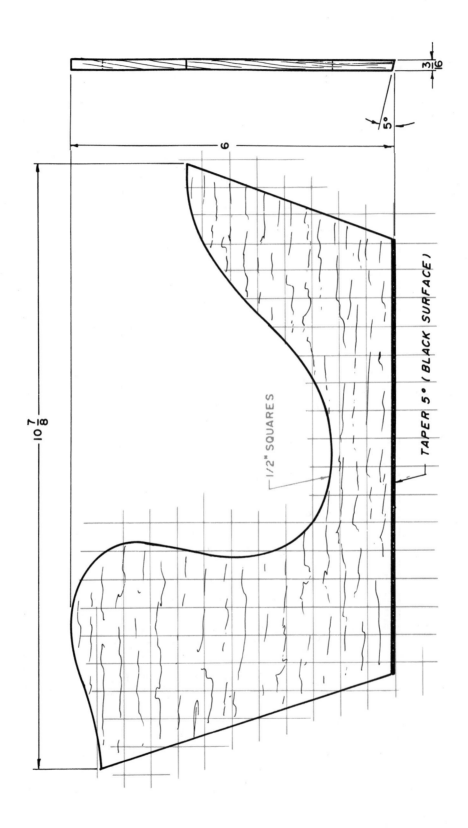

TAPER 5° (BLACK SURFACE)

1/2" SQUARES

6

10 7/8

5°

3/16

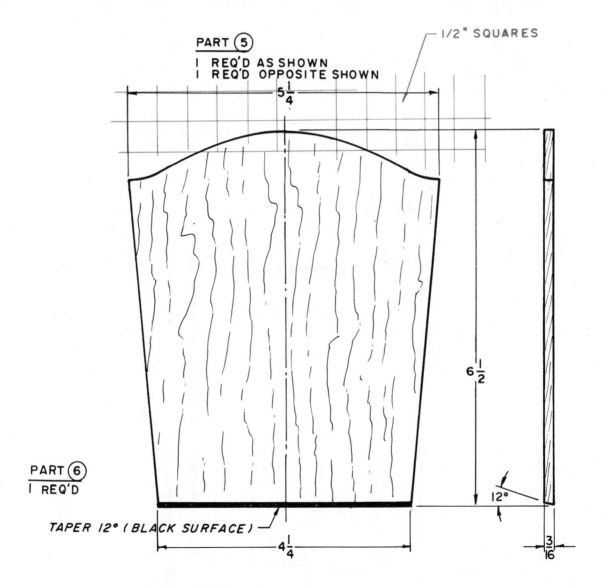

PART ⑤
I REQ'D AS SHOWN
I REQ'D OPPOSITE SHOWN

1/2" SQUARES

$5\frac{1}{4}$

$6\frac{1}{2}$

PART ⑥
I REQ'D

12°

TAPER 12° (BLACK SURFACE)

$4\frac{1}{4}$

$\frac{3}{16}$

# Assembly

Assemble the bottom rail section as shown, using the two rails (part 1), the two braces (part 2), and the step (part 3). Take care to keep the rails parallel to each other, and the braces at 90 degrees to the rails. After the glue has set, sand the top surface of the rail assembly, using sandpaper wrapped around a flat piece of wood, in order to provide a flat surface for the sleigh bottom (part 4).

Assemble the sleigh body as shown, using the two sides (part 5), the back (part 6) and the front (part 7), keeping everything square. After the glue has

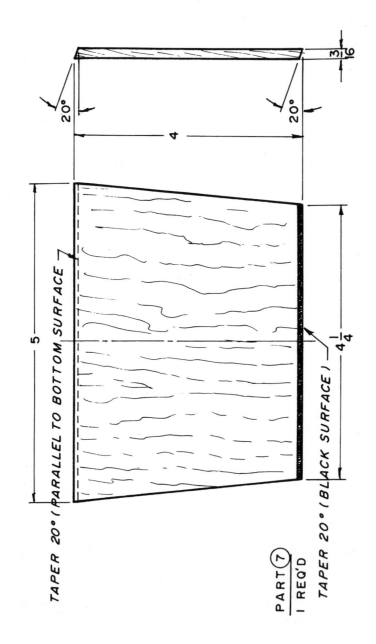

TAPER 20° ( PARALLEL TO BOTTOM SURFACE )

TAPER 20° ( BLACK SURFACE )

PART ⑦
I REQ'D

5

4

4 1/4

3/16

20°

20°

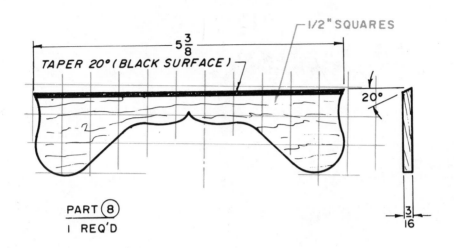

5 3/8

1/2" SQUARES

TAPER 20° (BLACK SURFACE)

20°

PART (8)
1 REQ'D

3/16

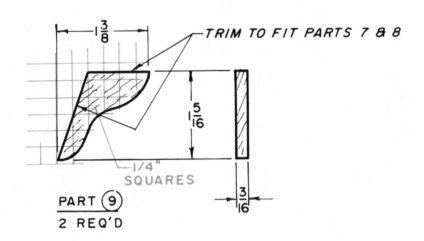

1 3/8

TRIM TO FIT PARTS 7 & 8

1 5/16

1/4"
SQUARES

PART (9)
2 REQ'D

3/16

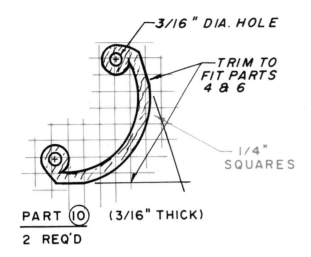

3/16" DIA. HOLE

TRIM TO
FIT PARTS
4 & 6

1/4"
SQUARES

PART ⑩ (3/16" THICK)
2 REQ'D

1/4" SQUARES

PART ⑪ (3/16" THICK)
2 REQ'D

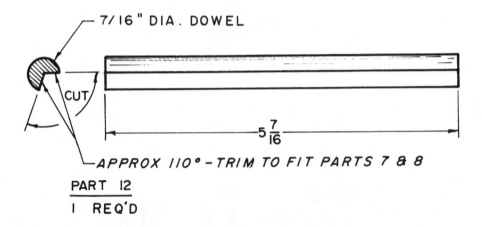

7/16" DIA. DOWEL

CUT

APPROX 110° – TRIM TO FIT PARTS 7 & 8

$5\frac{7}{16}$

PART 12

1 REQ'D

set, sand all surfaces and corners. Again, using sandpaper wrapped around a piece of wood, sand the bottom surface of the body in order to provide a flat surface for the sleigh bottom (part 4). Do not round any edges.

Glue the complete body assembly to the base, locating it as noted in the SIDE VIEW. Take care to exactly position the base (part 4) as indicated on the drawing, with the front facing the front of the rail assembly. (I glued mine backwards and had to take it all apart, so don't make that mistake.) Glue the bottom rail assembly to the bottom (part 4), again taking care to glue it in the correct position, facing front.

Assemble all the remaining parts as illustrated, and let it completely set. Carefully sand the sleigh all over using a fine-grit paper and clean all surfaces in preparation for finishing.

## Finishing

Paint the entire sleigh with either a surface sealer or with coat of varnish. Any color combination can be used, but I painted my sleigh body assembly bright red, the rail assembly gloss black, and all other trim yellow. If you are good at pinstriping, the sleigh body and rail assembly could be pinstriped for that added effect. Now all you have to do is to find Santa for his sleigh. Merry Christmas!

# Toy Train

A FAVORITE TOY THROUGHOUT THE YEARS HAS BEEN THE TOY TRAIN—ESPECIALLY the old steam train. Look through any woodworking magazine and you will find toy trains for sale, plans to build toy trains from scratch, and toy train kits. The interesting thing about *this* toy train is that it can be made from your wood scraps. You need only a small piece of wood, ³⁄₁₆ inch thick, 5½ inches wide, and 21 inches long; a 1¼-inch-diameter dowel, 9⅝ inches long; 1⅛-inch-diameter dowel, ¾ inch long, and a ¾-inch-diameter dowel, 6 inches long. Actual time to cut out, turn, and assemble this project is minimal—the train can easily be made in a weekend. The painting process takes the longest time, unless you use lacquer or some other fast-drying paint.

The toy train illustrated is used only as a decoration because the wheels are glued and nailed in place. In order to make it into a toy, the wheels will have to be made to turn. This is done by simply drilling a hole in each wheel slightly larger than the nail diameter and not gluing them in place. Extreme care should be taken so the nails cannot come loose, and possibly be swallowed by a child. You should also use lead-free paint.

## Instructions

Select a straight-grained, knot-free piece of hardwood, any type will do. Plane it down to a thickness of ³⁄₁₆ inch. Sand both sides smoothly with fine paper.

## MATERIALS LIST

| Part No. | Name | Size | Req'd. |
|---|---|---|---|
| 1 | Base Large | $\frac{3}{16}$ × 2 - $4\frac{1}{4}$ Long | 1 |
| 2 | Base Small | $\frac{3}{16}$ × 2 - $3\frac{1}{4}$ Long | 3 |
| 3 | Axle | $\frac{3}{16}$ × $\frac{3}{16}$ - 2 Long | 9 |
| 4 | All Round Parts | $1\frac{1}{4}$ Dia. × $9\frac{5}{8}$ Lg | 1 |
| 5 | Whistle | $\frac{1}{4}$ Dia. × 1 Long | 1 |
| 6 | Loco Side | $\frac{3}{16}$ × $1\frac{1}{4}$ - 2 Long | 2 |
| 7 | Loco Front | $\frac{3}{16}$ × $1\frac{1}{4}$ - 2 Long | 3 |
| 8 | Loco Top | $\frac{3}{16}$ × $1\frac{3}{4}$ - $1\frac{7}{8}$ Lg | 1 |
| 9 | Wheel - Large | $\frac{3}{16}$ Thick - $1\frac{1}{8}$ Dia. | 2 |
| 10 | Wheel - Small | $\frac{3}{16}$ Thick - $\frac{3}{4}$ Dia. | 16 |
| 11 | Tender - Side | $\frac{3}{16}$ × $1\frac{1}{2}$ - $2\frac{3}{4}$ Lg | 2 |
| 12 | Tender - Front | $\frac{3}{16}$ × $1\frac{1}{2}$ - $1\frac{1}{4}$ Lg | 1 |
| 13 | Tender End | $\frac{3}{16}$ × 1 - $1\frac{1}{4}$ Long | 3 |
| 14 | Box Car Side | $\frac{3}{16}$ × 1 - $2\frac{3}{4}$ Long | 2 |
| 16 | Caboose Side | $\frac{3}{16}$ × $2\frac{1}{8}$ - 2 Long | 2 |
| 15 | Caboose Side | $\frac{3}{16}$ × $\frac{3}{8}$ - 1 Long | 4 |
| 17 | Caboose Top | $\frac{3}{16}$ × $1\frac{7}{8}$ - $2\frac{5}{8}$ Lg | 1 |
| 18 | Caboose Top | $\frac{3}{16}$ × $\frac{3}{8}$ - $1\frac{3}{16}$ Lg | 2 |
| 19 | Caboose Top-End | $\frac{3}{16}$ × $\frac{3}{8}$ - $\frac{5}{8}$ Lg | 2 |
| 20 | Caboose Top | $\frac{3}{16}$ × $1\frac{3}{8}$ - $1\frac{5}{8}$ Lg | 1 |
| 21 | Caboose End | $\frac{3}{16}$ × $\frac{3}{4}$ - 1 Long | 2 |
| 22 | Eye | Small | 3 |
| 23 | Hook | Small | 2 |
| 24 | Tack - Brass | $\frac{5}{8}$ Long | 18 |

Joint one edge on one side and cut the board to just over 5½ inches wide. Square the ends and make the board 21 inches long.

Carefully lay out all parts as illustrated in the cutting plan layout, using a square.

*Note:* a ³⁄₁₆-inch space has been included between parts to allow for a standard saw blade width. Be sure to check yours. If it is wider, leave more space accordingly.

Carefully locate and drill all the ¼-inch-diameter holes as shown. This will save you from having to make very tight turns by hand or with your band saw, and will help make all turns the exact same size. Cut the board in two as noted by "1st CUT" on the drawing. Make the other three long cuts in the order illustrated.

Carefully cut each part slightly beyond the layout lines. You can sand them down to exact size later. Multiple parts must all be exactly the same size, so try to make them as close as possible. Sand all parts, keeping all edges sharp and all corners square. Lightly number each part in order to keep track of each one. The small wheels (part 10) are cut from a ¾-inch-diameter dowel, and the large wheels are cut from a 1⅛-inch-diameter dowel. It is a good idea to use a stop-gauge on your saw so all wheels are the exact same thickness. Carefully locate and drill a ³⁄₆₄-inch-diameter hole in the center of each wheel for the brass tack or brad (part 24).

Parts 4 and 5 must be turned on a lathe to size and shape as shown. Sand all over and separate all parts. Using a V-block, locate and drill the ⅜-inch-diameter and ⅛-inch-diameter holes in the boiler (part 4), taking care to keep them in line with each other.

Cut or sand a flat spot directly under the two holes in the boiler. This flat spot must be ⁷⁄₁₆ inch down from the center of the boiler (refer to the drawing). Take care to keep everything even.

Using a router, make a small radius undercut in the three tops (parts 8, 17, and 20) as shown. If you do have a router bit this small, simply cut a 45-degree chamfer in place of the undercut radius.

Locate and drill ³⁄₆₄-inch-diameter holes in the center of the axles. These holes are used to secure the wheels in place.

The train is now ready to assemble.

# Assembly

Dry-fit all parts to ensure correct fits. Carefully glue together the following parts, keeping everything square as possible. Use rubberbands for clamps where needed.

*Note:* the parts are listed starting from the *front* of the train to the rear.

Glue the loco sides (part 6) to the loco front (part 7). Glue the tender side (part 11) to the tender front (part 12) and tender end (part 13).

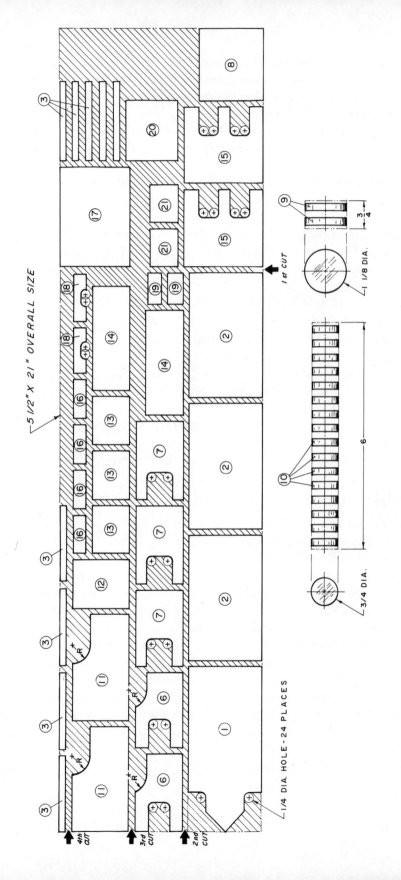

3/4 DIA.

6

1 1/8 DIA.

3
4

1/4 DIA. HOLE - 24 PLACES

1st CUT

5 1/2" X 21" OVERALL SIZE

2nd. CUT

3rd CUT

4th CUT

Glue the box car sides (part 14) to the tender ends. Glue the caboose sides, (part 15) to the loco fronts (part 7). Next, glue two pair of caboose sides (part 16) and tender ends (part 13), and glue the caboose tops (part 18) to the caboose top-ends (part 19).

Locate and glue all axles (part 3) to the large base (part 1) and small bases (part 2). Finally, glue the smokestack (part 4) and the whistle, part 5 to the boiler, part 4.

Allow these subassemblies to completely set. Afterward, sand all sides, edges, and ends as one complete unit of each subassembly. Take care to keep everything square and sharp.

Again, starting from the front of the train to the rear, glue all round parts in place (parts 4 and 5) and the subassembly of parts 6 and 7. Locate the loco sides (part 6) ½ inch *in* from the end of the large base (part 1), as illustrated. Add the loco top (part 8).

Glue the subassembly of parts 11 and 12 to the subassembly of parts 2 and 3. Center it on the small base (part 2).

Glue the subassembly of parts 13 and 14 to the subassembly of parts 2 and 3. Again, center it on the small base (part 2).

Next, glue the subassembly of parts 7 and 15 to the subassembly of parts 2 and 3. Center on the small base. Add and center the two subassemblies (parts 13 and 16) on each end.

Attach the caboose top (part 17), the subassembly (parts 18 and 19)—attach the caboose top, part 20.

Except for adding the wheels, this completes the assembly of the train.

# Finishing

Let your imagination take over at this point: be as creative as you can be. I painted my train bright candy-apple red with yellow striping and black wheels. Use a high-gloss paint that dries in a reasonable time. I am not an expert in pinstriping (as you can see), but it does not have to be perfect. Try to have some kind of a straight support to support your hand while pinstriping straight lines. Thin your paint slightly and use a *very* thin, high-quality paintbrush. Practice your pinstriping on a scrap piece of wood until you feel fairly competent. Paint the wheels and, after they dry, add them to the train. If they are to turn, drive the nails in just enough so that the wheels can move freely.

Starting from the front of the train, add very small hooks to the rear of each car and eyes to the front of each car. Check that the train can be coupled together easily. If the train is for a child, you might want to epoxy the hooks and eyes in place so there is no chance of them coming out.

Your train is now complete. Have fun. Be a kid again!

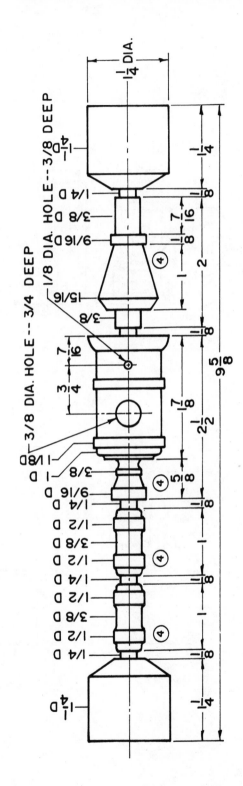

COLORS

CARS – BRIGHT RED

BASE / ALL TRIM – BRIGHT YELLOW

WHEELS – BLACK

1/8 DIA.

1/4 DIA.

3/8 D  3/16 D  1/4 D

1/8  3/4  3/8

⑤

1 1/4 DIA.

1/8 DIA. HOLE -- 3/8 DEEP

3/8 DIA. HOLE -- 3/4 DEEP

1/8 DIA. HOLE -- 3/4 DEEP

1 1/4 D

1/4 D  3/8  9/16 D  15/16  3/8  7/16  3/4  1 1/8 D  3/8  9/16 D  1/4 D  1/2 D  3/8 D  1/2 D  1/4 D  1/2 D  3/8 D  1/2 D  1/4 D  1 1/4 D

1 1/4  1/8  7/16  1  2  1/8  2 1/2  1 7/8  5/8  1/8  1  1/8  1  1/4

9 5/8

④  ④  ④  ④

147

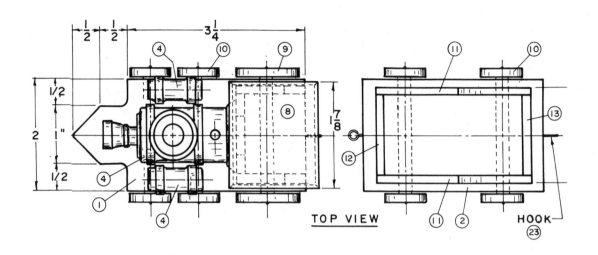

TOP VIEW

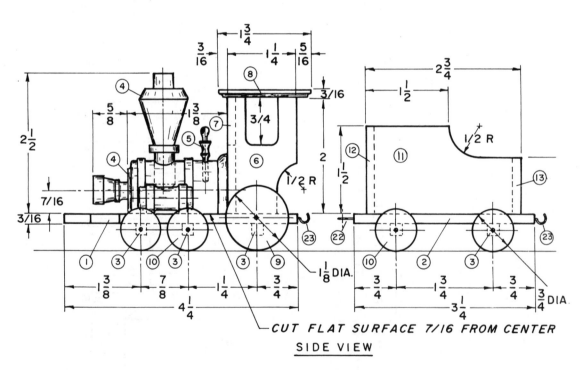

CUT FLAT SURFACE 7/16 FROM CENTER

SIDE VIEW

HOOK

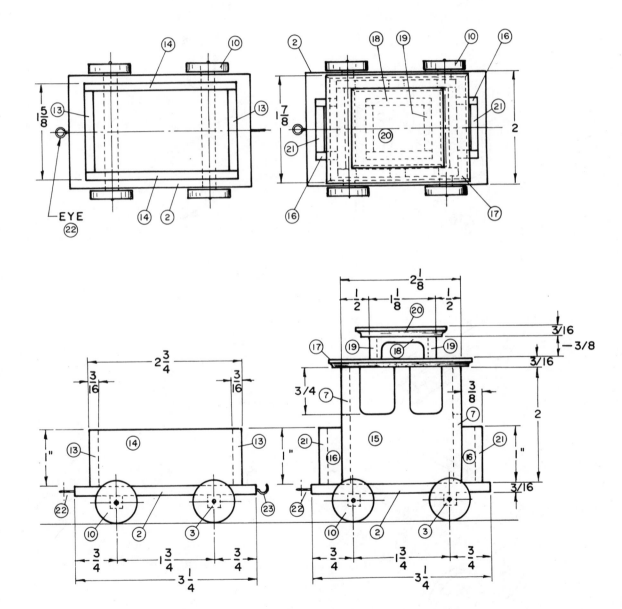

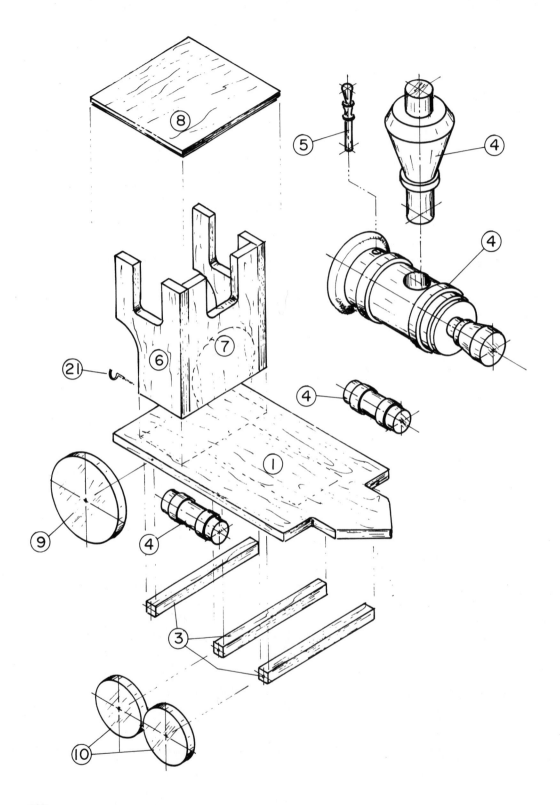

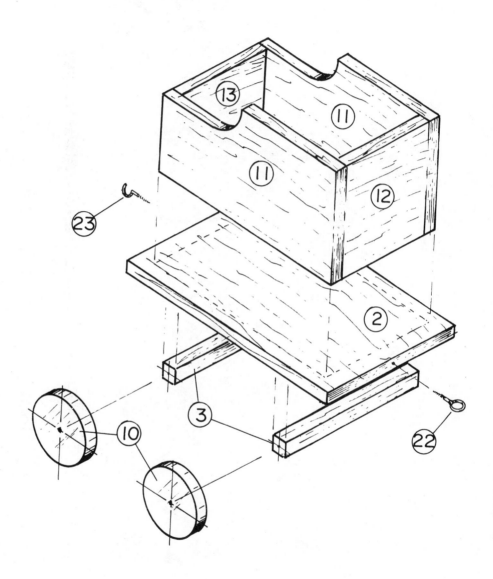

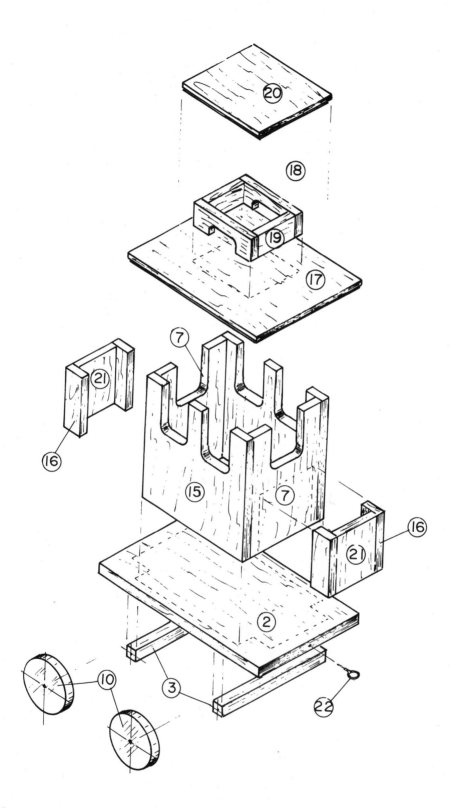

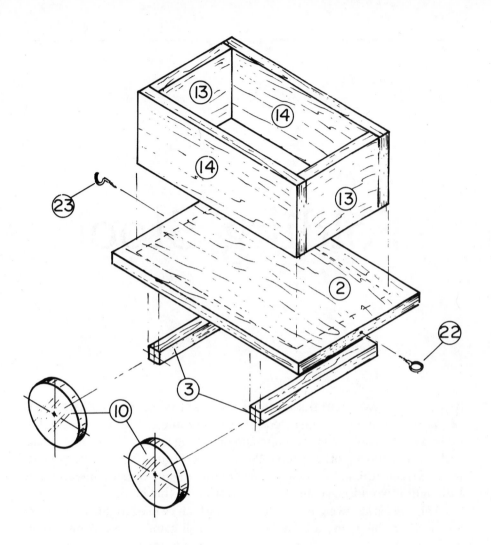

# Folding Stool

WHILE ON VACATION THROUGH THE MIDWEST LAST SUMMER, I CAME ACROSS this fascinating folding stool. It was very unusual in the way it folded up into itself. I couldn't stop folding and unfolding it; it was like doing a magic trick. After showing other people these stools, I found almost everyone did the exact same thing. I don't know where the original design came from, but I thought it would make an excellent project for this book.

This stool is lightweight, easy to carry, and can be used for many occasions: a concert on the green, a Little League baseball game, or an all-day county auction. I have two in the trunk of my car, ready for use.

The stool in the photograph has been painted two different colors only in order to illustrate how the two subassemblies come together around the center dowel (part 6). The individual parts for the stool are easy to make, but assembly does take a little thought. It is somewhat of an optical illusion at first glance.

## Instructions

Start by carefully cutting the individual parts to size per the Materials List. In making duplicate parts such as these, I find it best to make up jigs, so that all parts are exactly the same size and shape. It is especially important to maintain the 6 5/8-inch dimension on the four long legs (part 1). It is also important to make all the rounded ends exactly round and all the same size.

# Assembly

The stool is made up of two individual assemblies, held together by two center dowels. Start by studying the illustrations for STEP 1 and STEP 2. Be sure you fully understand where everything goes before beginning.

Assemble the parts as illustrated in STEP 1. Be sure to maintain the 11-inch and the 9½-inch dimensions (*oversize slightly*), as noted. Also be sure to keep the long legs, parallel to each other and square to the seat boards (parts 4 and 5). All dowels should be fitted for free motion. Be sure all dowels are flush with the side boards and do not extend out whatsoever, as they will interfere with folding up the stool. Note the dowels are held in place with finishing nails through the long legs only. They are allowed to rotate freely around the seat support (part 2).

Assemble the parts as illustrated in STEP 2. This assembly fits *into* the first assembly, so it is important that you maintain the 9½-inch outside and the 8-inch outside dimensions (*undersize slightly*), as noted. Be sure to keep the long legs parallel to each other and square to the seat boards. Note the dowel (part 7) is held in place with finishing nails through the long legs only. They are allowed to freely rotate around the seat support (part 2). Do not add the two center dowels (part 6) in place at this time. These dowels join the two assemblies together after finishing.

# Finishing

Any kind of finish can be used on this project, from a stain and varnish to a painted finish. However, I recommend that you apply the finish before joining the two subassemblies. Also wax the entire stool with a paste wax beforehand, to ensure a smooth folding and unfolding motion.

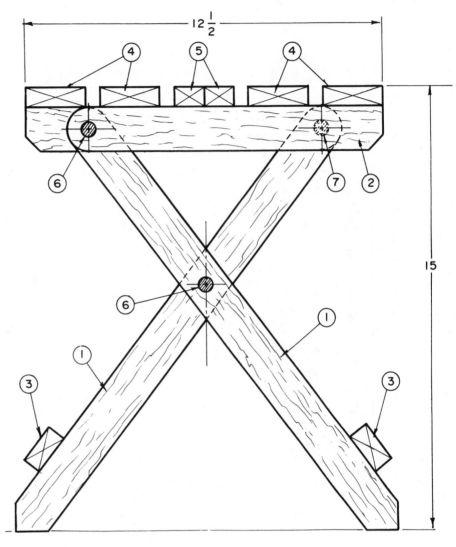

FRONT VIEW

159

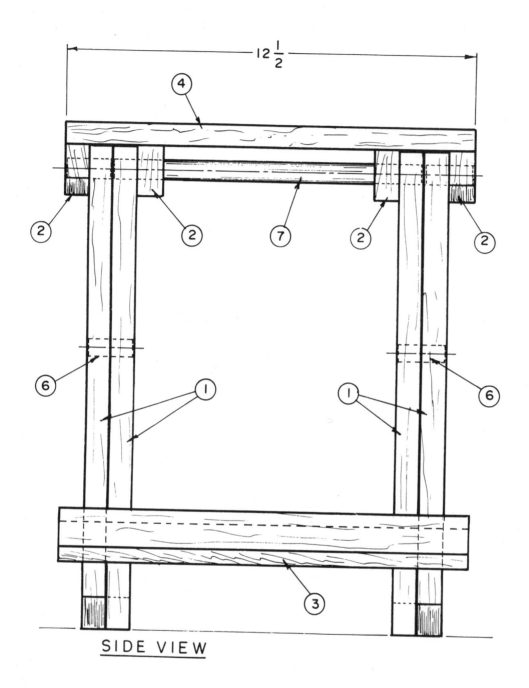

$12\frac{1}{2}$

SIDE VIEW

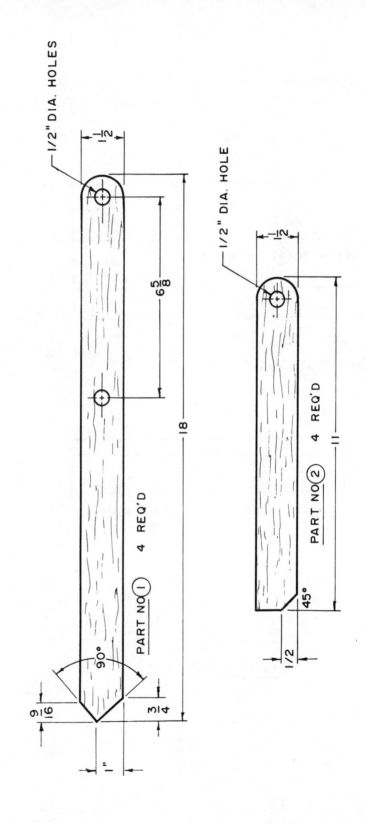

1/2" DIA. HOLES

1/2" DIA. HOLE

PART NO ① 4 REQ'D

PART NO ② 4 REQ'D

18

6 5/8

1/2

90°

9/16

3/4

1"

11

45°

1/2

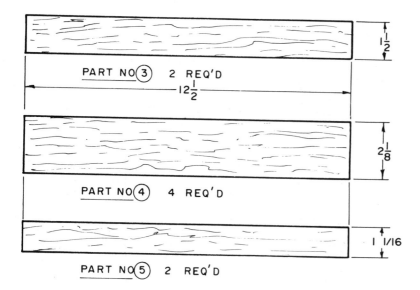

PART NO ③ 2 REQ'D

$1\frac{1}{2}$

$12\frac{1}{2}$

PART NO ④ 4 REQ'D

$2\frac{1}{8}$

PART NO ⑤ 2 REQ'D

1 1/16

(ALL PARTS 3/4" THICK)

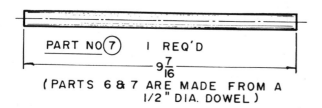

PART NO ⑦ 1 REQ'D

$9\frac{7}{16}$

(PARTS 6 & 7 ARE MADE FROM A
1/2" DIA. DOWEL)

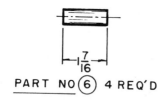

$1\frac{7}{16}$

PART NO ⑥ 4 REQ'D

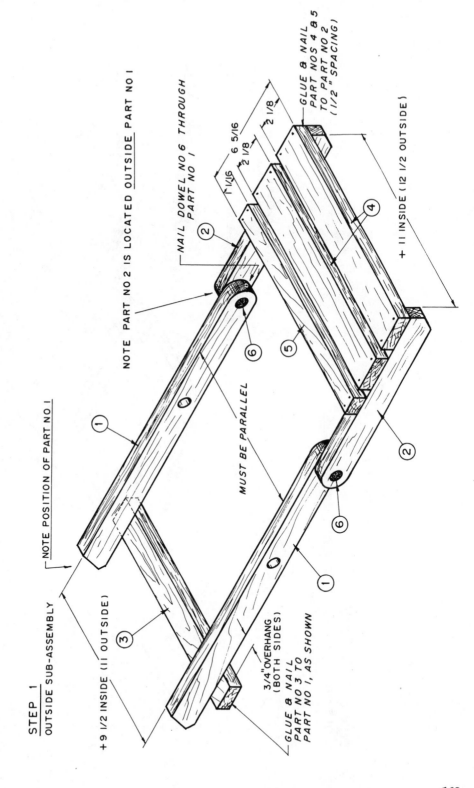

STEP 1
OUTSIDE SUB-ASSEMBLY

NOTE POSITION OF PART NO 1

NOTE PART NO 2 IS LOCATED OUTSIDE PART NO 1

NAIL DOWEL NO 6 THROUGH
PART NO 1

GLUE & NAIL
PART NOS 4 & 5
TO PART NO 2
( 1/2 " SPACING )

2 1/8

6 5/16

2 1/8

1 1/16

+ 11 INSIDE ( 12 1/2 OUTSIDE )

MUST BE PARALLEL

+ 9 1/2 INSIDE ( 11 OUTSIDE )

3/4 "OVERHANG
( BOTH SIDES )

GLUE & NAIL
PART NO 3 TO
PART NO 1, AS SHOWN

1    2    3    4    5    6

163

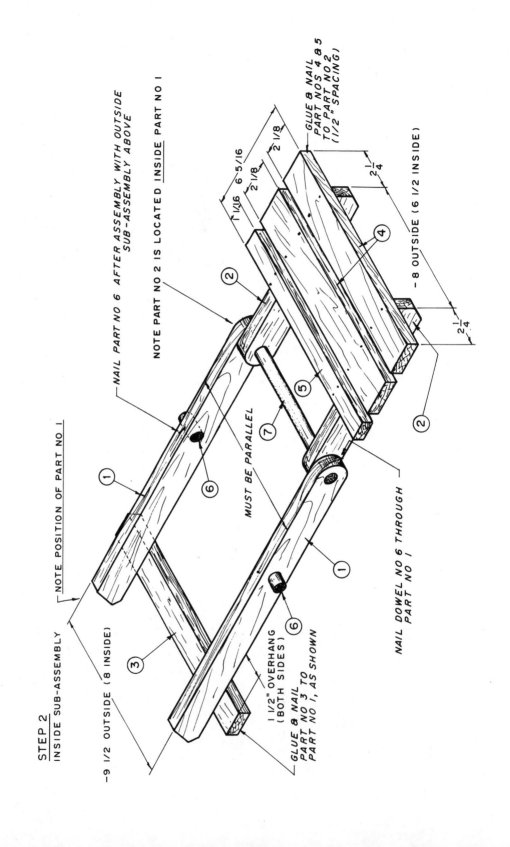

STEP 2
INSIDE SUB-ASSEMBLY

NOTE POSITION OF PART NO I

NAIL PART NO 6 AFTER ASSEMBLY WITH OUTSIDE
SUB-ASSEMBLY ABOVE

NOTE PART NO 2 IS LOCATED INSIDE PART NO I

GLUE & NAIL
PART NOS 4 & 5
TO PART NO 2
( 1 I/2" SPACING )

2 I/8
2 I/8
6 5/16
2 I/8
1 I/16

2 1/4

- 8 OUTSIDE ( 6 I/2 INSIDE )

2 1/4

MUST BE PARALLEL

NAIL DOWEL NO 6 THROUGH
PART NO I

- 9 I/2 OUTSIDE ( 8 INSIDE )

I I/2" OVERHANG
( BOTH SIDES )

GLUE & NAIL
PART NO 3 TO
PART NO I, AS SHOWN

164

# Coasting Sled

DURING THE FIRST HALF OF THE EIGHTEENTH CENTURY, MOST SLEDS WERE BUILT by the father or grandfather of the family, a local woodworker, or sometimes by the local blacksmith. These first sleds were not used as toys; they were used only for utilitarian purposes. As people began to accept the idea of children's playtime, the sled's function shifted from a transportation vehicle to a toy.

By the middle of the eighteenth century, companies starting to commercially build sleds for sale. By 1850 or so, it was said there were over twelve companies manufacturing coasting sleds in this country.

During the winter of 1860, Henry Morton, of West Sumner, Maine, built over 50 sleds to be sold in his hometown. He found the demand for sleds so great that he established a company to build only coasting sleds. His company builds coasting sleds even today.

As sleds became more and more in demand and more companies started to manufacture sleds, competition became very fierce. Companies began adding all kinds of special features to the sleds. Most were gaily decorated with bright colors and gold stripes. These wonderful sleds had a heavy coat of varnish added over the paint so the stripes would not wear away.

This project is an exact copy of an early coasting sled I found in Rhode Island a few years ago. It is fun to make, and will surely bring back a lot of memories for years to come. It is a rather simple project with only six parts— two of which are identical.

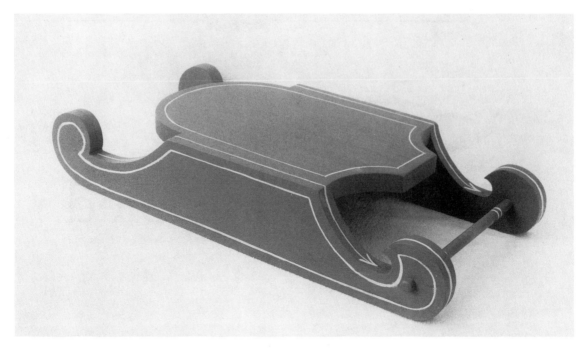

Coaster sleds such as this one should be very solid, so use a hardwood such as oak or rock maple.

# Instructions

Study the drawings carefully, so you fully understand how the sled is made and assembled before starting.

Measure out and cut all parts per the Materials List. If necessary, glue up material for the wide boards if you do not have the correct width. Follow by sanding the boards using a fine paper. This will save you from having to do it later, after the parts are cut to shape.

On a thick piece of paper of cardboard, 4 inches wide × 22 inches long, draw a 1-inch grid. Transfer the shape of the rail (part 1) point-by-point to the paper.

─────────────── **MATERIALS LIST** ───────────────

| Part No. | Name | Size | Req'd. |
|----------|------|------|--------|
| 1 | Rail | ¾ × 4 – 22 Long | 2 |
| 2 | Top Board | ¾ × 8½ – 14 Long | 1 |
| 3 | Pull | ½ Dia. – 10½ Long | 1 |
| 4 | Brace | ¾ × 1 – 8½ Long | 2 |

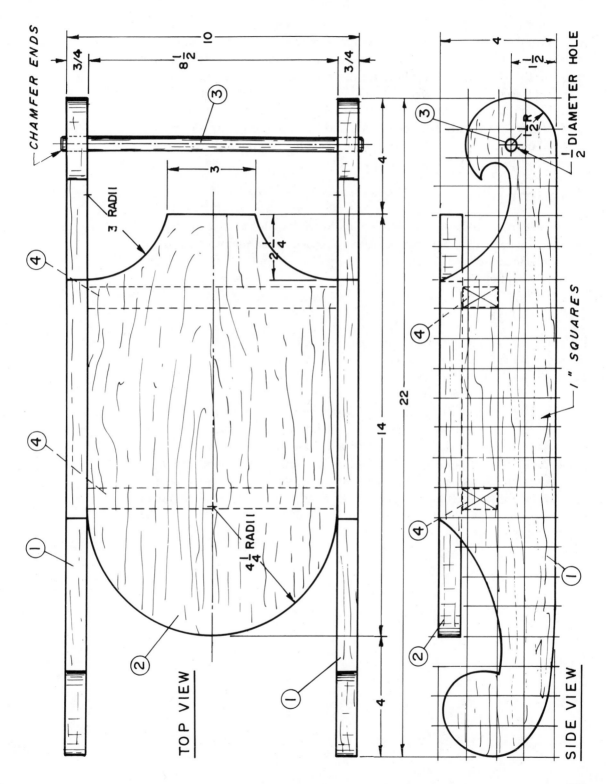

CHAMFER ENDS

10

3/4

$8\frac{1}{2}$

3/4

③

3 RADII

3

$2\frac{1}{4}$

④

④

①

$4\frac{1}{4}$ RADII

②

①

4

4

14

22

4

TOP VIEW

4

$1\frac{1}{2}$

③

$1\frac{1}{2}$ R

$\frac{1}{2}$ DIAMETER HOLE

④

1" SQUARES

④

②

①

SIDE VIEW

167

Tack the two rails together with two finishing nails on each end—out of the way of the cuts—and transfer the shape from the paper to the wood. Then cut out the two rails as a pair while the parts are still attached together. Locate and drill the ½-inch-diameter hole for the pull (part 3), as shown.

Sand the edges of the rails, still nailed together, so you will have an *exact* pair. Be sure to keep the edges sharp. Now separate the parts and set aside.

On a piece of wood, 8½ inches wide and 14 inches long, lay out and cut the top board (part 2). Sand the edges, still keeping all edges sharp. Cut the two braces (part 4) to size and sand all over.

# Assembly

Dry-fit all parts to make sure everything fits correctly. Glue and clamp the sled together, keeping everything square. After the glue has set, remove the clamps, and using square cut nails, nail the sled together. Do not set the nail heads, as they should be seen.

# Finishing

Distress your sled slightly to simulate years of use. Use any odd objects to make the distress marks—don't be afraid to even scratch your sled here and there. Lightly resand after distressing.

Next, apply a coat of undercoat paint all over. The original sled was painted a bright blue with yellow pinstriping. Don't be afraid to try your hand at pinstriping. Your pinstriping does *not* have to be exact and perfect. It will still look like the original sled. The sled shown here was my first attempt at pinstriping. It is not perfect, but it *does* look handmade. The trick is to use a long pinstriping brush and to thin your paint slightly. Practice on a piece of scrap wood until you get the hang of it. Keep a rag or cotton swab with thinner on it handy to wipe off any goofs. Apply a coat of varnish over the sled, let dry thoroughly, and the project is done.

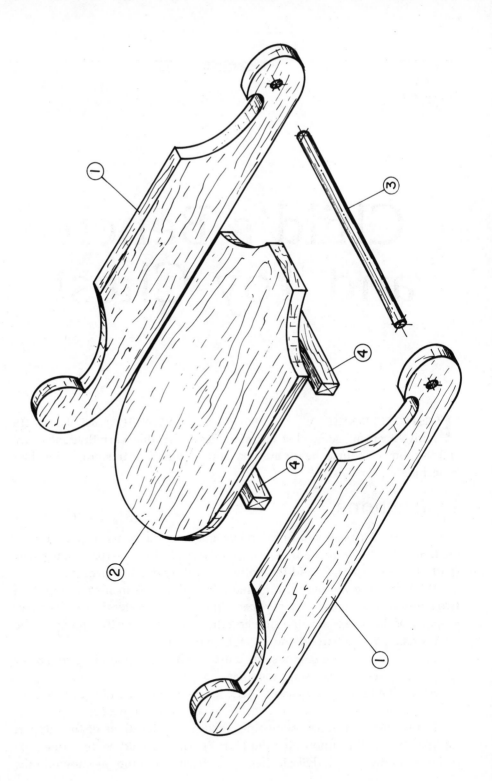

# Child's Bench
# and Toy Chest

THIS PROJECT DOUBLES AS A CHILD'S BENCH AND A TOY CHEST. BECAUSE OF ITS Early American, somewhat Victorian, design, it adds warmth to most any child's room. Of course, hearts are very popular today, so this project just had to include a heart.

## Instructions

Study the drawings so you fully understand how the bench will be assembled. Start by gluing up the wide backboard (part 1), the side (part 2), the skirt (part 3), the lid (part 4), and the bottom board, (part 7), if necessary.

While you are waiting for the glue to set, draw a 1-inch-square grid on two or three large pieces of heavy paper. On this grid, transfer the shapes point-by-point of the backboard, the side and the skirt. Transfer the shapes to the appropriate pieces of wood and carefully cut them out.

Because an exacting pair of sides must be cut, it is a good idea to tape or temporarily tack the two sides together.

Sand all edges and surfaces. Check for overall sizes and squareness.

Notch the sides, ¾ inch × 9 inches as shown for the skirt.

In the *interior* surfaces of the sides, lay out the locations of the support top (part 8) and the support bottom (part 7). They should be positioned 9½ inches from the floor and 5½ inches apart, from top to top, as shown in the

## MATERIALS LIST

| Part No. | Name | Size | Req'd. |
|---|---|---|---|
| 1 | Backboard | ¾ × 30 – 34½ Long | 1 |
| 2 | Side | ¾ × 12½ – 35 Long | 2 |
| 3 | Skirt | ¾ × 9 – 36 Long | 1 |
| 4 | Lid | ¾ × 10½ – 34⅜ Long | 1 |
| 5 | Backstop | ¾ × 2 – 34½ Long | 1 |
| 6 | Bottom Board | ¾ × 11 – 34½ Long | 1 |
| 7 | Support Bottom | ¾ × 1 – 11¾ Long | 2 |
| 8 | Support Top | ¾ × 1 – 11 Long | 2 |
| 9 | Brace – Seat | ¾ × 1 – 33 Long | 1 |
| 10 | Hinge | 2 × 2 Brass | 2 |

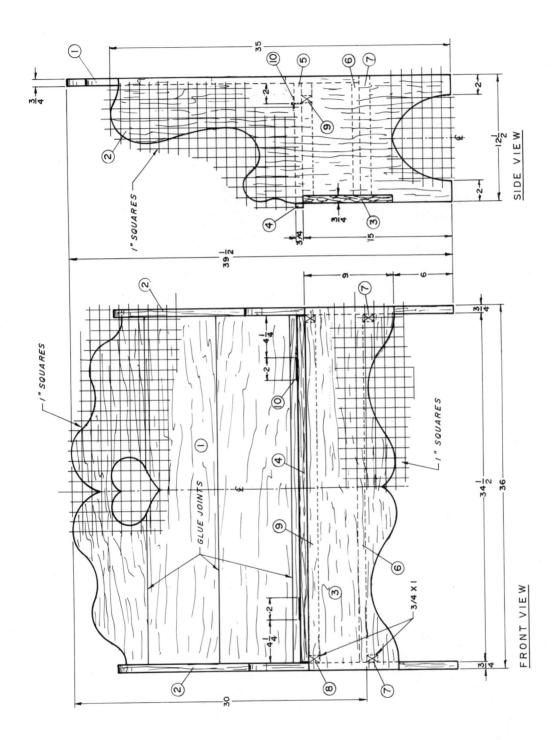

SIDE VIEW

FRONT VIEW

1" SQUARES

GLUE JOINTS

3/4 X 1

exploded view. The top edge of the top support should be positioned at the top of the notch as shown in the SIDE VIEW. Note that the support top (part 8) is positioned *in*, ¾ inch from the back edge to allow for the backboard, part 1. Be sure that they are square with the back (90 degrees) and *parallel* to each other. Check that the two side subassemblies and the supports (parts 7 and 8) line up exactly and make an exact pair.

## Assembly

Dry-fit all parts to ensure correct fit. Adjust if necessary.

Glue and nail the backboard to the two sides, and add the bottom board (part 6).

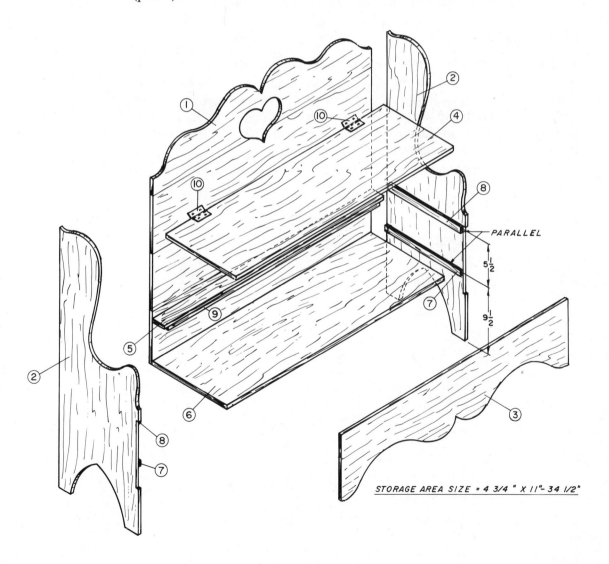

STORAGE AREA SIZE = 4 3/4 " X 11"- 34 1/2"

*Note:* Part 6 is also placed ¾ inch from the back edge of part 2.

Add the backstop (part 5) to the backboard. Then add the seat brace to the backstop. Notice that the seat brace is placed along the *front* edge of the backstop (see SIDE VIEW for details).

Glue and nail the skirt in place. Check that everything is square and flush.

Check that the bench sits flat on the floor and does not rock. Adjust if necessary.

Check that the lid fits correctly and that there is a little space all around. Attach the hinges (part 10) to the lid (part 4), and attach the lid with the hinges to the backstop.

Sand all over and "break" all edges slightly. Then round the front edge of the seat (part 4). The bench is now ready to be finished.

# Finishing

As this bench will be used by young children, it is extremely important that you do not paint the bench with a paint containing lead. As this bench has a somewhat Early American flare, it should be painted with rustic color. Choose a color to match or blend with the room the bench will be placed in. Remove the hinges and lid before painting. You might wish to paint the interior of the toy box a different color for contrast.

*Note:* the storage area is 4¾ inches deep, 11 inches wide, and 34½ inches long.

# IV

# *Projects with a Heart*

# Projects with a Heart

TODAY, HEARTS SEEM TO BE IN FASHION. EVERYPLACE YOU LOOK YOU SEE ITEMS for sale that feature a heart or two. Here are seven rather simple projects: Magazine Rack, Spice Wall Box, Wall Shelf, Child's Sled, French Bread Box, Silver Tray, and Window Box—each of which can easily be made in a weekend. I choose these seven simple projects because they seem to be popular items in local stores and in various mail-order sales catalogs throughout the country.

Rather than give directions for each of the seven projects, simple instructions are given that actually apply to all seven.

## Instructions

As with any project, study the plans carefully so that you fully understand how everything is assembled before starting. If you plan to paint your project, selection of knot-free wood is not essential; however, if you plan to stain your project, choose knot-free, straight-grained wood. All seven of these projects can be made of a softwood or a hardwood. They will be nice in either.

Note that the heart in all seven projects is exactly the same size and shape, so you could make two or three of these projects and they will all match (mix and match if you wish). Also, because the same heart size and shape is used, only *one* heart shaped pattern will be necessary. Use a compass to swing the required arcs as shown. If you have a 1⅝-inch-diameter drill size, drill the two

| Project | Part No. | Name | Size | Req'd. |
|---|---|---|---|---|
| Magazine Rack | 1 | End | ¾ × 11 – 30 Long | 2 |
| | 2 | Shelf | ¾ × 11 – 15 Long | 4 |
| Spice Wall Box | 1 | Front | ¾ × 9 – 8 Long | 1 |
| | 2 | Side | ¾ × 9 – 6⅝ Long | 2 |
| | 3 | Back | ¾ × 8 – 15 Long | 1 |
| | 4 | Bottom | ¾ × 5½ – 6½ Long | 1 |
| Wall Shelf | 1 | Backboard | ¾ × 5 – 21 Long | 1 |
| | 2 | End Brackets | ¾ × 5 – 6¼ Long | 2 |
| | 3 | Shelf | ¾ × 6½ – 27 Long | 1 |
| | 4 | Peg | ⅝ Dia. – 2½ Long | 2 |
| Sled | 1 | Top Board | ¾ × 10 – 22 Long | 1 |
| | 2 | Runners | ¾ × 4 – 28 Long | 2 |
| | 3 | Brace | ¾ × 1¼ – 8½ Long | 2 |
| | 4 | Handle | ¾ Dia. × 10¾ Long | 1 |
| French Bread Box | 1 | Backboard | ½ × 7½ – 32 Long | 1 |
| | 2 | Side | ½ × 6¼ – 28 Long | 2 |
| | 3 | Front | ½ × 7 – 24 Long | 1 |
| | 4 | Lid | ½ × 7½ – 7½ Long | 1 |
| | 5 | Stop | ½ × ½ – 5⅝ Long | 1 |
| | 6 | Bottom | ¾ × 5½ – 6 Long | 1 |
| Silver Tray | 1 | Side | ½ × 3½ – 14 Long | 2 |
| | 2 | End | ½ × 3½ – 7½ Long | 2 |
| | 3 | Center Board | ½ × 7 – 13 Long | 1 |
| | 4 | Bottom | ½ × 7 – 13 Long | 1 |
| Window Box | 1 | End | ¾ × 7 – 7½ Long | 2 |
| | 2 | Side | ¾ × 4 – 20 Long | 2 |
| | 3 | Bottom | ¾ × 6¼ – 8½ Long | 1 |

1⅝-inch holes and cut out the bottom half of the heart. This will eliminate cutting the two tight corners at the top of the heart and will make it almost exact.

Referring to the Materials List, cut all wood to size. Keep everything parallel and square as you proceed. Be sure multiple parts are exactly the same size.

Each of the seven projects requires a pattern or two to be laid out. On a sheet of thick paper, draw a 1-inch grid slightly larger than the area required. Lay out the required shape, point-by-point, from the drawing to the paper. Transfer this shape to the wood and carefully cut it out. If you want a matched pair of parts, either tack or tape the parts together, cut them out, and sand the edges as a *pair* before separating the parts. This will ensure an exact pair of parts.

Cut all dadoes and rabbets to size as required.

Dry-fit all parts to make sure that everything is correct and will go together correctly. Adjust the parts to fit if necessary. It might be a good idea to sand all surfaces of each piece before assembly, but take care to keep all edges sharp.

Glue and nail all parts together, checking that everything is square and true. After the glue has set, set the nails and putty as required.

Sand all over, keeping all corners rather sharp. Clean all over with a tack rag and your project is ready to be finished.

# Finishing

Any of these projects can be either painted or stained and varnished. If anyone in your house is good at tole painting, all of these projects make great tole painting projects. You might want to take up tole painting yourself. It becomes fairly easy with practice and will add a lot to your project. There are many excellent books out that explain tole painting step by step. If you goof, or just don't like your tole painting, you can always repaint over it. No one will ever know.

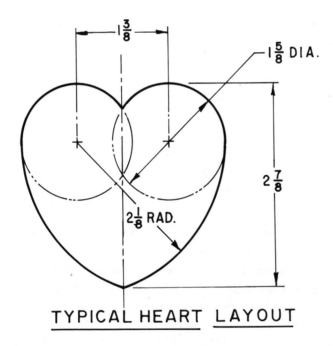

TYPICAL HEART LAYOUT

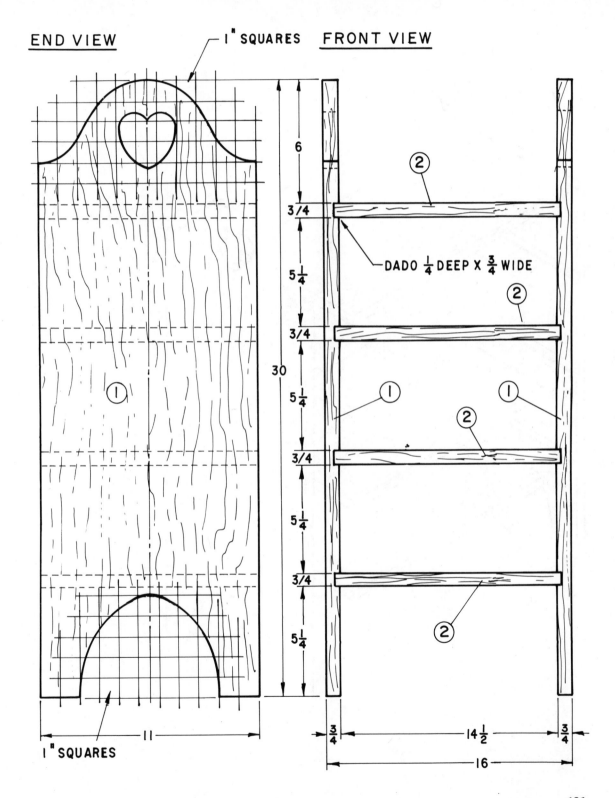

END VIEW

1" SQUARES

FRONT VIEW

6

3/4

DADO ¼ DEEP X ¾ WIDE

5¼

3/4

30

5¼

3/4

5¼

3/4

5¼

11

1" SQUARES

¾

14½

¾

16

181

# MAGAZINE RACK

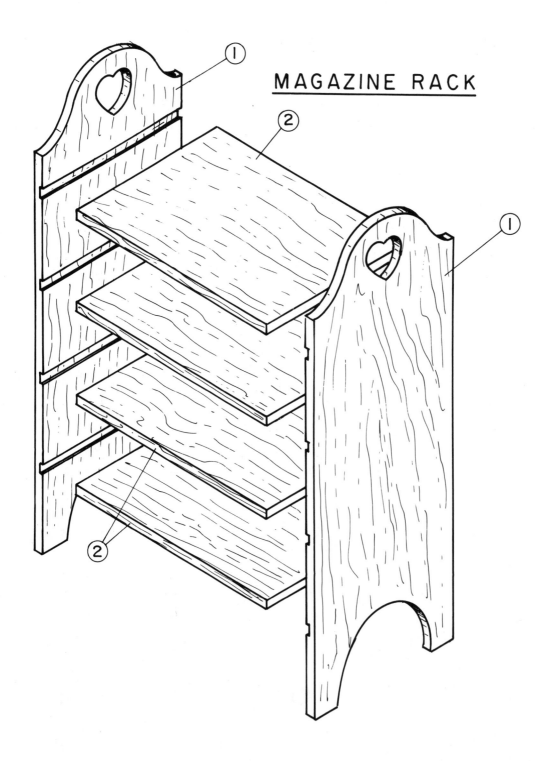

183

# SPICE WALL BOX

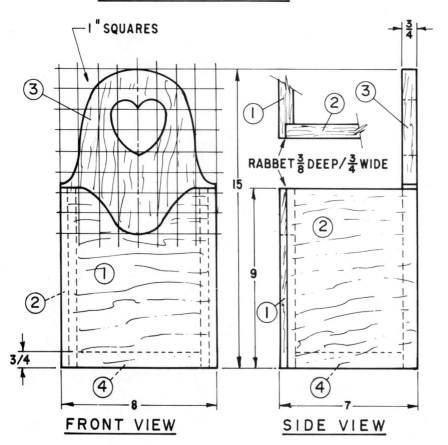

1" SQUARES

RABBET $\frac{3}{8}$ DEEP/$\frac{3}{4}$ WIDE

15

9

3/4

8

FRONT VIEW

7

$\frac{3}{4}$

SIDE VIEW

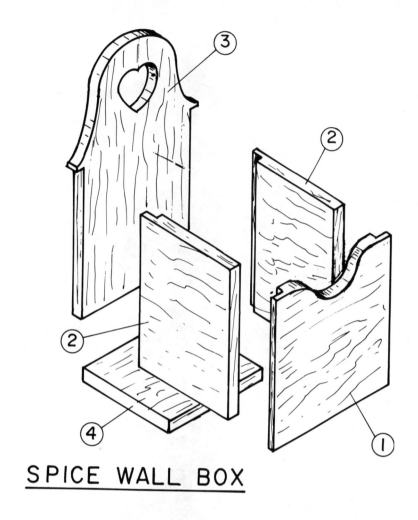

# SPICE WALL BOX

186

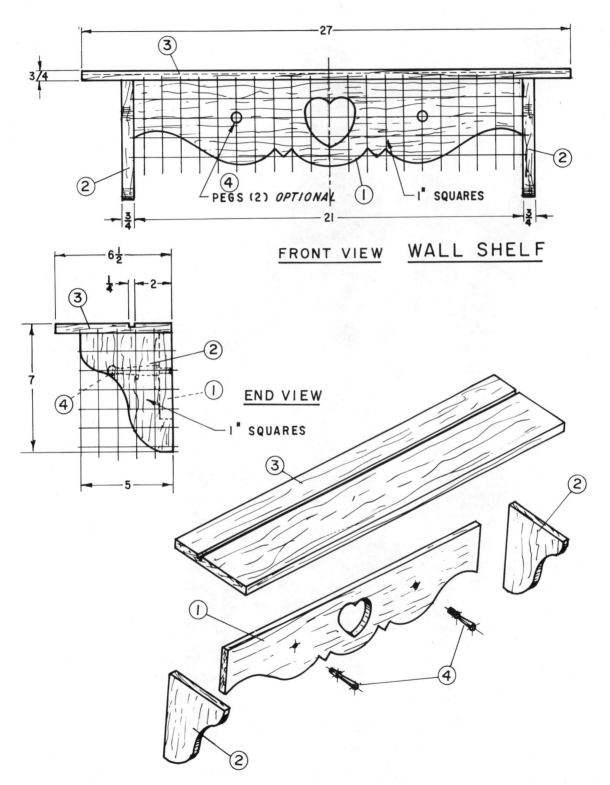

27

3/4

③

④ PEGS (2) *OPTIONAL*

② ②

21

3/4  3/4

① ① ⃝ 1" SQUARES

FRONT VIEW   WALL SHELF

6½

¼  2

③

②

7

④ ①

5

END VIEW

1" SQUARES

③

②

①

④

②

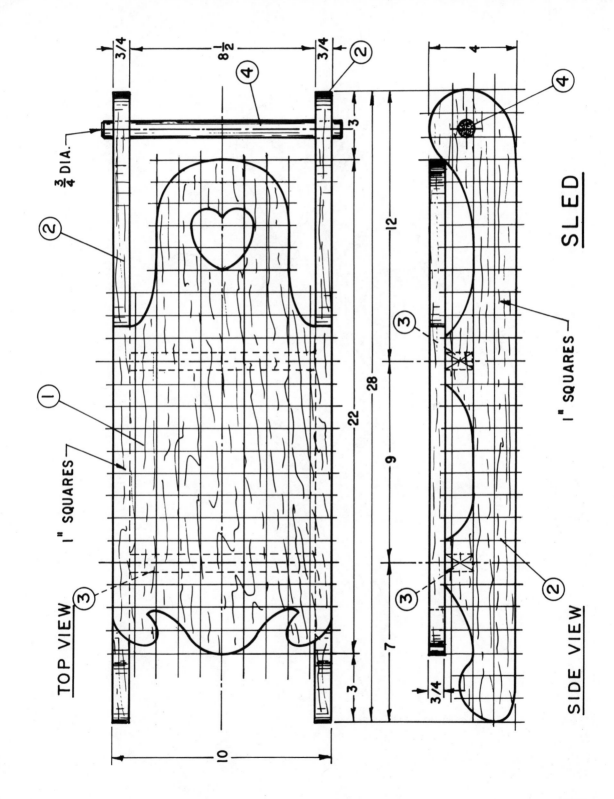

3/4 · 8½ · 3/4

④

②

$\frac{3}{4}$ DIA.

②

3

4

④

12

②

① I" SQUARES

③

③

28

9

③

22

③

②

I" SQUARES

7

**TOP VIEW**

10

3

3/4

**SIDE VIEW**

**SLED**

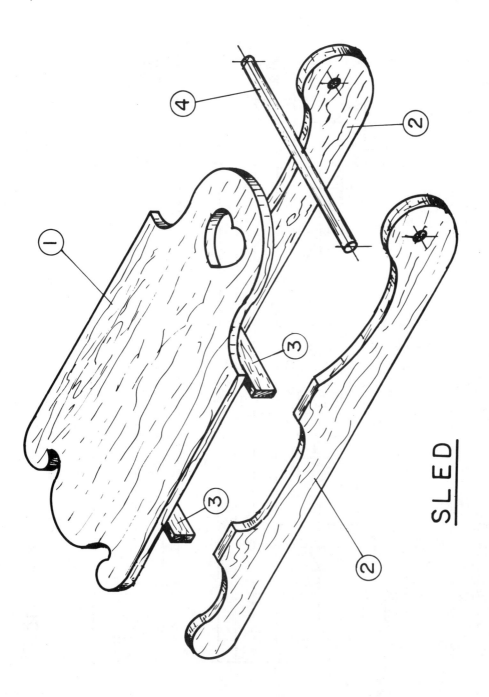

SLED

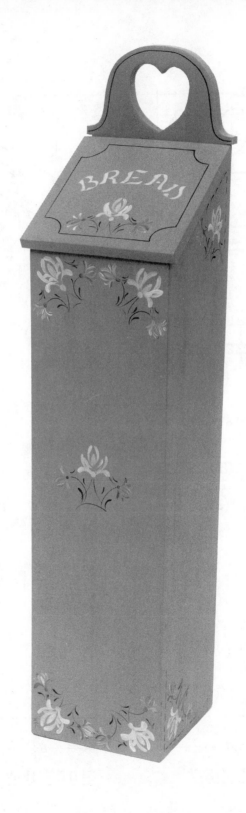

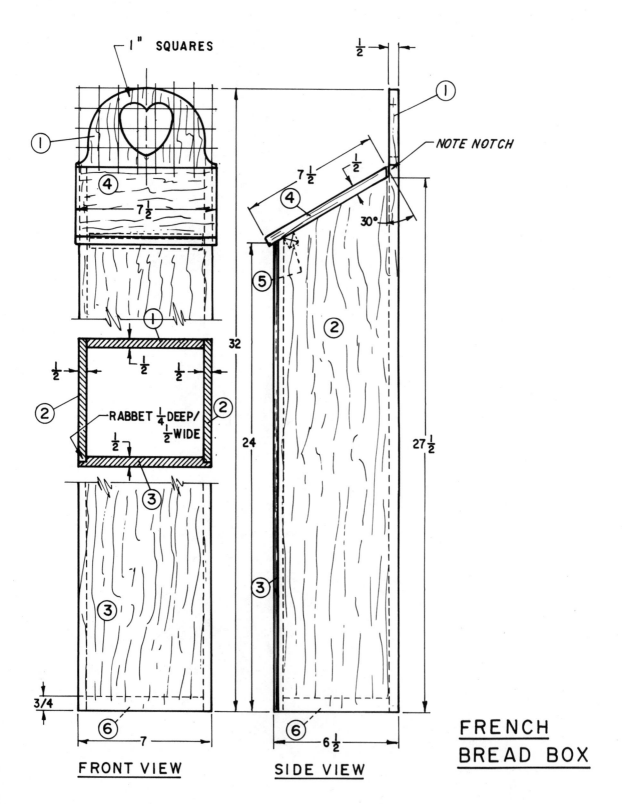

1" SQUARES

½

①

NOTE NOTCH

①

7½

½

④

30°

④

7½

⑤

②

RABBET ¼ DEEP/
½ WIDE

32

½    ½    ½

②    ②

½

24

27½

③

③

②

③

③

3/4

⑥    7    ⑥    6½

FRONT VIEW    SIDE VIEW

FRENCH
BREAD BOX

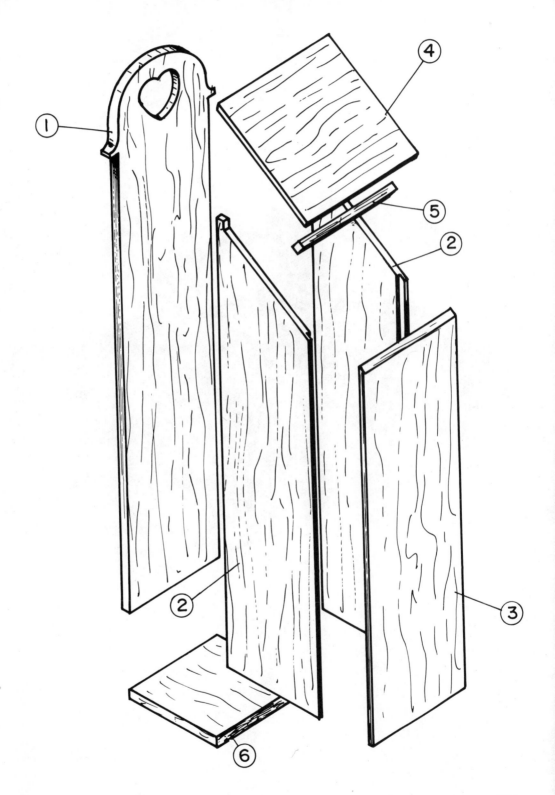

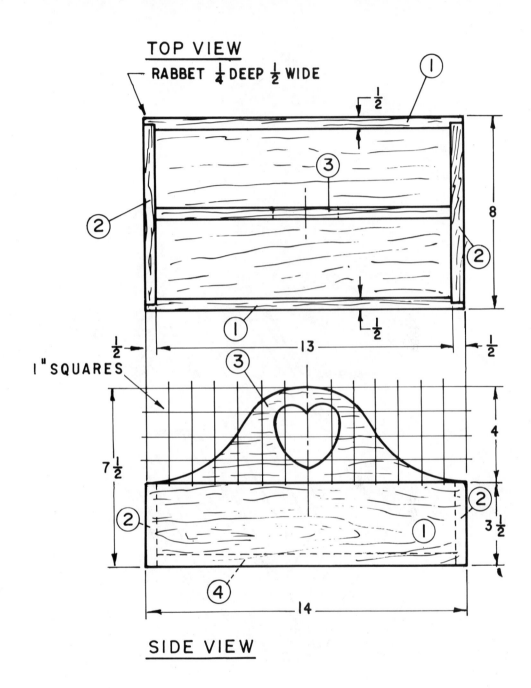

TOP VIEW

RABBET $\frac{1}{4}$ DEEP $\frac{1}{2}$ WIDE

①

③

②

②

8

$\frac{1}{2}$

$\frac{1}{2}$

①

$\frac{1}{2}$

13

$\frac{1}{2}$

1" SQUARES

③

4

$7\frac{1}{2}$

②

②

①

$3\frac{1}{2}$

④

14

SIDE VIEW

# SILVER TRAY

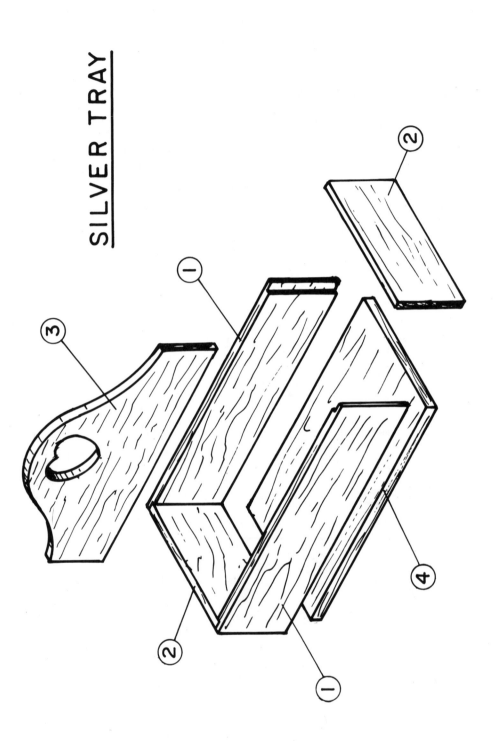

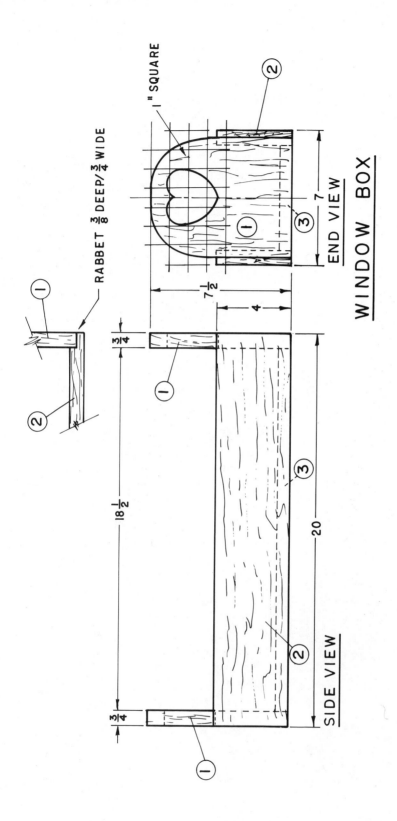

RABBET $\frac{3}{8}$ DEEP/$\frac{3}{4}$ WIDE

1" SQUARE

END VIEW

7

7$\frac{1}{2}$

4

18$\frac{1}{2}$

$\frac{3}{4}$

$\frac{3}{4}$

20

SIDE VIEW

# WINDOW BOX

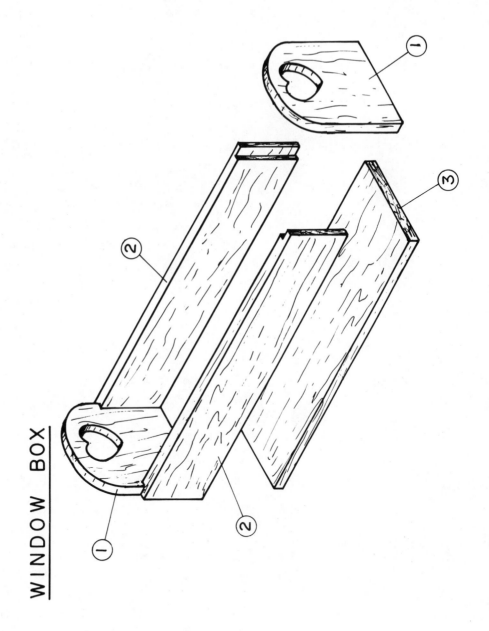

WINDOW BOX

# V
# *Weekend Projects*

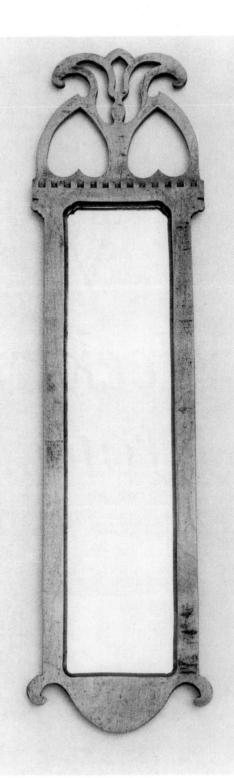

# Hall Mirror

THIS HALL MIRROR IS A TAKEOFF OF A VERY EARLY 1775 COURTING MIRROR. Courting mirrors were given to a young lady by a young man as a display of affection. It was said if the young lady smiled upon receiving the courting mirror, it was taken as an acceptance of marriage.

This version has been lengthened about three times to bring it in keeping for a hall mirror. The top and bottom design has been taken directly from an original mirror that was about 17 inches in overall length. If you would like a copy of an original courting mirror, reduce the 42-inch overall length to 17 inches.

Notice the unusual dentil work, it is cut out exactly as you would make progressive cuts for a box joint. If you do not know how to make box joints, check the instructions from any good woodworking book. This is even easier as there are no mating parts to worry about.

## Instructions

Study the drawings carefully so you fully understand how the mirror goes together. The exploded view shows how it is assembled.

Cut all parts to overall size per the Materials List. Try to choose a hardwood with a nice grain pattern. The backboard (part 5) can be made of pine.

| Part No. | Name | Size | Req'd. |
|:---:|:---|:---|:---:|
| 1 | Top Section | ½ × 11 – 10 Long | 1 |
| 2 | Bottom Section | ½ × 11 – 33¼ Long | 1 |
| 3 | Side Board | ½ × 1¼ – 28¾ Long | 2 |
| 4 | Bottom Board | ½ × 1¼ – 11 Long | 1 |
| 5 | Backboard | ⅜ × 6⅞ – 28¾ Long | 1 |
| 6 | Mirror | ⅛ × 6⅝ – 28⅝ Long | 1 |
| 7 | Nail (Sq.–Cut) | ¾ Long – Finishing | 12 |

On a piece of paper, lay out a ½-inch grid and transfer the shape of the mirror to the grid for both the top section (part 1) and the bottom section (part 2). Note the given diameters. Carefully locate all center points, as holes will be drilled first before cutting out.

Starting with the top section, locate and drill the four 2-inch-diameter holes, the four ⅝-inch-diameter holes, the one ½-inch-diameter hole, and the two, ⅜-inch-diameter holes. Cut out the remaining interior shape. Cut the exterior shape and sand all over, keeping all edges sharp. Be sure that the grain of the wood is going up and down to match the bottom section (part 2).

To make the bottom section (part 2), cut the thirteen ¹³⁄₃₂-inch notches of the dentil work in the top area, using the same steps as you would normally follow to make a box joint.

Center your pattern around the two outer teeth of the dentil work and transfer the pattern to the wood.

Locate and drill the six ¾-inch-diameter holes and the two ½-inch-diameter holes. Cut the interior area out. If you have a router bit with a ⅛-inch radius and follower, rout out the interior edge as shown. If you do not have a router bit that will make the interior edge shape, simply rasp and sand a rounded edge all the way around. Cut the exterior shape, and sand all edges.

Cut the bottom board (part 4) to size, using the bottom section (part 2) as a pattern.

Chamfer all edges of the backboard as shown. Leave about ¹⁄₁₆-inch edge all around the backboard. This part will be fitted to the actual opening later to suit.

# Assembly

Glue the top section (part 1) to the bottom section (part 2). Note that there is a 1¼-inch overlap between parts.

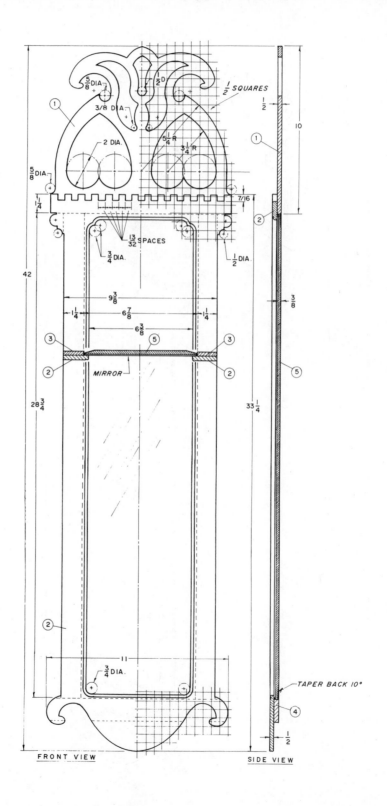

FRONT VIEW

SIDE VIEW

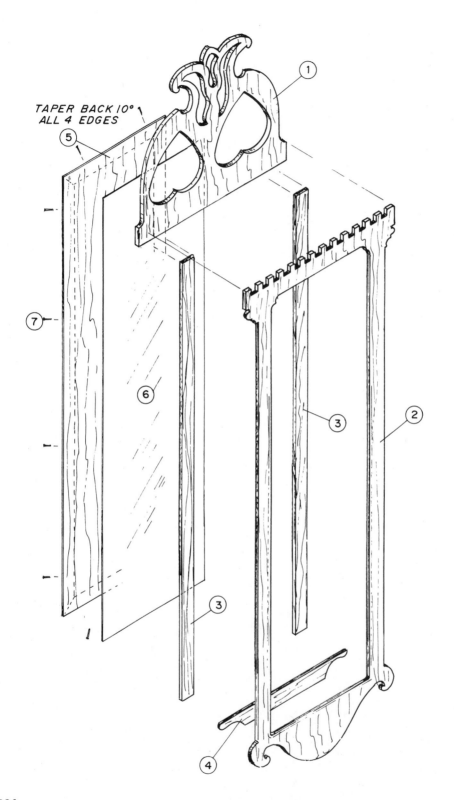

TAPER BACK 10°
ALL 4 EDGES

Nail the bottom board (part 4) to the bottom section (part 2). Do *not* glue these parts together, as the grain is going different directions and the bottom section will warp.

Add the two side boards (part 3) with glue, keeping the outer edges in line as shown.

Use a piece of mirror, cut to size, to check the actual opening *after* you assemble the mirror. Make the mirror about ⅛ inch *smaller* than the finished opening.

# Finishing

Finish the mirror as you would any project. Use a stain of your choice. A satin finish is more in keeping with the mirror's overall design and time-period, but a high gloss would be fine. Apply a coat or two of paste wax.

The mirror is held in place with the backboard. The backboard is tacked in place with twelve, short, square-cut or finishing nails. They are lightly tacked in place at an angle approximately the same as the chamfer of the backboard. *Take care not to crack the mirror.*

Add two small eyelets on both sides where the top and bottom sections are joined. Use a picture frame wire between the eyelets to hang the mirror.

All that remains is to go out and find a young lady whom to give this mirror. Be sure to watch for a telling smile.

# Scandinavian Bookshelf

THE SCANDINAVIAN BOOK/DISPLAY SHELF SHOWN IS 48 INCHES LONG AND 42 inches high. It was designed to fit a 4-foot module system. Standing alone it is simple and functional—an ideal weekend project for beginning to intermediate woodworkers. You can adjust the lengths of the pieces to suit available wall lengths.

## Instructions

Because it is so strong, solid red oak is a good wood to use. The unsupported span of shelf, nearly 4 feet, requires a sturdy wood to keep the shelf from sagging under a full load of books. You can use weaker woods, provided you shorten the length of the bookshelf so that this unsupported span is reduced. Clear white pine, for example, should not be used in shelf spans exceeding 30 inches. Lower-grade, large-knot pine may only be able to span 24 inches without sagging.

The ¾-inch-thick shelf parts may be purchased already surfaced on four sides, and all the same width, for convenience.

Glued-up boards are also acceptable and are as strong or stronger than solid stock.

Use dowels to help align stock when gluing edge-to-edge. Apply glue to the edge of the boards, but not on the dowels, nor in the dowel holes. This would restrict the wood from expanding or contracting during changes in humidity. Edges should fit tight together without light showing through.

| Part No. | Name | Size | Req'd. |
|---|---|---|---|
| 1 | End Boards | ¾ × 8½ – 42 Long | 2 |
| 2 | Shelf | ¾ × 8½ – 49 Long | 4 |
| 3 | Backboard | ¾ × 4 – 48½ Long | 1 |
| 4 | Kick Board | ¾ × 3 – 48½ Long | 1 |
| 5 | Screw – Flathead | No. 8 – 1½ Long | 8 |
| 6 | Plug – Wood | Size to Suit | 8 |

It seems no matter how straight the boards are jointed and how carefully they are ripped, they never seem to end up exactly the same width when the shelf is assembled. This is because few boards are really flat when ripped on the table saw. Boards that are cupped become slightly wider when they are forced flat in the dado joint. To remedy this, lightly hand-plane the wide board down after assembly.

The backboard (part 3) and kick board (part 4) are ripped to width after the sides (part 1) and shelves (part 2). The combined width of both the kick board and the backboard is designed to be cut from one shelf-size board so there is a minimum of waste.

The radial-arm saw is the best tool to cut the parts to length. Once the radial-arm saw is adjusted for square cuts, it may be easily set up for multiple operations. Set the saw up to square one end of each shelf, and then slide the shelf to the other side of the table for the second cut. Use a stop-block clamped to the radial-arm saw fence on the second cut, so that all shelves are exactly the same length. In three settings the cutting is done. The shelves (part 2) are cut at 47 inches, the kick board and the backboard at 46½ inches, and the sides (part 1) at 42 inches. Check to be sure the corresponding parts are square and the same length.

Next, lay out the dado locations in the end parts. Although the dadoes may be cut by hand, or with dado blades on the table or radial-arm saw, you can also use a router for this operation. A ¾-inch dado bit will leave a clean, flat-bottomed cut ready to be glued and assembled. The router, coupled with a simple homemade jig, is safer and more accurate than other methods. Another plus is the router's ability to follow the contour of a slightly cupped end board. The dado remains the same depth across the entire width. Keeping the dadoes consistently at a ¼-inch depth across a slightly cupped end board will allow the board to be pulled flat during assembly.

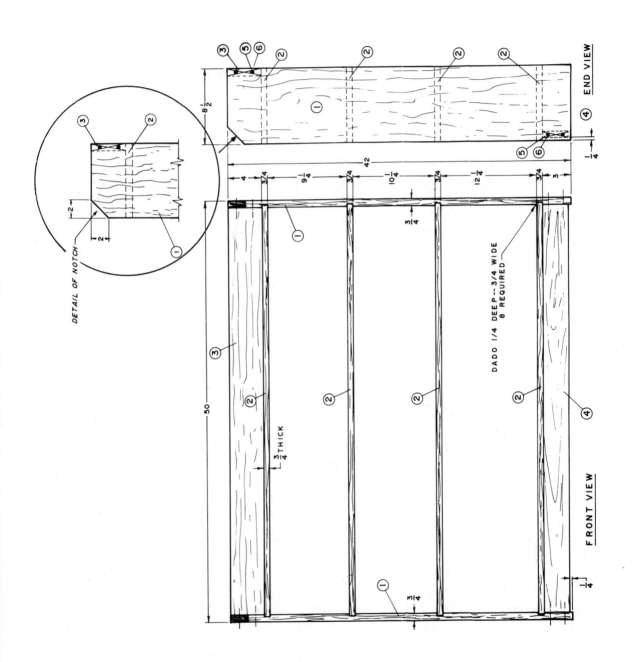

DETAIL OF NOTCH

END VIEW

FRONT VIEW

DADO 1/4 DEEP--3/4 WIDE
8 REQUIRED

3/4 THICK

A simple double-track jig to guide the router is clamped to the end board to ensure the router does not wander during the cutting operation. Cutting the dadoes is a safe, accurate, and easy operation with the jig guiding the router and both hands on the router handles.

To make the double-fence router jig, rip four pieces of scrap stock $\frac{1}{2} \times 2 \times 12$ inches. Glue and screw the pieces as shown. The only trick to the jig is to be sure the inside edges of the track are straight and the ends are screwed square to the track parts. The distance between the tracks is determined by the base of the router. The easiest way to make the jig is to fasten one track square to both end pieces and use the base of the router to space the second track from the first. The length of the track may be made to fit snugly to both sides of the end parts, or it may be longer to make an all-around jig for many other projects. All that is needed is that one end of the square track be clamped securely on the edge of the stock being machined.

When the first $\frac{1}{4}$-inch-deep cut is made, the bit travels through the stock and right across the end of the jig, leaving a shallow dado in the jig itself. This shallow dado cut in the jig is used to align future dadoes, when the jig is moved and clamped for the next cut. Always start the router cut in the far side of the stock, and pull the router toward the end of the jig. The end of the jig,

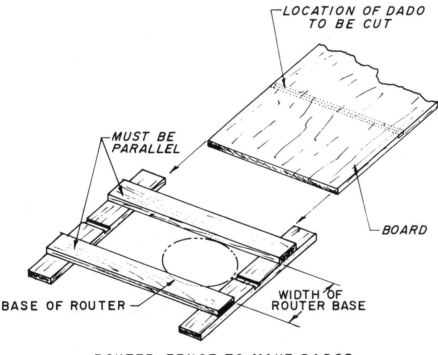

ROUTER FENCE TO MAKE DADOS

clamped against the stock, will keep the edge of the stock from splitting when the router bit exits.

After the end boards are dadoed, cut the top front angle of each board. Remember there is a definite right and left side here. Check the shelf fit in the dadoes. If they are tight at this point, sand only lightly the end of each shelf, so as not to decrease the thickness of the shelf board. Keep the dadoes snug for the strongest fit. Sand or plane all parts prior to assembly.

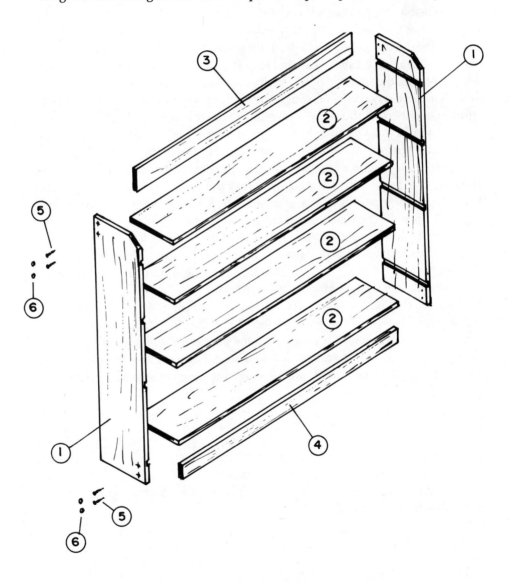

# Assembly

The shelves are now assembled with glue and screws. The screw holes are predrilled in the end boards first. The screws are countersunk to allow for plugs. After the holes are predrilled, lay masking tape down on both sides of the dadoes in the end boards. The tape will protect the sides from glue squeezing out during assembly.

The easiest way to assemble the shelves is on a wide bench with the shelves and end boards on edge. A power screwdriver is especially handy for this. Glue all the dadoes in one end board, then insert the shelves and secure with screws one shelf at a time. Then move to the second side. Dense woods like oak will require that the end of the shelves are also predrilled as the end boards were. For these woods drill through the counter bore holes in the end boards during assembly for the screw holes in the shelf boards.

As soon as the second side is in place, check the squareness of the case by measuring across the diagonals from opposite corners on the face of the bookcase. If the diagonals do not measure the same, the case is out-of-square. The case is squared with a bar clamp across the end boards of the bookcase. The bar clamp is placed in the same direction as the longest diagonal and snugged up until the diagonals measure the same.

When the case is square, insert the top brace and kick board and screw in place. The kick board is designed not to touch the floor. The small gap left beneath the kick board will keep the bookcase resting square on the end boards in case there is a slight hump in the floor.

Remove the masking tape after assembly. Cut plugs for the screw holes, and glue in place with the grain of the plug following the grain in the end boards. Careful selection of plugs by color and grain will make the plug almost unnoticeable after sanding and finishing. Let the plugs stand proud of the finish surface. Later, sand, file, or shave the plugs to the finished surface. Now finish sand.

# Finishing

The bookcase illustrated was finished with four coats of Watco Golden Oak oil finish, each applied 1 day apart. The third and fourth coat was wisk sanded smooth with 360 paper and then a coat of wax applied. To maintain the finish use a fine furniture polish.

# Wooden Thread Jaw Clamp

A VERY GOOD FRIEND OF MINE, JERRY ERNCE, MADE A BEAUTIFUL PAIR OF wooden thread jaw clamps for me as a gift. They were so beautiful, I suggested Jerry try doing a write-up on instructions on how to make them for a magazine article. I told him I would do the camera-ready artwork for it if he would. He did the write-up and it was published. I think this wooden jaw clamp project is such a wonderful project, I asked Jerry if I might add them to this book. What follows is a copy of that article:

I know you have seen one or more of these old-style, wooden thread, handmade clamps at every flea market you have ever gone to. I always marveled at how the old craftsman of yesterday ever got anything together with them, after having used the chrome steel clamps of today. Two years ago I bought a wood thread maker threadbox. Eager to try it, I made a toy clamp for my 5-year-old grandson. I was so impressed with its strength that I made two larger clamps for myself.

Today, I can't seem to keep them in my shop, as everyone that sees them just *has* to have one. It seems I am always making one or more for myself just so I have a workable clamp or two myself. They are fun to make and, of course, you *never* have enough wood clamps around the shop! Also, the pride of using a fine tool you have made yourself that works well instills a lot of confidence in your own work. These clamps make a wonderful gift, even for those who don't usually use them. Many are hung on office or den walls as decorations, yet they add nostalgia to just about any room.

215

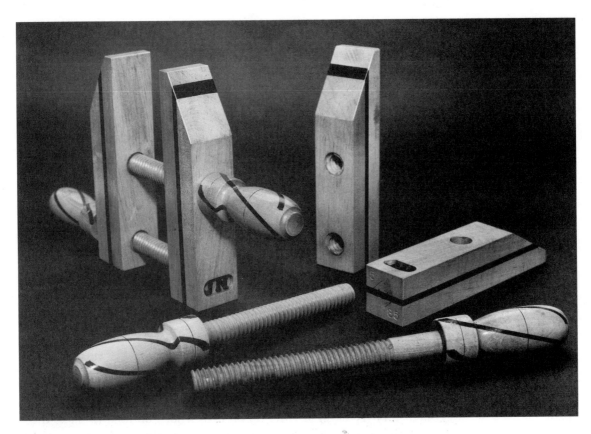

## Tools Required

A ¾-inch threadbox for threading, a drill press for drilling straight clean holes, and a wood lathe for turning the handles are the only tools actually required. If you don't have a lathe, square handles will do. (My threadbox is made by *Conover Woodcraft Specialties Inc.*, 18125 Madison Road, Parkman, OH 44080. I have been very pleased with it.)

## Selecting Material

Hardwoods are a must here, although some are better than others. You will have to experiment and use what works best for you. Oak and maple both make good jaws, but I like the maple better than the oak. I have also made some out of poplar and had good luck with it. Poplar is lighter than the other two and has held up very well in my shop. Whatever wood you choose, be sure it is close-grained.

The dowels I use are the standard birch dowels from any supply house. Choose only straight-grain dowels, without any sign of knots. A word of caution here: 99 percent of all dowels you buy are oversize. This will have to

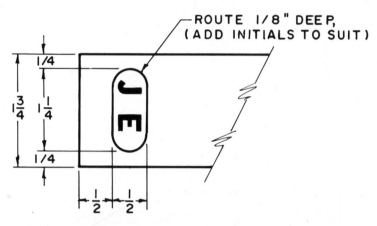

ROUTE 1/8" DEEP, (ADD INITIALS TO SUIT)

**VIEW OF BOTTOM (OPTIONAL)**

FIGURE 1

be corrected before you start making threads. Don't just sand them to size, as the sand will quickly dull your threadbox when you thread the dowel. If you take care in selecting your dowels you probably can eliminate this problem.

The more-advanced woodworker may elect to turn the dowel and handle as one piece. If so, remember that the last two turns or so for the threads will most likely have to be cut by hand. The threadbox knife is set in from the face of the tool and will jam up against the turned handle. Initials (see Fig. 1) are optional but really add that personal touch. They can be purchased from *Paxton's Beautiful Wood Store*, 5420 S. 99th E., Tulsa, OK 74146.

## Instructions

Start with the jaws. Select stock and cut as indicated in Figs. 5 and 6. Measure and mark the center of the clamps for the center hole. Now measure 1 inch from the rear of the clamp and locate the center for the other screw hole. Before drilling the holes, note that only one of the jaws actually has threads (refer to Figs. 2 and 5). This jaw will have two ⅝-inch-diameter holes in it, to allow for the threads, and the other jaw (Fig. 6) will have two ¾-inch diameter clearance holes in it.

Before drilling the threaded jaw, countersink the holes with a ⅞-inch-diameter bit, ¹⁄₁₆ inch deep, in on both sides of the jaw at the hole locations (Fig. 5). This will keep the hole from splintering when you later make the threads. Then drill the two ⅝-inch-diameter holes completely through and carefully tap the holes using a ¾-inch-diameter tap. Use a lot of wax as you tap the hole, and be sure to back out of the hole often to clear the chips as the wax will not let them fall away. It is *very* important that you start absolutely straight when you drill into the hole with the tap.

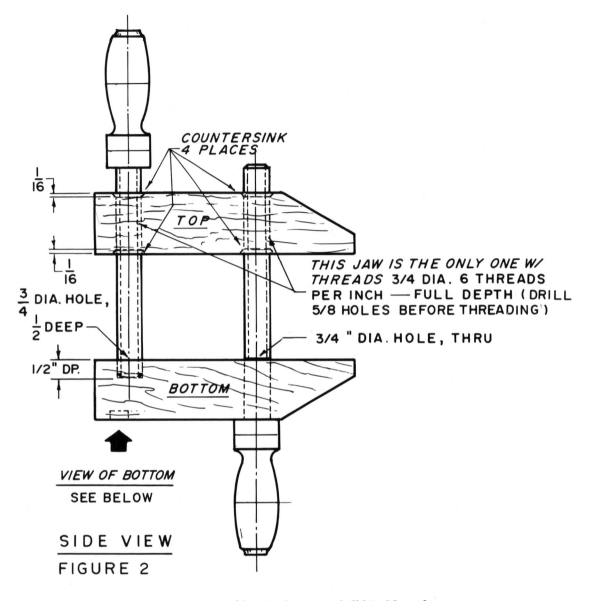

COUNTERSINK
4 PLACES

TOP

THIS JAW IS THE ONLY ONE W/
THREADS 3/4 DIA. 6 THREADS
PER INCH — FULL DEPTH (DRILL
5/8 HOLES BEFORE THREADING')

3/4 " DIA. HOLE, THRU

$\frac{1}{16}$

$\frac{1}{16}$

$\frac{3}{4}$ DIA. HOLE,
$\frac{1}{2}$ DEEP

1/2" DP.

BOTTOM

VIEW OF BOTTOM
SEE BELOW

SIDE VIEW
FIGURE 2

Next, drill the other jaw, using a ¾-inch-diameter drill bit. Note that one of the clearance holes, the one on the end, is drilled only ½ inch deep (see Figs. 2 and 6).

Select the material for the handle and drill a ¾-inch-diameter hole into it 2 inches deep and turn it on the lathe per Fig. 1.

Cut the dowel to length, making sure there is at least 2 inches extra that will be inserted into the handle (see Figs. 4 and 7). Mark off on the blank dowel where everything will be located. Don't forget the bearing surface on the center screw *plus* the 2 inches for the handle.

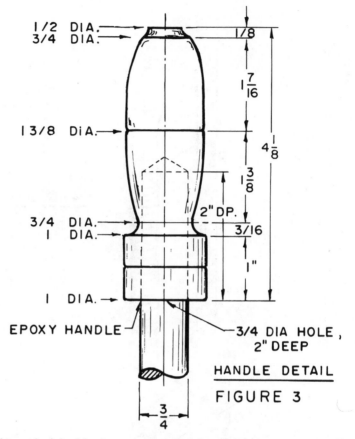

1/2 DIA.
3/4 DIA.

1/8

$1\frac{7}{16}$

1 3/8 DIA.

$4\frac{1}{8}$

$1\frac{3}{8}$

2" DP.

3/4 DIA.
1 DIA.

3/16

1"

1 DIA.

EPOXY HANDLE

3/4 DIA HOLE,
2" DEEP

HANDLE DETAIL

FIGURE 3

$\frac{3}{4}$

On the end of the blank screw dowels, the end that goes up into the handle, cut a spiral groove with a wood file or saw to allow the epoxy glue to go around and squeeze out as you push the finished dowel into the handle. Cut the threads on both dowels, stopping at your marks. Glue the handle onto the threaded dowels. Work slowly and allow time for the glue to move out, then clean away the excess glue. Fitting the handle too quickly could cause the glue to split it. White or yellow glue will not take the clamping pressure these little clamps will produce, so epoxy must be used. I use about ½ teaspoon per handle of Elmer's Epoxy, made by Borden.

# Finishing

Finish as you desire. I use a spray-coat of lacquer on my clamps, but any good finish process would do. I use three coats of lacquer and rub between each coat with 0000 steel wool. Do not, however, rub the threads. The lacquer adds some strength to the threads, helps seal them, and keeps the wax from soaking into the threads. Apply wax to all bearing surfaces and all threaded surfaces and work in well.

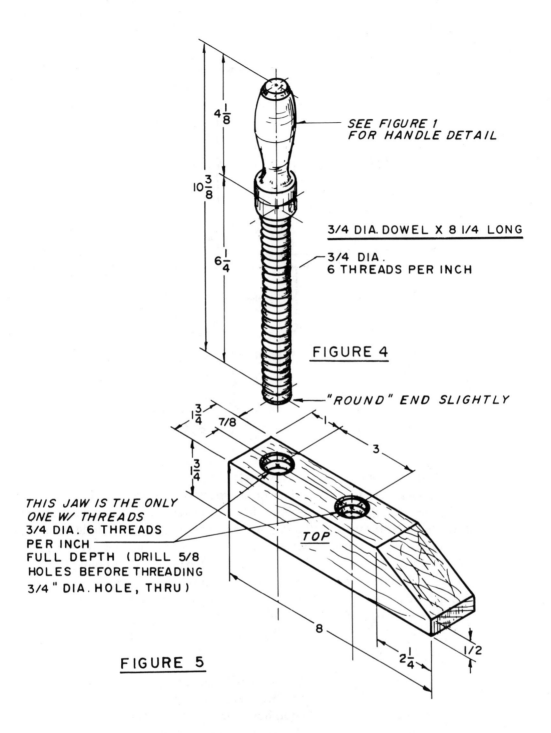

4 1/8

10 3/8

6 1/4

SEE FIGURE 1
FOR HANDLE DETAIL

3/4 DIA. DOWEL X 8 1/4 LONG

3/4 DIA.
6 THREADS PER INCH

FIGURE 4

"ROUND" END SLIGHTLY

3/4

7/8

1 3/4

1

3

THIS JAW IS THE ONLY
ONE W/ THREADS
3/4 DIA. 6 THREADS
PER INCH
FULL DEPTH ( DRILL 5/8
HOLES BEFORE THREADING
3/4" DIA. HOLE, THRU )

TOP

8

2 1/4

1/2

FIGURE 5

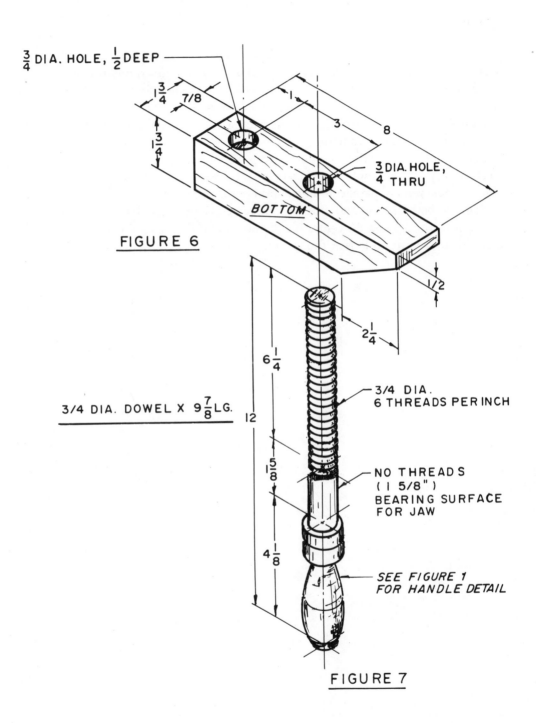

$\frac{3}{4}$ DIA. HOLE, $\frac{1}{2}$ DEEP

$1\frac{3}{4}$

7/8

$1\frac{3}{4}$

1

3

8

$\frac{3}{4}$ DIA. HOLE, $\frac{3}{4}$ THRU

*BOTTOM*

FIGURE 6

1/2

$2\frac{1}{4}$

$6\frac{1}{4}$

3/4 DIA. DOWEL X $9\frac{7}{8}$ LG.

12

3/4 DIA.
6 THREADS PER INCH

$1\frac{5}{8}$

NO THREADS
( 1 5/8" )
BEARING SURFACE
FOR JAW

$4\frac{1}{8}$

*SEE FIGURE 1
FOR HANDLE DETAIL*

FIGURE 7

221

# Helpful Hints

After you have made one or two of these clamps, let your mind go and experiment. I find that by laminating up different colors of scrap hardwood you can make some beautiful clamps. I was asked to make a set for Mr. Tage Frid a while back and I made his of rosewood. When I turned the handles, I put on a 1-inch-diameter piece of brass tubing on the front of the handles which made a striking addition.

People unfamiliar with this type of clamp will naturally pick them up and start turning just one handle. You must resist this habit. The jaws of this kind of clamp must remain parallel to one another at all times. To use them, hold the clamp by both handles and spin the jaws to open large enough to be placed over your work. Tighten the center handle first and then the end handle. Reverse this procedure to loosen the clamp.

# Picnic Table

O F ALL THE PROJECT PLANS I HAVE DESIGNED AND DRAWN THROUGH THE YEARS, the picnic table is the one project I have the most requests for. It seems *every* woodworker worth his salt builds his or her own picnic table. After all, how would it look for an avid woodworker to go out and buy a picnic table? Everyone who has asked for the plans, wants a different length, so to accommodate everyone, these drawings illustrate how to build a picnic table ranging in length from 72 inches (6 feet) long, to 96 inches (8 feet) long. This is done by a kind of drawing called a "tab drawing". Note the SIDE VIEW— there are listed three dimensions within brackets. Decide which length table you want to make: 6, 7, or 8 feet. If you choose the 7-foot length, you will find it is the *center* dimension; therefore, use all center dimensions. This affects only parts 5, 6, and 7. Also, be sure to use the *center* dimensions indicated in the Materials List for parts 5, 6, and 7.

The overall design of this public table was taken from a table you will find if you ever visit a Vermont State park or one of the many rest stops along the interstate highways of Vermont. The photograph is of an actual 6-foot picnic table from Vermont. Note in the photograph that they have the table chained and padlocked.

The picnic table is a simple project and can easily be made in a weekend. Before starting, carefully study the drawings provided in order to have a good idea as to exactly how it is made and put together before proceeding. It is a

good idea to decide which length table you want to make and cross out the extra dimensions you do not need. This will eliminate confusion or errors when you are actually cutting the parts to size.

# Instructions

Here in the Northeast, straight grain fir or pine is usually used. In the western states, I would assume a local wood, such as redwood, would be best to use. Whatever kind of wood you choose, try to get pressure-treated lumber if possible, as your table will last much longer if you do. Try to obtain the exact sizes as indicated in the Materials List so you will have the least amount of waste and the lowest cost.

Carefully measure, check, and cut the legs, (part 1), seat support (part 2), top brace (part 3), and top brace (part 4) to the exact sizes and angles given. Be sure to use the correct dimension for the table length you are building. Do not forget to cut the top brace (part 4) on a 30-degree angle as illustrated. Note this is the SIDE VIEW of the top brace.

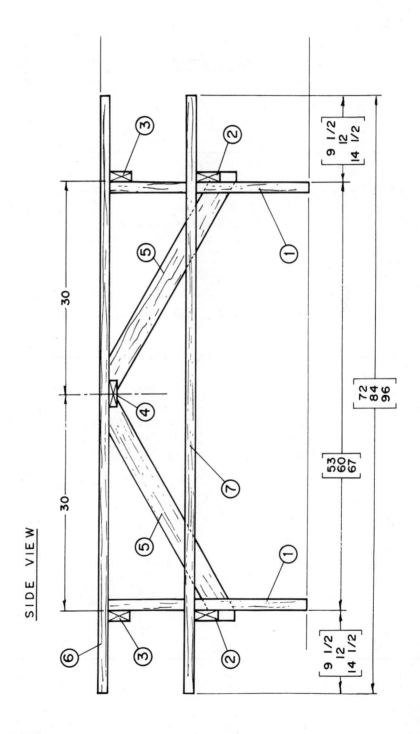

SIDE VIEW

# END VIEW

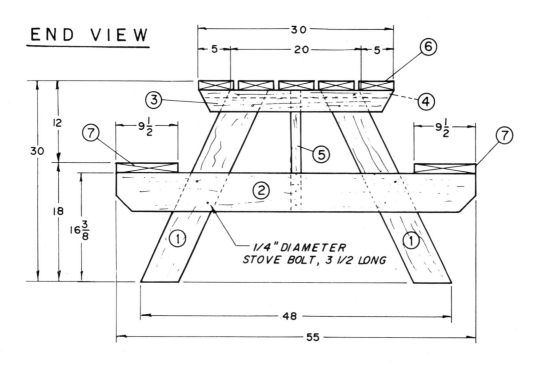

1/4" DIAMETER
STOVE BOLT, 3 1/2 LONG

## MATERIALS LIST

| Part No. | Name | Size | Req'd. |
|----------|------|------|--------|
| 1 | Leg | 2 × 6 – 34¾ Long | 4 |
| 2 | Seat Support | 2 × 6 – 55 Long | 2 |
| 3 | Top Support | 2 × 4 – 30 Long | 2 |
| 4 | Top Brace | 2 × 4 – 30 Long<br>– 30 | 1 |
| 5 | Leg Brace | 2 × 6 – 33 Long<br>– 36½<br>– 72 | 2 |
| 6 | Top | 2 × 6 – 84 Long<br>– 96<br>– 72 | 5 |
| 7 | Seat | 2 × 10 – 84 Long<br>– 96 | 2 |

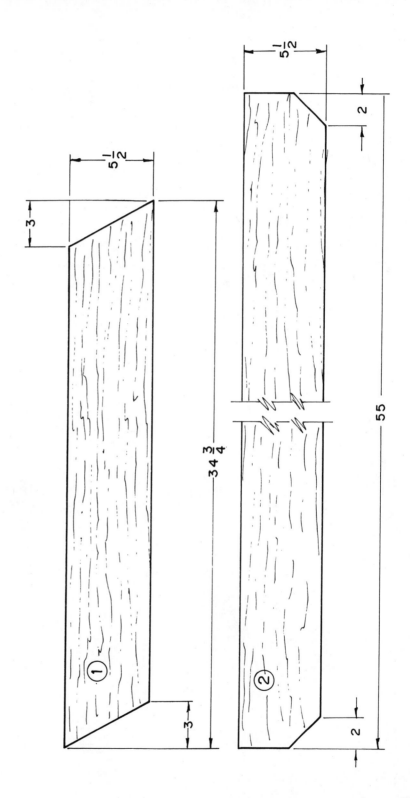

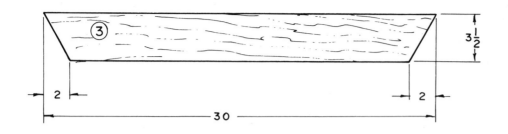

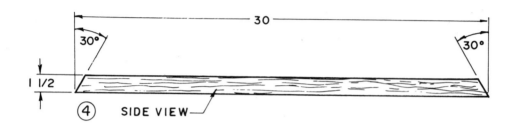

SIDE VIEW

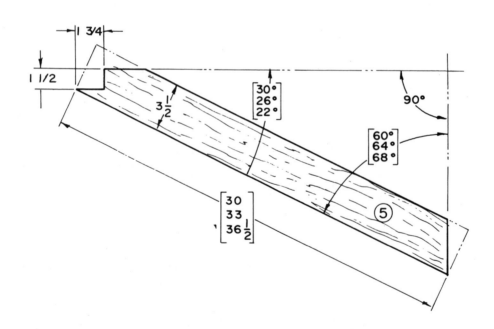

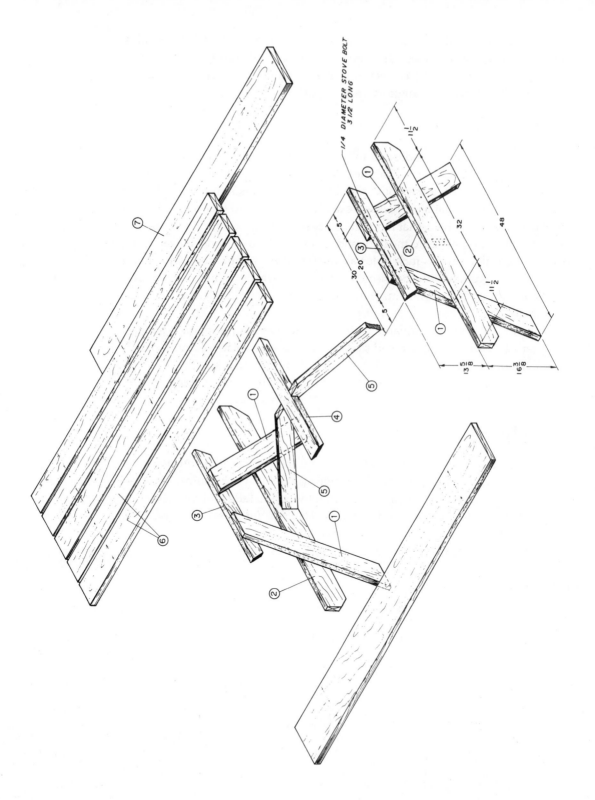

1/4 DIAMETER STOVE BOLT
3 1/2 LONG

229

The chamfer on the tabletop and seat can be cut after the final assembly of the table if you wish. Take extra care in laying out and cutting the leg braces (part 5). Be sure to use the correct angles and maintain the 90-degree angle as shown. The 90-degree angle is very important.

# Assembly

Using the dimensions as indicated in the end view, carefully lay out the two ends, using parts 1, 2, and 3. Nail them together using 10-d nails as required. Stand the sides up on a flat floor, side-by-side, and check that the sides are *exactly* alike. Check that all angles are exactly the same and that both ends are the same size. Also check that the seat supports and the top supports are parallel to each other, parallel to the floor and to the exact dimensions. If everything checks out, drill nine $^{15}\!/_{16}$-inch holes as illustrated through parts 1 and 2, and bolt the legs together with the ¼-inch stove bolts, washers, and nuts—round heads out, nuts and washers in. (Stove bolts are sometime referred to as carriage bolts.)

Keeping everything square, assemble the remaining parts together. Number 12, 2½-inch-long flathead screws can be used in place of the 10-d nails and actually look much better. (It will take about 48 screws.)

*Note:* It might be easier to install the leg brace with the table upside down. Again, recheck everything to ensure everything is square.

# Finishing

If you used pressure-treated wood, allow the table to weather outdoors for 2 months or so and apply a coat of exterior oil stain of your choice. The time delay will allow the green color of the treated wood to fade and the new stain to penetrate a little deeper into the wood. *Do not paint pressure-treated wood*, as this tends to make it rot under the paint.

All you need now is a basket lunch and a bunch of ants.

# Folding
# Picnic Table

T HE SMALL FOLDING STOOL IS UPSCALED TO A RUGGED TABLE AND AND BENCH
that also folds flat for storage and transport. No more sitting at dirty, wet
picnic tables. No more watching, as your picnic table weathers and rots outside
all year. Fold and store this furniture away from inclement weather, and it
will easily outlast other wooden deck furniture.

When folded, the table is 5 ½-×-38 ½-×-48 inches and the benches measure
4-×-27½-×-48 inches. The units have a built-in carrying handle and can be
hung on a utility wall, clean and dry for the next use. The length of the table
and benches is only 4 feet, so the unit can easily be transported in a small station
wagon, and still be large enough to seat four adults comfortably.

## Instructions

The picnic table and benches illustrated in the photograph are made of red
oak. Red oak is strong and beautiful, but somewhat disadvantaged by its heavy
weight. The table and benches can be constructed of many favorite woods;
however, strength and outdoor resistance to decay are important factors. The
wood chosen should be dry and reasonably straight-grained, to ensure minimal warpage after construction. In determining the choice of woods, keep in
mind the critical areas are the span of the boards in the bench seat, needed
to support an occasional enthusiastic eater, and the strength of the joint at the
dowel hinge.

The project is not difficult, but careful machining of the parts is essential for proper folding of the furniture. Folding action is hinged by wood dowels, eliminating the need for expensive hardware. Although there are 60 wooden parts to the table and bench set, there are only 6 different parts to each unit, including the dowel hinge. Because there are so many identical parts, jigs and fixtures become indispensible for speed and accuracy. In fact, once the jigs are built, it becomes easy to make multiple tables and benches. The jigs may be used later in other projects as well.

Start by machining the tops part (A) and the braces part (D) to the rectangular size on the Materials List. Follow suit with the supports part (B) and the legs part (C) except cut the lengths ½ inch oversize. Later, when the radius and hole is machined, they will be cut to finished length. Rip the stock on the table saw, and cross cut with a fence stop on the radial-arm saw or power miter box. Once the rectangular parts are made, the holes should be carefully located and drilled.

| Part | | Bench (Two) | | Table (One) | |
| Letter | Name | Size | Req'd. | Size | Req'd. |
| --- | --- | --- | --- | --- | --- |
| A | Top | 1 × 5½ – 48 Long | 4 | 1 × 5½ – 48 Long | 5* |
| B | Support | 1 × 2 – 10½ Long | 8 | 1 × 3½ – 27½ Long | 4 |
| C | Leg | 1 × 2 – 18¾ Long | 8 | 1 × 3½ – 38½ Long | 4 |
| D | Brace | 1 × 3 – 41 Long | 4 | 1 × 3½ – 35 Long | 2 |
| E | Dowel – Long | ¾ Dia. – 38 Long | 2 | 1 Dia. – 32 Long | 1 |
| F | Dowel – Short | ¾ Dia. – 2 Long | 12 | 1 Dia. – 2 Long | 6 |
| G | Nail for Dowel | 4d Finishing | 12 | 6d Finishing | 6 |
| H | Screw – Flathead | No. 8 – 2½ Long | 36 | No. 8 – 2½ Long | 36 |
| I | Screw – Flathead | No. 8 – 1½ Long | 4 | No. 8 – 1½ Long | 4 |

*Note*: All dimensions are based on full ¼ (1") thick material

* Rip-cut one into two boards 1 × 2¾ – 48 long.

As the stability of the furniture is quite dependent on reasonably tight dowel fitting, first check the dowels purchased with a hole drilled in scrap wood. Purchased dowels are notoriously different from the drill of the same size. Remember the bench parts require ¾-inch holes and the table parts 1 inch. To check the setup, flip a part and be sure the drill centers on the backside as well. When setting up the jig for the second hole in the legs, be sure to butt the top hole end against the jig fence. This will ensure that both holes in all of the legs are the same distance apart.

After the holes are drilled in the legs and supports, cut the radius in the end of these parts. Lay a pattern on each part and draw the radius. Band saw off the waste, leaving the line. Trim to the line with the disk sander. The mating parts could be clamped together with a dowel in the holes for alignment and sanded until they match.

Next the angles are cut in the ends of the legs and supports. The radial-arm saw with the carriage arm angled and fence stops, or power miter box with similar fence stops are excellent tools for the job. If you are using a table saw, a long board screwed to the miter gauge with a fence stop will do. Now cut the dowels to size. If you are using thinner stock than specified, you will have to cut the 2-inch dowel parts to the thickness of two leg parts combined. Then, if desired, sand all parts before assembly. *Do not* sand the dowels, which fit the hole sizes.

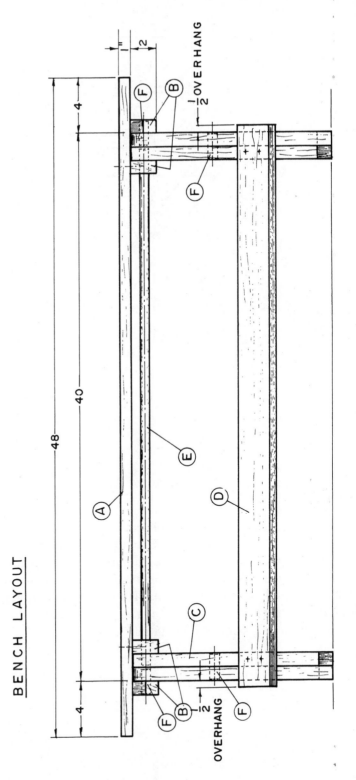

BENCH LAYOUT

SIDE VIEW

235

## BENCH LAYOUT

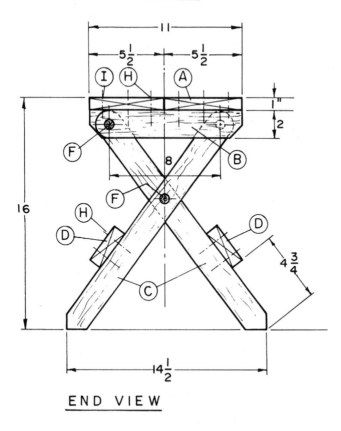

END VIEW

# Assembly

The same sequence is used to assemble both the table and benches. The units are assembled in the folded position. Study the drawing for the support (part B) and the leg (part C). Notice that each part on the drawings has a dot on one side of the part. The dots were placed there to aid in assembly. The dot side of the part will be referred to as the TOP OF THE PART. And dot side down will be the BOTTOM OF THE PART. It is suggested that the parts be marked accordingly before assembly to avoid mistakes.

Slide the legs and supports together on their dowels as shown. Referring to the drawing marked FIGURE 1 END VIEW OF FOLDED STOOL, working from left to right, place a short dowel between a support and leg, both top side up. Do not nail at this time. The next leg and support are placed bottom side up and secured by a long dowel at the top, and the second short dowel is placed between the two legs. Study the right side (designated as FIGURE 2) and place the legs and supports in their proper alignment. Now slide a cardboard spacer between all leg and support parts and clamp together. The cardboard spacers (posterboard thickness) will be removed after assembly, but for now they will ensure proper spacing for good folding operation.

## END VIEW

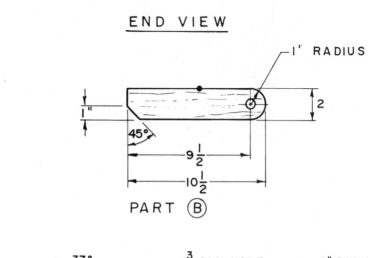

PART Ⓑ

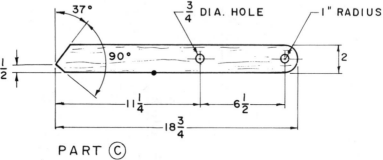

PART Ⓒ

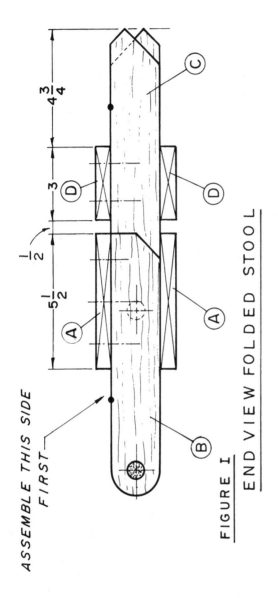

ASSEMBLE THIS SIDE
FIRST

FIGURE I

END VIEW FOLDED STOOL

238

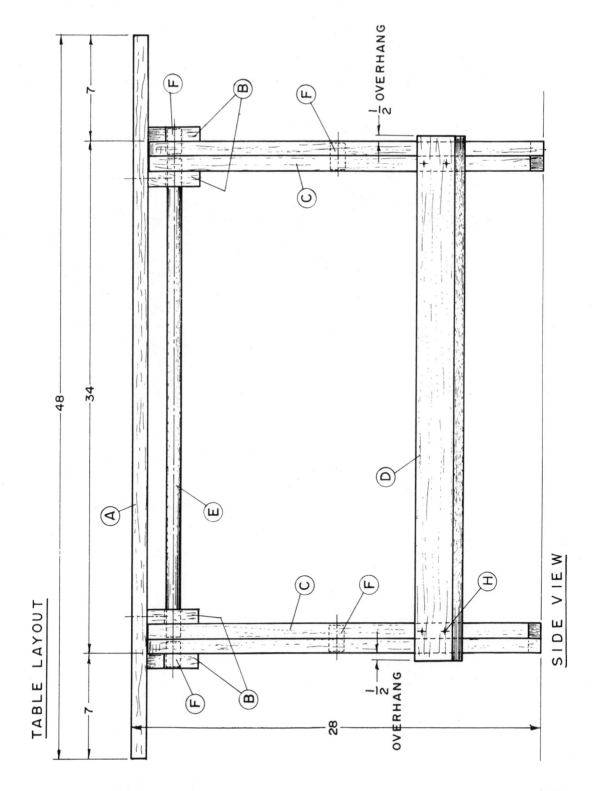

TABLE LAYOUT

SIDE VIEW

239

## TABLE LAYOUT

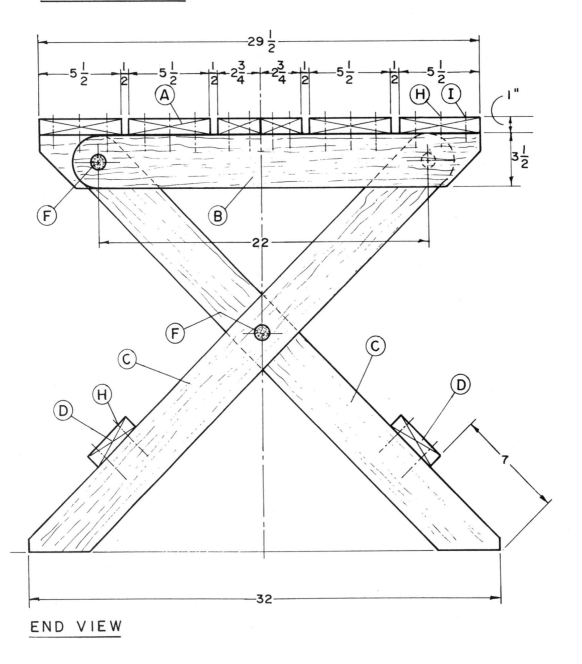

END VIEW

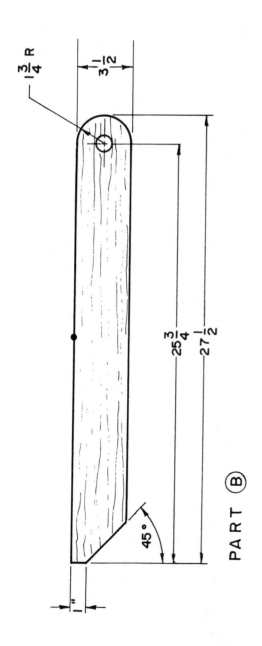

$1\frac{3}{4}$ R

$\frac{1}{3\frac{1}{2}}$

$25\frac{3}{4}$

$27\frac{1}{2}$

$45°$

$1''$

PART Ⓑ

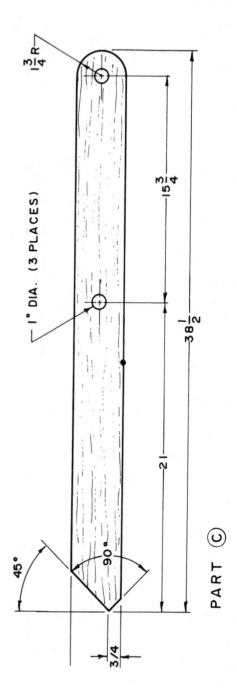

$1\frac{3}{4}$ R

1" DIA. (3 PLACES)

$15\frac{3}{4}$

$38\frac{1}{2}$

$21$

$45°$

$90°$

$3/4$

PART Ⓒ

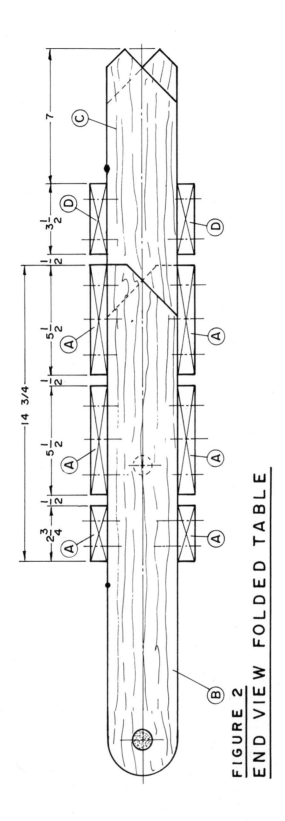

FIGURE 2
END VIEW FOLDED TABLE

242

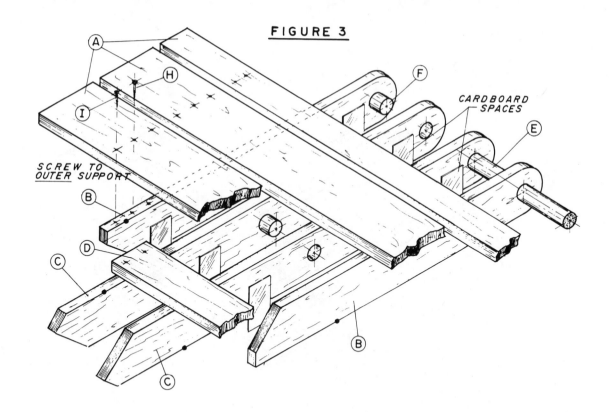

## FIGURE 3

CARDBOARD SPACES

SCREW TO OUTER SUPPORT

Now place the top part (A) and brace part (D) on the support and leg assembly. They will be marked and screwed in place. Use flathead No. 7 zinc-coated drywall screws, 2 ½ inches long, for all parts except in the outer-most location on the support. Here the screws are too long and will go through, so switch to No. 6 flatheads, 1½ inch screws in these locations. All parts must be predrilled to avoid splitting. The table illustrated has the screws countersunk and plugged; however, this is optional.

Study the drawing marked FIGURE 4 for the locations of the top parts and brace. Check for squareness. The top parts and brace should be at right angles to the legs and supports. Correct placement means the table or bench will set up flat. On the first side, screw the top part (S) and brace in the support and legs as shown in FIGURES 2 and 3. *When the table or bench is flipped to put on the tops and brace on the other side, refer to* FIGURE 4 *for drill locations.* Again, check for squareness of the parts before screwing the top parts and brace on the second side of the table or bench.

Once the screws are in place, the furniture should unfold to the useful position. The cardboard spacers will then fall out. Having satisfied yourself that everything is o.k., finishing nails can be placed through the leg or support and into the dowel in one side of each dowel location. This will keep the dowels

FIGURE 4

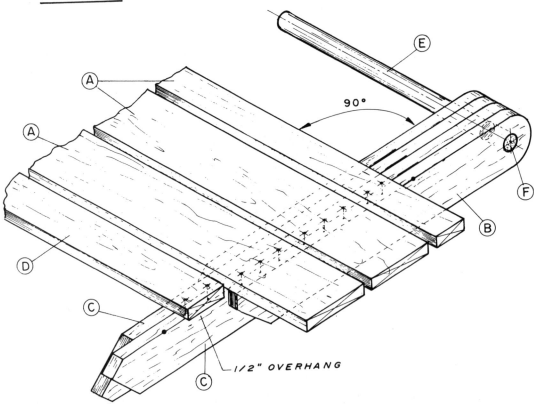

in place. Note that nails are *not* placed in all the leg and support positions because the matching parts need to rotate around the dowel for the hinging action of the furniture. Predrill even for the nails to avoid splitting of the dowels.

## Finishing

The red oak table and benches shown were finished with linseed oil. Oil has the advantages of easy application, lubrication of the dowel hinge parts, and ease of touch-up when wear shows. If you choose urethane for a finish, be sure to use a brand resistant to ultraviolet light. Paint is also attractive; however, if you use paint or urethane, a topcoat of wax should be applied, especially around the dowel locations. The wax will help in the folding action of the table or bench. While there is absolutely no guarantee this picnic table will ever be free of ants, I hope a modest weekend effort will yield years of happy picnics.

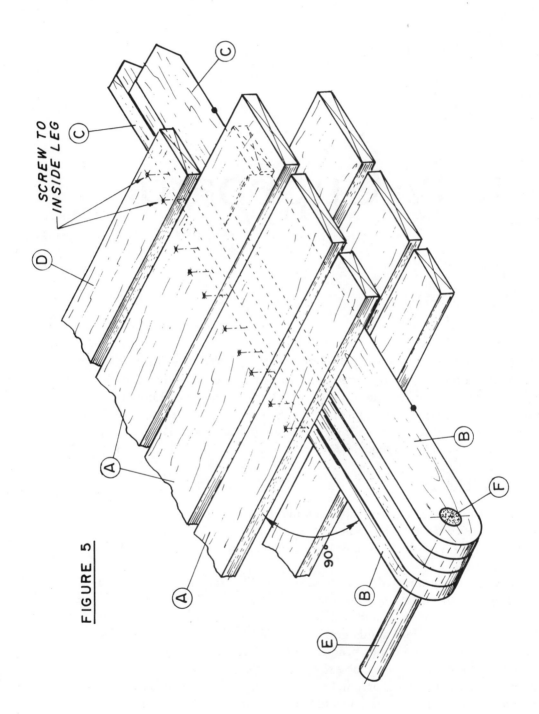

SCREW TO
INSIDE LEG

FIGURE 5

90°

245

# Jelly Cupboard

JELLY CUPBOARDS COME IN ALL SHAPES AND SIZES. HERE IN NEW HAMPSHIRE, MOST furniture stores carry two or three different jelly cupboards. Most, however, are low to the floor. The design presented here is somewhat different, in that it has long legs so the bottom shelf is 18¾ inches above the floor. It will save a lot of bending to retrieve things from the bottom shelf. The legs also make the jelly cupboard unique.

## Instructions

As always study the plans so you have an idea how it is to be assembled. Cut the wood to size per the Materials List. As standard 1-×-10-inch material is used, the only pieces that will have to be glued-up are the back (part 3) and the top (part 8).

Locate and make the dadoes in the sides (part 1) ¼ inch deep and ¾ inch wide as shown. Attach the shelves, (part 2) and the back. They could be simply glued in place, or glued and nailed. To this, add the two side rails (part 4). Do *not* cut out the legs at this time. They will be cut at a later time. Note you could add a ⅛-inch radius bead along the *inside* edges of the side rails, as shown. Do this before attaching to the case. Refer to the VIEW AT A-A to understand how the case is assembled. Notice that the backboard, overlaps the sides. In finer furniture, this would have been rabbeted to hide the joint.

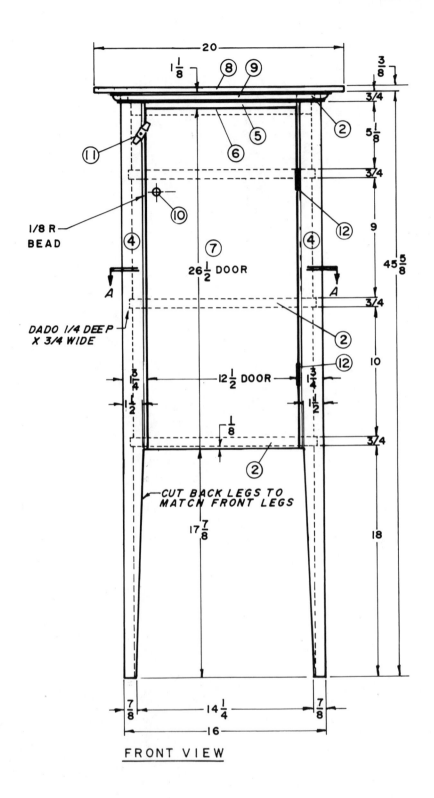

20

1⅛ ⑧ ⑨

3/8

3/4

②

5⅛

⑪

3/4

⑤

⑥

⑩

9

⑫

1/8 R
BEAD

④    ④

⑦

26½ DOOR

A        A

45⅝

3/4

②

DADO 1/4 DEEP
X 3/4 WIDE

12½ DOOR

1¾        1¾

⑫

10

1½        1½

⅛

3/4

②

CUT BACK LEGS TO
MATCH FRONT LEGS

17⅞

18

7/8        7/8

14¼

16

## FRONT VIEW

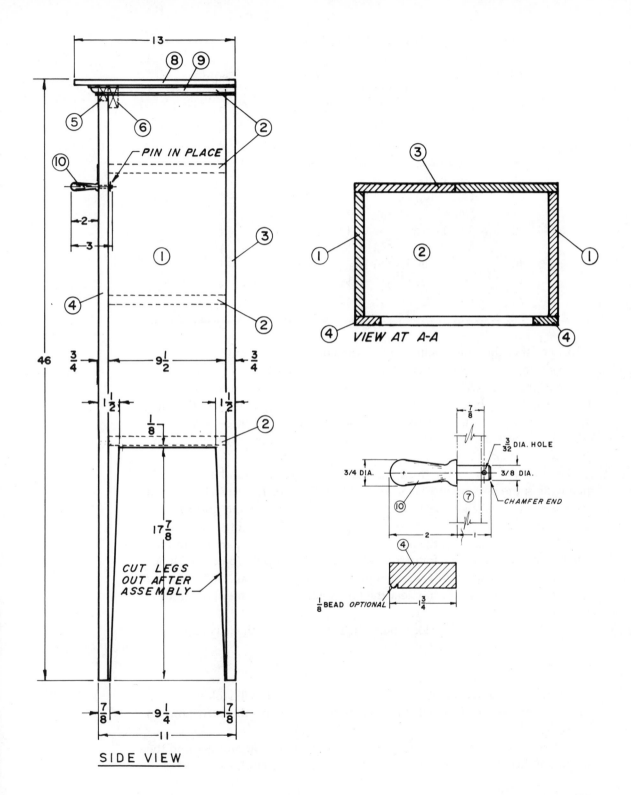

13

⑧ ⑨

⑤
⑥
② 

PIN IN PLACE

⑩

②

$\frac{3}{4}$

② 

②

③

①

④

②

46

$\frac{3}{4}$   9$\frac{1}{2}$   $\frac{3}{4}$

1$\frac{1}{2}$   1$\frac{1}{2}$

$\frac{1}{8}$

②

17$\frac{7}{8}$

CUT LEGS
OUT AFTER
ASSEMBLY

$\frac{7}{8}$   9$\frac{1}{4}$   $\frac{7}{8}$

11

SIDE VIEW

③

①   ②   ①

④   VIEW AT A-A   ④

$\frac{7}{8}$

$\frac{3}{32}$ DIA. HOLE

3/4 DIA.   +   3/8 DIA.

⑩   ⑦   CHAMFER END

2   1

④

$\frac{1}{8}$ BEAD OPTIONAL   1$\frac{3}{4}$

| Part No. | Name | Size | Req'd. |
|---|---|---|---|
| 1 | Side | ¾ × 9½ – 45⅝ Long | 2 |
| 2 | Shelf | ¾ × 9½ – 15 Long | 4 |
| 3 | Back | ¾ × 8 – 45⅝ Long | 2 |
| 4 | Side Rail | ¾ × 1¾ – 45⅝ Long | 2 |
| 5 | Top Rail | ¾ × 1⅛ – 12½ Long | 1 |
| 6 | Dust Stop | ¾ × 1⅝ – 14½ Long | 1 |
| 7 | Door | ¾ × 12½ – 26½ Long | 1 |
| 8 | Top Board | ⅜ × 13 – 20 Long | 1 |
| 9 | Molding | ¾ × ¾ – 50 Long | 1 |
| 10 | Door Pull | ¾ Dia. × 3 Long | 1 |
| 11 | Door Lock | ½ × ¾ – 2 Long | 1 |
| 12 | Hinge | 1½ × 2 | 2 |

Check that the unit is square in all directions at this time.

Add the top rail (part 5) and the dust stop (part 6).

Sand the two sides and the front surface keeping all edges sharp.

Attach the top board (part 8) with glue and finishing nails. Set and putty the nails. Add the molding (part 9). Fit and attach the front piece and add the two side pieces. Cut the two side pieces a little long and trim to size *after* adding them to the case.

Lay out the legs on the front sides and back. Notice that they all are ⅞ inch wide at the bottom and 1½ inches wide at the top. They also are ⅛ inch *below* the bottom shelf (refer to the drawing). Cut the legs out and sand all edges with a sanding block in order to keep the legs straight.

Fit the door (part 7) to the opening. Mortise the hinges (part 12) into the side rails as shown. Check for correct fit. Add the door pull, (part 10). Notice that it is held in place with a wooden peg or a square-cut nail. Be careful *not* to locate it directly over or too near the top shelf, as it will interfere with the door closing.

Locate and add the door lock (part 11). This completes the jelly cupboard.

# Finishing

Jelly cupboards can be stained or painted—either way, it will look very nice. Finish the cupboard whichever way you choose, following all instructions on the container.

All you have to do now is to get out of the wood shop and get into the kitchen and cook 150 jars of jelly to fill your new jelly cupboard.

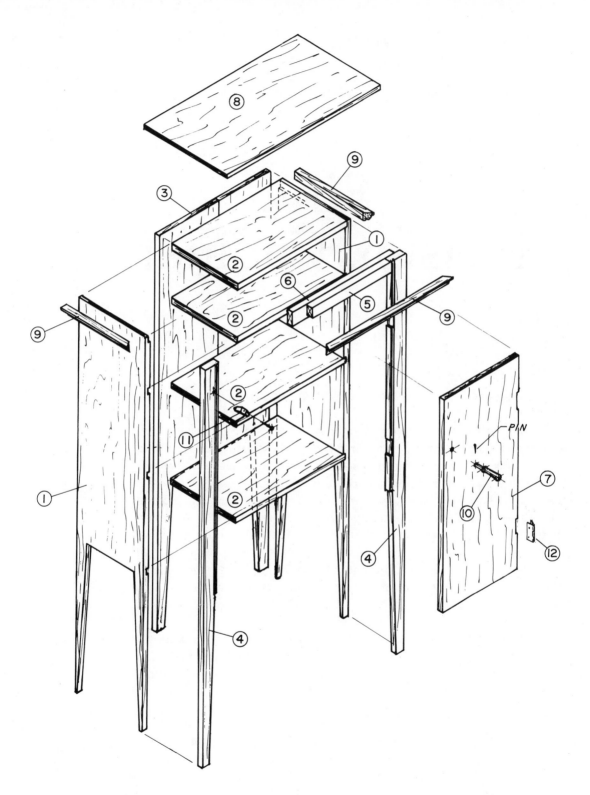

# Dry Sink/
# Television Cabinet

MANY YEARS AGO, EARLY AMERICAN HOMES DID NOT HAVE INDOOR PLUMB-ing and made do with a dry sink—a washstand for the bowl and water pitcher, with storage spaces below. Originals of these rare pieces are very expensive and sought after by collectors. Today, these rather unusual and unique dry sinks can be very functional again by hiding a television set and VCR, while they add warmth and charm to the home.

For over 30 years, my wife, Joyce, and I have collected antiques. Not the formal, expensive kind, just the "country" type of around 1875 or so. Although our house is a *new* split cape, Joyce stenciled the walls of the house to further add to the eighteenth-century atmosphere. For years, sitting smugly on an antique table, surrounded by our antique furnishings, was the plastic, simulated-wood encased television set. To make things worse, a year or 2 ago, we added a VCR. Having no good place to put the VCR, it was finally put under the television set—accenting the whole mess even *more*!

While looking through one of the those country home-type magazines, I spotted an original dry sink and thought, "Why not hide the dumb television set inside one of those?" By lengthening the width of the sides a little, I came up with this design. The result is a "new" old-style dry sink that hides the television, VCR, *and* all the VCR tapes.

Everyone who has seen the new dry sink seems to like it, as I have had requests to build three or four more just like this one. If you have such a problem with your television set, perhaps you would like to build one of these also.

# Instructions

Before beginning, carefully measure your television, as this dry sink will not take all 13- to 19-inch television sets. When measuring, measure from top to bottom, side to side, and front to back. When measuring from front to back, be sure to include the knobs in the front of the set and add at least ½ inch extra. As this dry sink is designed and dimensioned, it will take only a television set 16 inches high, 21 inches wide and 17½ inches deep. Any set slightly larger in size will mean changing some of the dimensions accordingly. The overall design, however, should not be affected too much.

As with any woodworking project, carefully study all drawings so that you fully see and understand how the dry sink is put together. The parts are numbered approximately in the recommended order that it is to be made.

## MATERIALS LIST

| Part No. | Name | Size | Req'd. |
|---|---|---|---|
| 1 | Side | $3/4 \times 17^1/4 - 44^1/4$ Long | 2 |
| 2 | Shelf | $3/4 \times 17^1/4 - 24$ Long | 3 |
| 3 | Backboard | $1/2 \times 8^1/2 - 44^1/4$ Long | 3 |
| 4 | Stiles | $3/4 \times 2 - 29^3/4$ Long | 2 |
| 5 | Top Trim | $3/4 \times 1/2 - 23^1/2$ Long | 1 |
| 6 | Dust Stop | $1/4 \times 1^1/2 - 25$ Long | 1 |
| 7 | Doors | $3/4 \times 10^1/2 - 29^3/4$ Long | 2 |
| 8 | Narrow Top | $3/4 \times 12^1/8 - 27^3/4$ Long | 1 |
| 9 | Moulding Stock | $3/4 \times 1^1/4 - 84$ Long | 1 |
| 10 | Door Pulls | $3/4$ Dia. Dowels | 2 |
| 11 | Door Lock | $3/4 \times 3/4 - 2^1/2$ Long | 1 |
| 12 | Hinge (Brass) | $1^1/2 \times 2$ | 4 |
| 13 | Bottom Skirt | $3/4 \times 3^3/4 - 25$ Long | 1 |
| 14 | Top Shelf | $3/4 \times 18^3/4 - 25$ Long | 1 |
| 15 | Door Battens | $3/4 \times 2 - 9$ Long | 4 |

Start by gluing-up the sides (part 1), shelves (part 2), and top shelf (part 14). After the glue has set, cut all boards to overall sizes, taking care to keep all corners at exactly 90 degrees. Carefully lay out and cut the 1/4-inch-deep, 3/4-inch-wide dadoes in the *inside* surfaces of the sides. Again be sure to keep all dadoes at 90 degrees. Lay out 1-inch squares on a sheet of cardboard and transfer the pattern of the sides to the cardboard for a pattern. Transfer this pattern to the sides *as a pair*—a right-hand side and a left-hand side. Cut the 1- × -3-inch notch out of the shelves for the wires from the television and VCR.

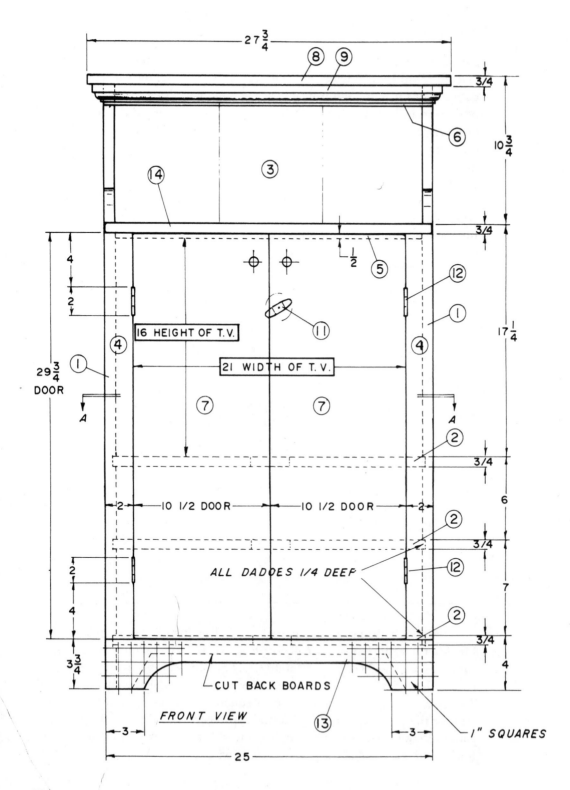

27 3/4

⑧ ⑨

3/4

⑥

10 3/4

③

⑭

3/4

1/2 ⑤

④

⑫

16 HEIGHT OF T.V.

① ⑪

17 1/4

21 WIDTH OF T.V.

④

⑦ ⑦

②

3/4

2 10 1/2 DOOR 10 1/2 DOOR 2

6

29 3/4 DOOR

①

②

3/4

A A

2 ALL DADOES 1/4 DEEP ⑫

7

4

②

3/4

3 3/4 CUT BACK BOARDS 4

FRONT VIEW

⑬

3 3 1" SQUARES

25

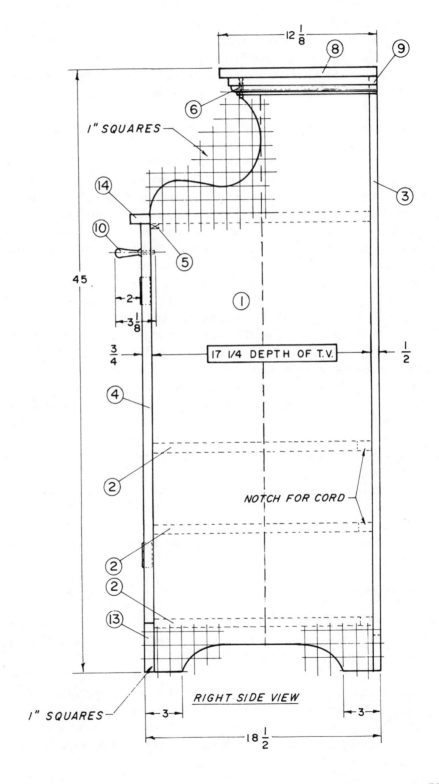

12 1/8

⑧

⑨

⑥

1" SQUARES

⑭

⑩

⑤

③

45

②

17 1/4 DEPTH OF T.V.    1/2

3/4

④

2

3 1/8

NOTCH FOR CORD

②

②

⑬

1" SQUARES

*RIGHT SIDE VIEW*

3

3

18 1/2

Glue and nail the shelves and the top shelf to the sides, taking care to keep everything at 90 degrees. For authenticity, I would suggest using 2-inch square-cut nails. Add the top board (part 8).

Cut to size the backboards, and rabbet the sides. Note the two outer parts have butt joints and rabbeted sides, and one has two rabbeted sides. Glue and nail the two *outer* boards in place and screw the center board in place for removal to install the television and VCR sets later. *Do not glue the center backboard.*

Cut the legs (part 4) and bottom skirt (part 13) to size, cutting the legs into part 13 as shown. Glue and nail in place. Check that everything is 90 degrees. Add the dust stop (part 5) and another top board (part 6). Next, add the molding (part 9), taking care to cut 45-degree angles where the parts meet.

Cut to size the doors (part 7) and the battens (part 15). Check the television set and note the locations of the knobs in the front of the set and the shelves. Take care to locate the door battens *above* or *below* the knobs on the set so they will not interfere with closing the doors. Take care not to locate the door battens over a shelf. Battens in old pieces such as this were usually nailed through from the front into the batten and cinched (bent) over.

Locate the brass hinges (part 12) 4 inches up and 4 inches down from the edges of the door as illustrated. Notch the doors and leg to accept the hinges. Carefully attach the doors in place and check for a good fit.

The door pulls (part 10) are simply turned or carved from a 3/4-inch-diameter dowel as shown. As they were originally made by hand, they do not have to match each other exactly. Locate and drill two 3/8-inch-diameter holes, 2 inches down and about 1 inch in, as illustrated. Like the originals, these door pulls are held in place by a small square-cut nail inserted through the 3/32-inch-diameter holes in the door pulls.

Cut or carve out the door lock (part 11) and attach it to the right-hand door with brass screws as shown. (Again, this was originally somewhat crude and therefore, does *not* have to be exact.) This locks the left-hand door. The right-hand door is held closed and locked by a small hook and eye located inside the right-hand door and below the top shelf.

# Finishing

Most dry sinks were stained but a few were painted. If you choose to paint yours, try to choose an Early American color, such as those from the suggested supplier list provided (see Appendix A).

To make my dry sink look old, I distressed it before applying the stain and finish, then sanded all over. Be sure to wipe clean before applying the stain coat. Any early color stain would be good, I used an Ipswitch pine stain followed by three coats of satin-finish tung oil. To add that 150-year-old effect, I wiped on a wash coat of black paint (slightly thinned), which I wiped off right away, leaving the black paint in the corners and in all the distressed marks. Do not let the dry sink finish become too shiny—it should have a satin finish. If it does get too shiny, simply rub the piece with number 0000 steel wool.

After the tung oil has dried, apply a coat of lemon oil. Do not wax over tung oil.

Remove the center backboard (part 3) and install the television set and VCR. With the center board removed, it is very easy to route the connectors from one set to the other, and to route the wires down and out to the electrical power outlet. Then replace the center board.

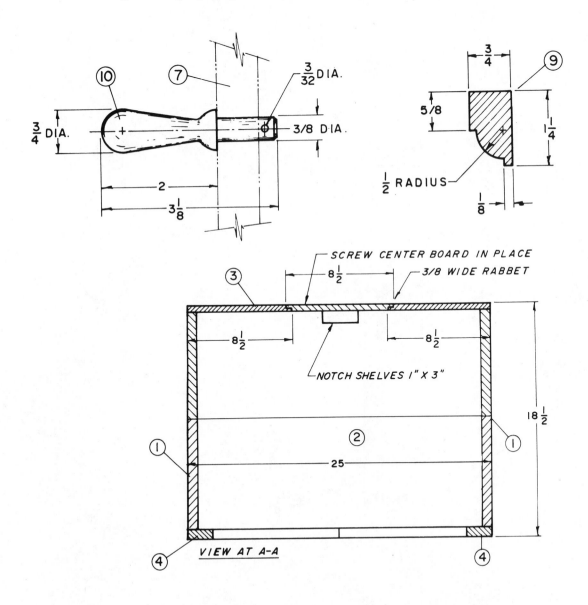

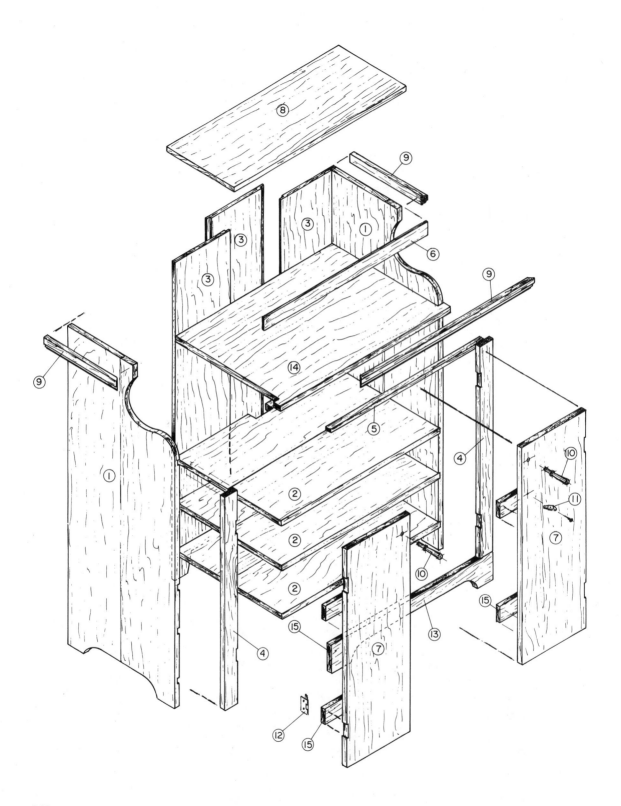

# Chest of Drawers

As its name implies, this is a chest containing thirteen drawers. If you have always avoided projects with a drawer or two in the past, now is the time to "bite the bullet" and learn how to make drawers. Each step in making a drawer is fully illustrated, in order to simplify the project. Drawers are actually easy to make—think of them as nothing more than a box without a lid. In fact, a drawer with a lip all around, such as these drawers have, can be somewhat sloppy and still look all right, as the lip will hide any imperfections. After you have made these thirteen drawers, *you* will be the expert on drawer-making.

This chest is not a copy of an original chest of drawers: rather, it is a combination of many originals. I picked and chose various features of many different chests and even part of an apothecary chest. If I had it to do again, however, I would have added an inch to the depth of the chest, in order to have an inside drawer size of 8½ × 11 inches, so it could be used as a paper storage area.

The entire project, including the drawers is actually easy to make and can be made in a weekend or two. Hopefully, the step-by-step illustrations will speed up the project. After all pieces are made to size and sanded all over, the project should go together like a kit.

Because there are ten drawers that must be identical, you should try to make and use as many cutting jigs as possible, so the multiple parts will be exactly the same size and shape.

# Instructions/Case Assembly

Cut all parts (1 through 5) to overall sizes. Dado the two sides (part 1) as illustrated, taking care to make a matching right-hand and left-hand pair. Glue-up the back (part 2), if necessary, and cut out the feet as illustrated.

Cut enough $3/4\text{-}\times\text{-}1$-inch and $3/4\text{-}\times\text{-}2^{1}/4$-inch material to make up the three subassemblies (parts 3, 4, and 5). Simple butt joints could be substituted if you do not care to make the illustrated tongue-and-groove joints.

Sand all surfaces of all parts, and carefully assemble as illustrated. Take care to keep everything exactly square or the drawers probably will bind. Cut out the notches for the legs of the sides, as illustrated on the skirt detail. Lay out and cut along the dash line. Again, sand all over keeping all edges sharp and square. Sand the front surface of the case where all dado joints join.

## MATERIALS LIST

| Part No. | Name | Size | Req'd. |
|---|---|---|---|
| 1 | Side | $3/4 \times 9^{1}/2 - 45^{1}/2$ Long | 2 |
| 2 | Back | $1/2 \times 13 - 45^{1}/2$ Long | 1 |
| 3 | Dividers | $3/4 \times 1 - 7^{3}/8$ Long | 20 |
| | | $3/4 \times 1 - 13$ Long | 20 |
| 4 | Top Divider | $3/4 \times 1 - 7^{3}/8$ Long | 4 |
| | | $3/4 \times 1 - 13$ Long | 4 |
| | | $3/4 \times 2^{1}/4 - 7^{3}/8$ Long | 4 |
| 5 | Vertical Divider | $3/4 \times 1 - 7^{3}/8$ Long | 4 |
| | | $3/4 \times 1 - 3^{1}/2$ Long | 4 |
| 6 | Chest Subassembly | (All of the Above.) | |
| 7 | Top | $1/2 \times 11^{1}/2 - 16$ Long | 1 |
| 8 | Top Trim | $1/2 \times 1^{1}/4 - 11$ Long | 2 |
| | | $1/2 \times 1^{1}/4 - 15$ Long | 1 |
| 9 | Bottom Skirt | $3/4 \times 2^{3}/4 - 10^{1}/4$ Long | 2 |
| | | $3/4 \times 2^{3}/4 - 15^{1}/2$ Long | 1 |
| 10 | Drawer Side | $1/2 \times 3 - 9$ Long | 26 |
| 11 | Drawer Back | $1/2 \times 3 - 12$ Long | 12 |
| | | $1/2 \times 3 - 3^{1}/8$ Long | 3 |
| 12 | Drawer Bottom | $1/4 \times 8^{1}/4 - 12$ Long | 10 |
| | | $1/4 \times 8^{1}/4 - 3^{1}/8$ Long | 3 |
| 13 | Drawer Front | $3/4 \times 3^{1}/2 - 13$ Long | 10 |
| | | $3/4 \times 3^{1}/2 - 4^{3}/16$ Long | 3 |
| 14 | Drawer Assembly | Large. | 10 |
| 15 | Drawer Assembly | Small. | 3 |
| 16 | Finish Nail | (As Required.) | |

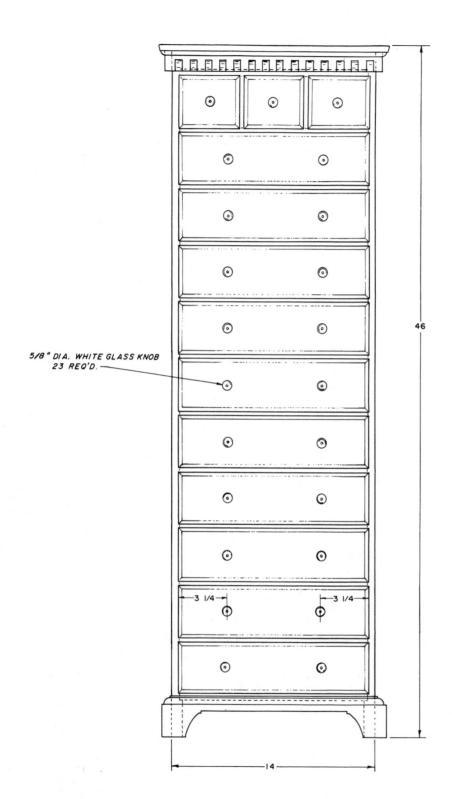

5/8" DIA. WHITE GLASS KNOB
23 REQ'D.

46

3 1/4

3 1/4

14

264

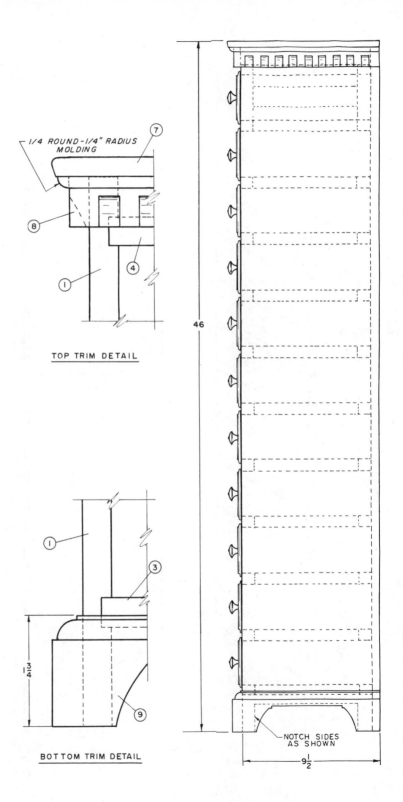

1/4 ROUND-1/4" RADIUS MOLDING

⑦

⑧

④

①

TOP TRIM DETAIL

①

③

$1\frac{3}{4}$

⑨

BOTTOM TRIM DETAIL

46

NOTCH SIDES AS SHOWN

$9\frac{1}{2}$

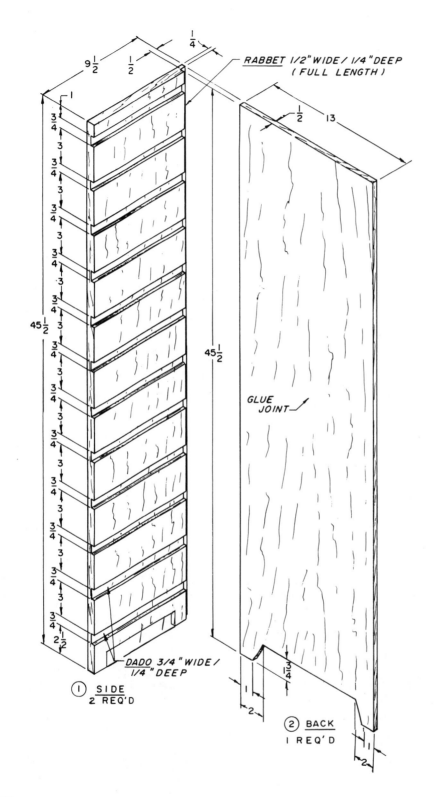

9½

½

¼

RABBET 1/2" WIDE/ 1/4 "DEEP
( FULL LENGTH )

1

¾
3
¾
3
¾
3
¾
3
¾
3
¾
3
¾
3
¾
3
¾
3
¾
3
¾
3
¾
3
¾

45½

45½

2½

½   13

GLUE
JOINT

DADO 3/4" WIDE/
1/4 "DEEP

① SIDE
2 REQ'D

¾
1
2

② BACK
1 REQ'D

1
2

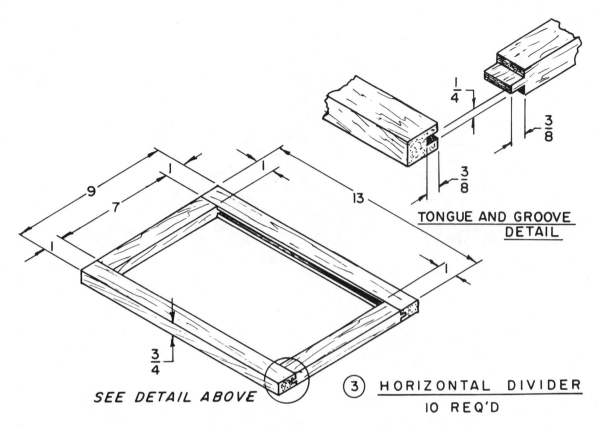

**TONGUE AND GROOVE DETAIL**

SEE DETAIL ABOVE

③ HORIZONTAL DIVIDER
10 REQ'D

Next, cut to size the top (part 7), as illustrated, and sand all over, especially the ends where the end grain is exposed. Attach the top, taking care to keep the back surface of the top flush with the back surface to the case.

Cut enough material for the top trim (part 8). Make the notches in the top trim exactly as if you were cutting a box joint, except do not cut through—simply cut the 3/4 inch in from the edge as shown. I would suggest making twice as much material as you actually need while the saw is set up, just in case you make a mistake in cutting the 45-degree mitered angles. Add the top trim to the case and sand the corners. Add the 1/4-inch radius molding trim (refer to top trim detail view).

Cut to size enough material for the bottom skirt (part 9). Cut the shape of the top surface as illustrated, using either a router or a shaper. If you do not have a router or shaper, commercial molding could be substituted. Cut to size, and miter the corners to fit the case. Before actually adding them to the case assembly, cut out the pattern for the legs per pattern, given in the 1/2-inch squares. Add the bottom skirt to the case assembly and sand all over. This completes the case assembly.

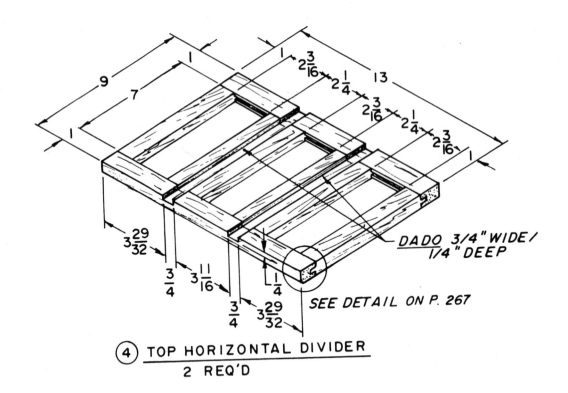

DADO 3/4" WIDE/
1/4" DEEP

SEE DETAIL ON P. 267

④ TOP HORIZONTAL DIVIDER
2 REQ'D

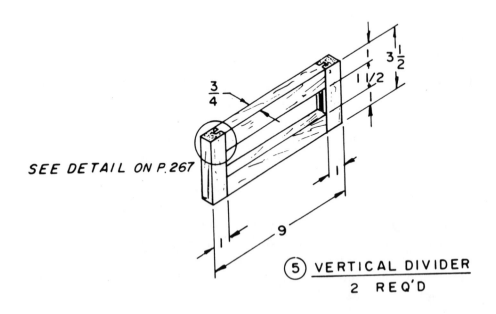

SEE DETAIL ON P. 267

⑤ VERTICAL DIVIDER
2 REQ'D

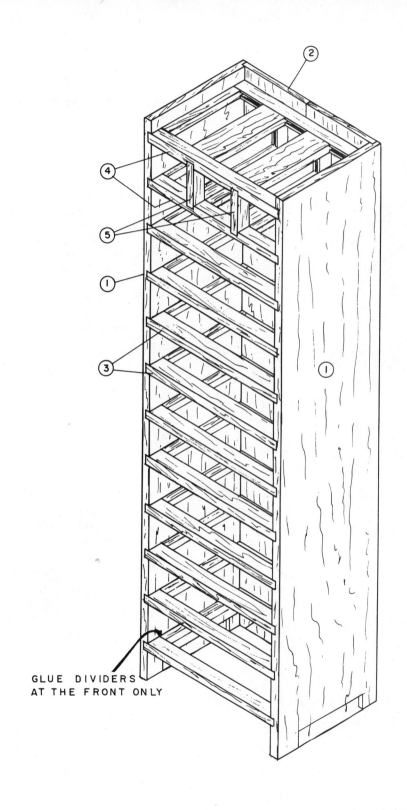

GLUE DIVIDERS
AT THE FRONT ONLY

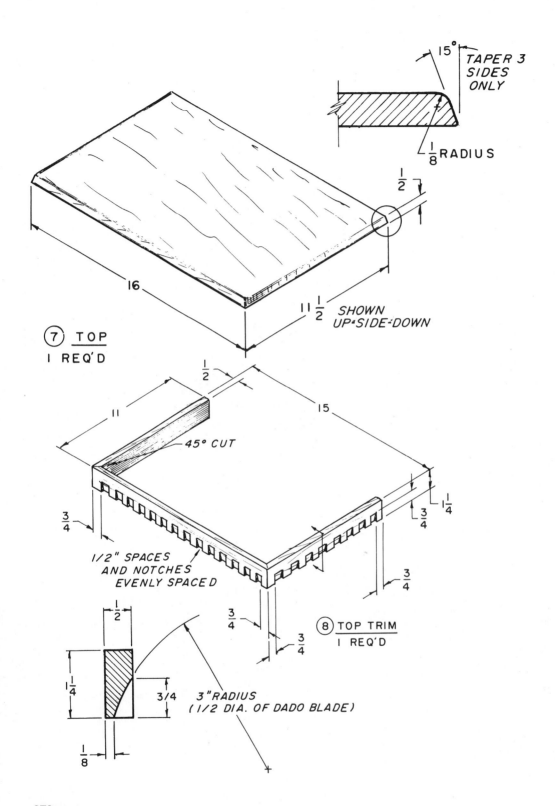

15°  TAPER 3 SIDES ONLY

$\frac{1}{8}$ RADIUS

$\frac{1}{2}$

16

11 $\frac{1}{2}$  SHOWN UP·SIDE·DOWN

(7) TOP
1 REQ'D

$\frac{1}{2}$

11

45° CUT

15

$\frac{1}{4}$

$\frac{3}{4}$

$\frac{3}{4}$

$\frac{3}{4}$

1/2" SPACES AND NOTCHES EVENLY SPACED

$\frac{3}{4}$

$\frac{3}{4}$

(8) TOP TRIM
1 REQ'D

$\frac{1}{2}$

$\frac{1}{4}$

3/4

$\frac{1}{8}$

3" RADIUS
(1/2 DIA. OF DADO BLADE)

270

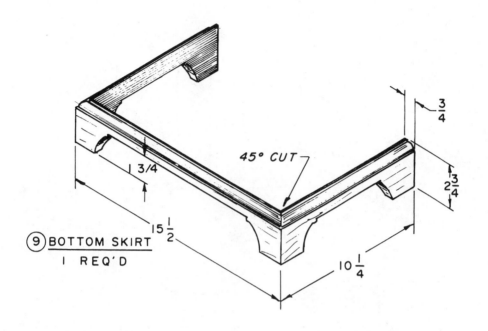

$\frac{3}{4}$

$1 \; 3/4$

45° CUT

$2\frac{3}{4}$

$15\frac{1}{2}$

⑨ BOTTOM SKIRT
1 REQ'D

$10\frac{1}{4}$

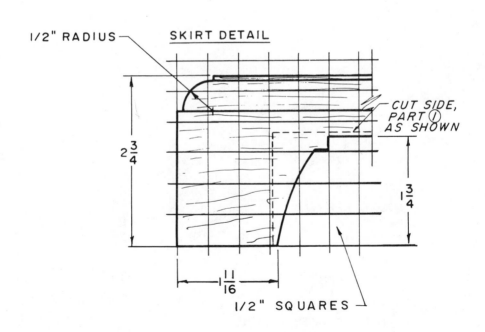

1/2" RADIUS

SKIRT DETAIL

CUT SIDE,
PART ① 
AS SHOWN

$2\frac{3}{4}$

$1\frac{3}{4}$

$1\frac{11}{16}$

1/2" SQUARES

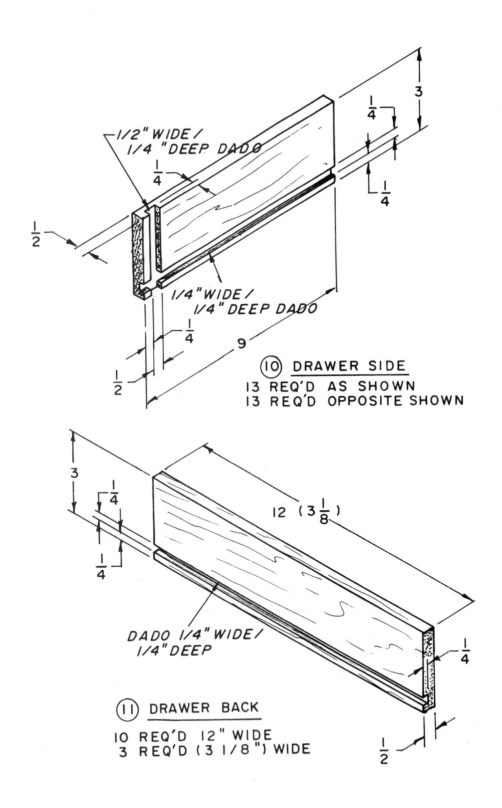

1/2" WIDE / 1/4" DEEP DADO

1/4

1/2

3

1/4

1/4

1/4" WIDE / 1/4" DEEP DADO

9

1/4

1/2

⑩ DRAWER SIDE

13 REQ'D AS SHOWN
13 REQ'D OPPOSITE SHOWN

3

1/4

1/4

12 ( 3 1/8 )

DADO 1/4" WIDE / 1/4" DEEP

1/4

⑪ DRAWER BACK

10 REQ'D 12" WIDE
3 REQ'D (3 1/8") WIDE

1/2

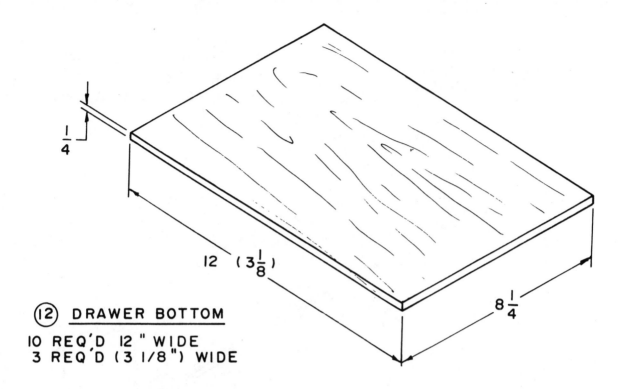

$\frac{1}{4}$

12 $(3\frac{1}{8})$

$8\frac{1}{4}$

(12) DRAWER BOTTOM

10 REQ'D 12 " WIDE
3 REQ'D (3 1/8") WIDE

## Instructions/Drawer Assemblies

One-half-inch material is specified for the drawer sides and back (parts 10 and 11), because 1/2-inch material can be readily found at any local lumber company. If you have a surface planer or access to one, I would recommend making the drawer sides and back of 5/16- or 3/8-inch-thick material, as this is more in keeping with the drawer sizes. If any other thickness is used, simply change a few of the given drawer dimensions to accommodate the thickness you use.

Cut all pieces for the drawers, as illustrated, for parts 10, 11, 12 and 13. Take care to make all pieces of matching sizes exactly the same size by using cutting jigs or saw stops wherever possible. It is extremely important that all identical parts be the same size and interchangeable. Cut as many pieces as possible with the same saw settings as you can. (For example, cut the 3-inch height of parts 10 and 11 with the same saw setting.)

In the event you cannot make the drawer lip shape (part 13), simply rabbet for the sides, top and bottom as shown, and leave the drawer fronts square. This will not take away too much from the project. Locate and drill holes for the drawer pulls in the drawer front. Sand all over, keeping everything square.

Dry-fit all drawers to check for accuracy. Check the drawer assembly for fit into the opening in the case. Fit to size if necessary. Glue and nail the drawer

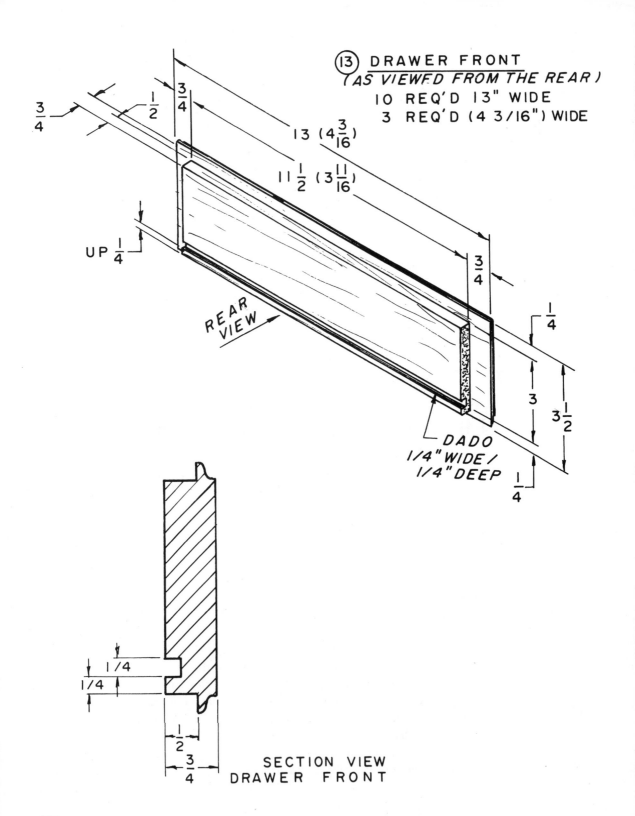

13 DRAWER FRONT
(AS VIEWED FROM THE REAR)
10 REQ'D 13" WIDE
3 REQ'D (4 3/16") WIDE

$\frac{3}{4}$

$\frac{1}{2}$

$\frac{3}{4}$

13 ($4\frac{3}{16}$)

$11\frac{1}{2}$ ($3\frac{11}{16}$)

$\frac{3}{4}$

UP $\frac{1}{4}$

REAR VIEW

$\frac{1}{4}$

3

$3\frac{1}{2}$

$\frac{1}{4}$

DADO
1/4" WIDE /
1/4" DEEP

1/4

1/4

$\frac{1}{2}$

$\frac{3}{4}$

SECTION VIEW
DRAWER FRONT

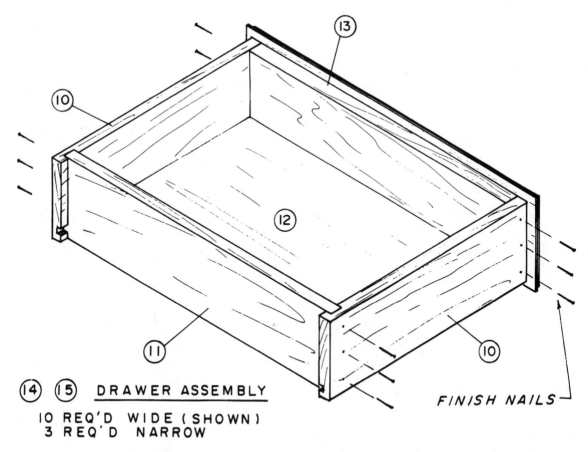

**DRAWER ASSEMBLY**

10 REQ'D WIDE (SHOWN)
3 REQ'D NARROW

FINISH NAILS

assemblies together, keeping everything square. Again, check the drawer assemblies in the openings of the case before the glue sets for proper fit. Adjust if necessary. After glue sets, sand all over.

## Finishing

Clean all surfaces with a tack rag and add any good grade of stain. (Whatever you use, follow the instructions on the container.) Then add knobs to the drawers and recheck for correct fits.

After you have completed this project, you should not be intimidated by *any* project that has drawers in it.

## Suppliers

The 5/8-inch-diameter drawer pulls (#2510-B) can be ordered from:

*Mason and Sullivan*
586 Higgins Crowell Road
West Yarmouth, Cape Cod, MA 02673

# VI

# *Antique Projects*

# Country
# Wall Shelf

I FOUND THIS EARLY AMERICAN WALL SHELF IN SOUTHERN NEW HAMPSHIRE. THE graceful, stepped curve of the sides and the large top of this unusual shelf will complement the pieces displayed on it. The original shelf, estimated to be made around 1840, was made of pine. I chose cherry for the reproduction and finished two shelf units, both by planing and scraping the surface. I made one to appear old, and another to look as the original had when it was new. The project is not difficult and can be finished in a weekend.

## Instructions

Parts A through E on the Materials List are listed as $1\frac{1}{16}$ inch thick. For woodworkers who do not have thickness machines, ¾ inch would do just fine. For those who want the shelf surface to appear as the original, a light hand-planing on ¾-inch stock would do the trick.

Start by cutting out the sides, top board, and shelves (parts A,B,C,D, and E). Next, lay out the side curve in part A, and then lay out the dado locations. In most cases, it is easier to cut the dadoes before cutting the side curve in part A, especially if you plan to use a table saw that requires a straight edge in contact with the miter gauge. I have found, however, that a router with a simple fence jig is the safest, easiest, and cleanest way to cut the dadoes.

| Part No. | Name | Size | Req'd. |
|----------|------|------|--------|
| 1 | Side | ¾ × 9¼ – 31 Long | 2 |
| 2 | Top Board | ¾ × 9¼ – 23 Long | 1 |
| 3 | Top Shelf | ¾ × 7⅞ – 23 Long | 1 |
| 4 | Middle Shelf | ¾ × 8 – 23 Long | 1 |
| 5 | Bottom Shelf | ¾ × 8½ – 23 Long | 1 |
| 6 | Facing Board | ¼ × 2⅝ – 24 Long | 1 |
| 7 | Top Molding | ½ × 1¾ – 50 Long | 1 |
| 8 | Bottom Molding | ½ × 2¼ – 50 Long | 1 |

The double-fence jig to guide a router can be made from scrap wood and easily aligned and clamped over the sides for the dado cuts. The double fence will not allow the router to wander as a single-fence system will invariably do, and if care is taken to secure the end pieces 90 degrees to the rails, the jig will cut dadoes at right angles to the edge.

Once the bit passes through the end of the jig, further cuts are easy to set up. Simply align the cut in the end rail of the jig to the dado layout lines in the stock to be cut. I make several jigs, cutting both ends of each jig with the different cutters I use. (One jig may have ¾-inch cut at one end and ½-inch cut at the other.) Lacking a ¹¹⁄₁₆-inch cutting bit, I used a ½-inch bit and made a second pass, unclamping the jig and moving it slightly.

After the dadoes are cut in the two A parts, stack them together with the dadoes to the inside. Masking tape will hold the parts together during the cutting operation without leaving nail holes. With a band saw, carefully cut out the waste, relief cutting where necessary.If a saber, or bow, saw is used to cut the curves, care must be taken to support the top and bottom shelf area where the grain runs across narrow areas.

# Assembly

After cutting, file, scrape, or sand the edges. Sand, plane, or scrape the flat sides of all parts A,B,C,D, and E before assembly. Trial-fit the shelves in the dado slots for proper fit.

Next, glue and clamp the shelves together. Shelves C and D are slightly wider than the length of the dado slot. Align them flush with the back, and plane the front flush slightly round. The top board (part A) and shelf (part E) will be covered with molding and should be flush with the front. After clamping, check the shelf for squareness and correct before the glue sets.

Cut the molding and front board (parts G,H, and F). Leave parts G and H full-length while cutting the molding profile. The profiles require three common cutters, the Roman Ogee (a rounding-over bit) and the cove bit. If a router is not available, specialty planes, scrapers, or table saw techniques can be used to closely follow the patterns.

When the shelf has dried and the clamps are removed, glue and nail the front board (part F) in place. The ends of the front board must be flush with the outside face of the sides, as the top molding will be installed on the front board and be mitered around the side of the shelf. Cut the miters and install the moldings (parts G and H). Glue the top moldings flush with the top board, and fit the bottom moldings flush with the top of the bottom shelf. The original had square nails in both the moldings and the shelf dadoes.

# Finishing

As an alternative to final sanding, I chose to scrape the shelves before applying the finish, as was the practice in 1840, before sandpaper. Scraper blades, properly edged, are faster and a good deal more quiet and dust free than sanding machines. Scraping leaves a smooth finish like the original. Finally apply your favorite finish. I used several coats of Watco Oil, which proved quite satisfactory.

The shelf that was made to look old or ''antiqued'' required several more steps. After the Watco Oil had dried, the shelf was distressed to suggest years of use. Marks and dents were made on the edges and tops of the shelves where perhaps objects had marred the shelf. Sharp corners were worn down. Layout lines for locating the nails were scratched into the sides. Square nails were counter-set slightly and the hole left open. Next, a wash coat of oil-based black paint, thinned 50 percent, was wiped on the entire surface of the shelf and then immediately wiped off. Black paint was left in the nail holes, surface depressions, cracks and corners, effectively accenting these areas. Then the shelf was waxed.

Beauty is in the eye of the beholder. These shelves with their graceful curves, whether they look new or old, will add elegance and charm to the objects displayed on them.

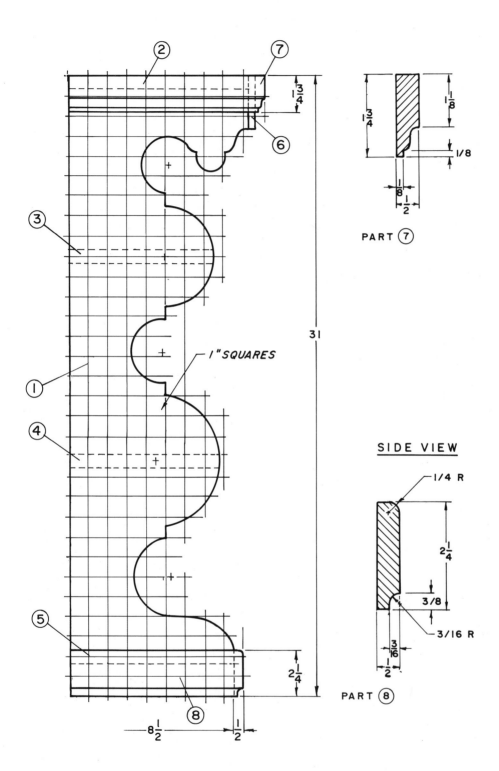

$1\frac{3}{4}$

⑥

PART ⑦

$1\frac{3}{4}$

$1\frac{1}{8}$

1/8

$\frac{1}{8}$

$\frac{1}{2}$

31

1" SQUARES

SIDE VIEW

1/4 R

$2\frac{1}{4}$

3/8

3/16 R

$\frac{3}{16}$

$\frac{1}{2}$

PART ⑧

$2\frac{1}{4}$

$8\frac{1}{2}$

$\frac{1}{2}$

282

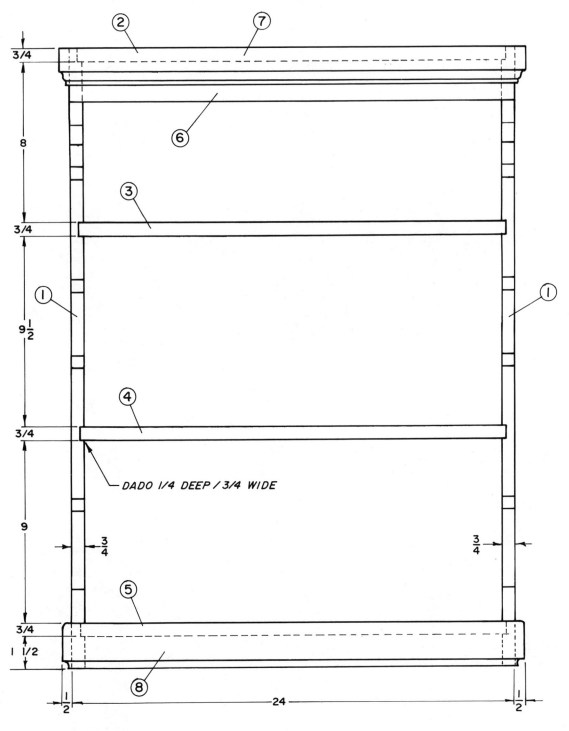

②　⑦

3/4

8

③

3/4

①　　①

9 1/2

④

3/4

DADO 1/4 DEEP / 3/4 WIDE

9

3/4　　3/4

⑤

3/4

1 1/2

⑥

⑧

1/2　　24　　1/2

FRONT VIEW

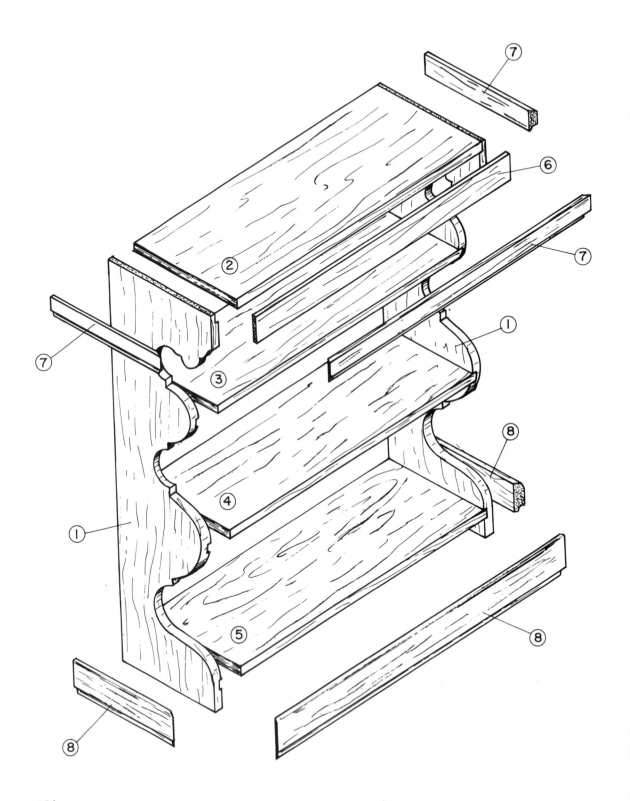

# Pipe Box

THERE PROBABLY WERE NEVER TWO PIPE BOXES MADE ALIKE: THEY RANGED FROM elegant to rather crude boxes. These boxes were usually made of thin ¼- to ⅜-inch-thick hardwood. Cherry, maple, mahogany, or walnut was usually the wood chosen, but pine was also sometimes used, especially on the more informal pipe boxes. The open top area was where the long stemmed clay pipes were stored and the drawer below was used to store the forbidden tobacco.

The pipe box shown here was found in a museum in Massachusetts and is dated about 1750 or so. It is somewhat unusual as it was made of pine and not as tall and thin as most pipe boxes of its day. Today, the pipe box can still be functional for other uses and will add the warmth of yesterday to any room.

## Instructions

Select a piece of pine ⅜ inch thick and 60 inches long for the box and drawer front, and a piece ¼ inch thick and 15 inches long for the drawer assembly (back, sides, bottom). Referring to the Materials List, cut all parts to overall size.

With light pencil marks, divide the top 8 inches of the backboard into ½-inch squares and transfer the shape to the wood. Carefully cut out and sand the backboard, taking care to keep sharp sharp edges. In the same manner, lay out and cut the top design of the two sides and the front board.

Next, locate and rabbet two ⅜-inch slots in the two side pieces. Make rabbets to within ⅜ inch from the back edge of the sides as shown. Then sand the two spacers.

Dry-fit all pieces to ensure correct and tight fits. Trim to fit if necessary. Lightly glue parts together and nail together with short square-cut nails. Be sure to drill small holes before nailing to avoid splitting the wood, especially near the edges. Sand all over, slightly rounding the front edge of the top, side, and front trim designs.

Fit the drawer front into the drawer opening. The assembly should have a snug fit at this time. Rabbet for drawer bottom and sides. Rabbet drawer back ⅛ inch wide for drawer bottom. Also rabbet drawer sides ⅛ inch wide for drawer bottom.

Bevel the four edges of the drawer bottoms at a 10-degree angle to fit into ⅛-inch rabbet groove as shown. (This was done on many early-made drawers and adds authenticity to your project.)

Dry-fit the drawer to ensure a correct and tight fit. You might have to trim a bit. Glue parts together. Then fit the drawer to the opening by sanding the sides and bottom. Drawer should open and close with a little friction, but should not be sloppy.

# Finishing

Stain to suit; an Ipswitch Pine stain is somewhat close to the original pipe box. If you wish to make your pipe box look aged, apply a clear sealer coat, slightly distress the surface, and apply a wash coat of 50 percent black paint and 50 percent paint thinner. Wipe on and wipe right off. Leave the black wash coat in the distress marks and scratches. Also try to leave some of the wash coat in the corners.

*Important:* experiment on some scrap wood to get the effect you want. Use two or three coats of top coat or tung oil to get a nonglossy finish. If your finish is too shiny, use #0000 steel wool to dull the finish. Apply a coat of lemon oil.

Don't forget, a new-looking antique does not look authentic. A copy of an antique should look old, so do try the distress and wash coat effect.

## MATERIALS LIST

| Name | Size | Req'd. |
|---|---|---|
| Backboard | 5¾" Wide × 16" Long | 1 |
| Sides | 4⅝" Wide × 8¾" Long | 2 |
| Front Board | 5¾" Wide × 5¾" Long | 1 |
| Spacers | 4¼" Wide × 6" Long | 2 |
| Drawer Front | 2⅝" Wide × 5¾" Long | 1 |
| Drawer Back | 3" Wide × 5½" Long | 1 |
| Drawer Sides | 3" Wide × 4" Long | 2 |
| Drawer Bottom | 3½" Wide × 5½" Long | 1 |

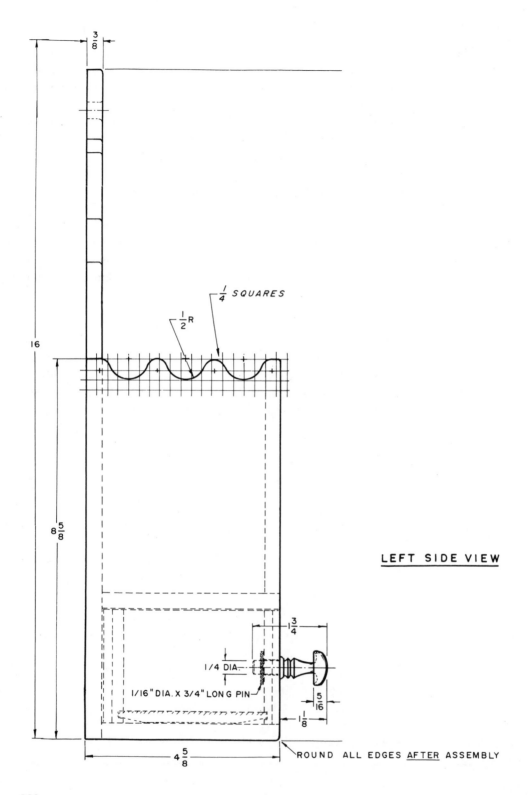

$\frac{3}{8}$

$\frac{1}{4}$ SQUARES

$\frac{1}{2}$ R

16

LEFT SIDE VIEW

$8\frac{5}{8}$

$1\frac{3}{4}$

1/4 DIA

5/16

1/16" DIA. X 3/4" LONG PIN

$1\frac{1}{8}$

$4\frac{5}{8}$

ROUND ALL EDGES AFTER ASSEMBLY

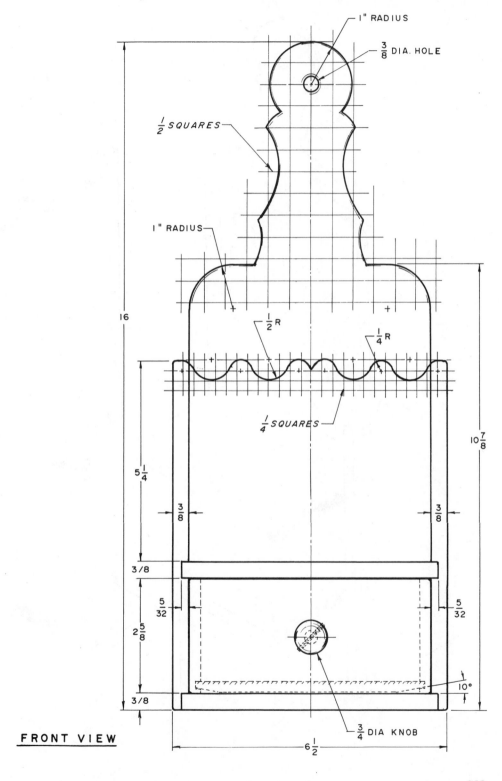

1" RADIUS

$\frac{3}{8}$ DIA. HOLE

$\frac{1}{2}$ SQUARES

1" RADIUS

16

$\frac{1}{2}$ R

$\frac{1}{4}$ R

$\frac{1}{4}$ SQUARES

$10\frac{7}{8}$

$5\frac{1}{4}$

$\frac{3}{8}$

$\frac{3}{8}$

3/8

$\frac{5}{32}$

$\frac{5}{32}$

$2\frac{5}{8}$

10°

3/8

**FRONT VIEW**

$\frac{3}{4}$ DIA KNOB

$6\frac{1}{2}$

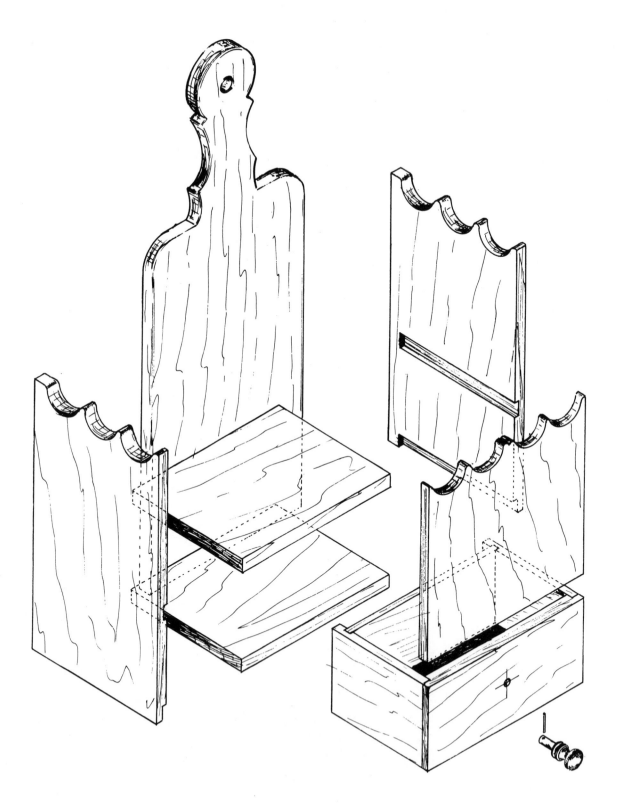

# Sleigh Bench

THIS IS A COPY OF A CHILD'S SLEIGH BENCH I FOUND IN THE PENNSYLVANIA AREA. Most copies of today are simplified versions with simple one-piece end boards. This copy with its stepped end, is more authentic, and, of course, much stronger, as the seat is supported by the legs. These sleigh benches were placed in the sleigh for the children to sit on and removed when not in use. I doubt if they would pass today's child-restraint laws.

The original was painted, as was this copy, with a simple country tole design.

## Instructions

Cut all parts to overall size per the Materials List. Sand all sides at this time.

On a piece of paper draw a 1-inch-square grid. Then lay out the leg (part 1), the side (part 2), and the side brace (part 4).

Locate and cut the ¼-inch-deep and ¾-inch-wide dado in the side, 2¼ inches up from the bottom, as shown. Cut the bottom end at 39 degrees. Be sure to make a matched pair, with the dado on one side and the slanted end on the other side.

Transfer the paper pattern to the wood for parts 1, 2, and 4. Cut the parts to size and sand all edges. Be sure to make two matching pairs of parts 1, 2, and 4.

On the side, round the top outside edge as shown. A router with a ¼-inch-radius cutter with a ball bearing follower works great for this. Be sure to stop as illustrated. If a router is not available, a rasp will do fine.

Cut the two braces (part 5) at an angle as shown, and sand all over, keeping sharp edges.

# Assembly

Dry-fit all parts to check for tightness. Adjust if necessary.

Glue and nail together the side members (parts 1 and 2). Keep everything square and straight. If you have them, use square-cut nails. Add the top board (part 3), and glue and nail it in place. Add the support (part 6) and the brace (part 5) with glue and nails.

Sand all over, keeping all edges rounded just slightly. You can countersink the nail heads or leave them exposed; many original antiques have exposed nail heads. Some early woodworkers puttied them with a white putty and let this show also.

# Finishing

This project can be either stained or painted—it looks good either way. If you choose to stain, apply a coat of your choice, following the instruction on the can. Then apply a light coat of Watco oil, tung oil, or some other topcoat.

If you paint the bench, apply a primer coat, followed by a color of your choice. To achieve an antique look, apply two coats of paint of a totally different color. For example, the first coat could be powder blue and the top coat Early American red. After the paint has dried, sand down through the topcoat in places you think the bench would normally have been worn—places such as the edges and bottom of the legs.

Apply a topcoat of a walnut stain and wipe off immediately. Leave the stain in the corners and in the nail holes. If you distressed and scratched your "antique" bench, leave the stain in the scratches and distress marks; this will really add years to your project.

If you wish, a simple tole painted design can be added to the side board. Don't be afraid to apply a light stain topcoat over the painting to give it that old look.

All you need now is a horse, a sleigh, and some snow, and your sleigh bench is ready for use.

―――――――――――――MATERIALS LIST―――――――――――――

| Part No. | Name | Size | Req'd. |
| --- | --- | --- | --- |
| 1 | Leg | ¾ × 9¾ – 11 Long | 2 |
| 2 | Side | ¾ × 9¾ – 9½ Long | 2 |
| 3 | Top Board | ¾ × 9¾ – 20½ Long | 1 |
| 4 | Side Braces | ½ × 2½ – 21½ Long | 2 |
| 5 | Brace | ¾ × 1½ – 9¾ Long | 2 |
| 6 | Support | ¾ × 1¾ – 9¾ Long | 2 |

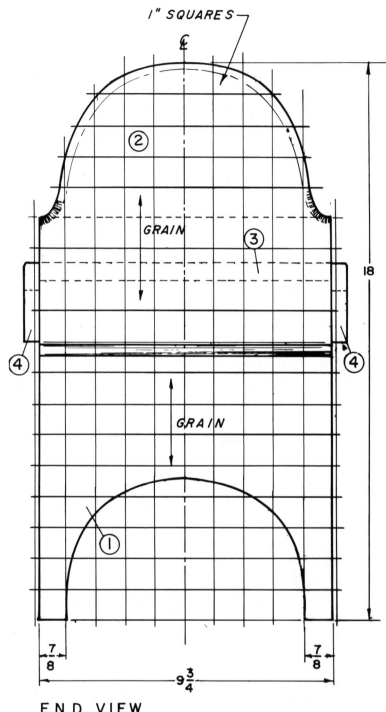

1" SQUARES

GRAIN

GRAIN

18

2

3

4    4

1

7/8    7/8

9 3/4

END VIEW

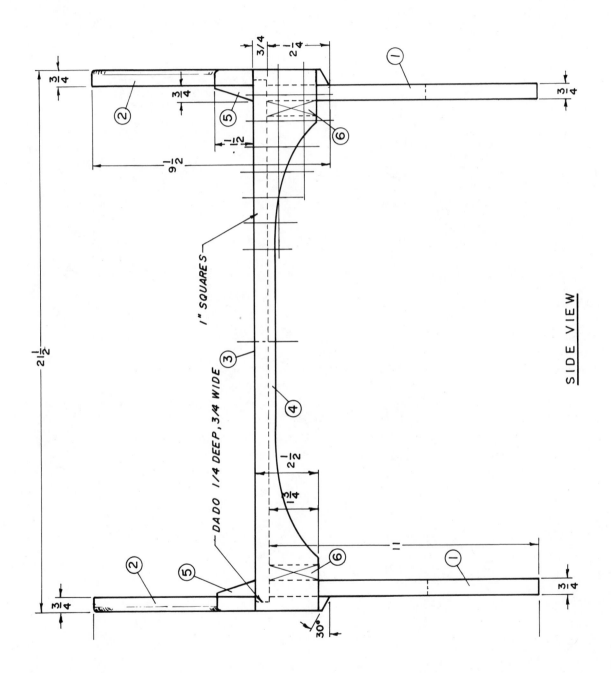

SIDE VIEW

295

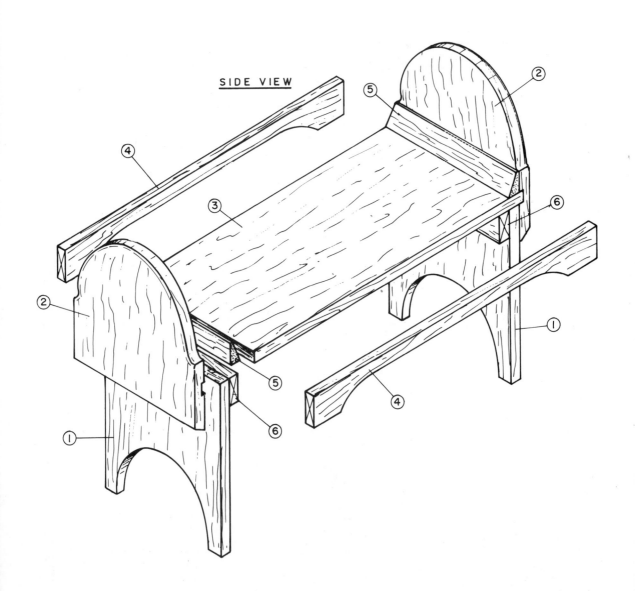

SIDE VIEW

# Candle Box

IN YEARS PAST, SMALL BOXES CAME IN MANY SHAPES AND FORMS. THEY WERE USED to store just about everything. Some had lids that hinged and others had sliding tops. This particular box is an exact copy of an old antique box that probably held candles. Candle boxes often were used to store jewelry and other valuables. This probably offered a great hiding place; who would look for jewelry in a candle box? The original box was found in an antique shop in southern New Hampshire and had a hefty price tag of $325.

A box like this is very simple to build, takes very little material, and does not take long to make. After having made eight or ten of these boxes myself, I find everyone who sees them seems to want one. Perhaps I should go into the business of making candle boxes. The actual dimensions can be changed to accommodate almost any size or particular need. Today, they make excellent documentary boxes.

The original candle box was made of maple, but it could be made of any kind of hardwood. The boxes can be stained and finished, or, like the original, painted. The original was painted an old powder-blue color and was well worn, as shown in the photograph.

## Instructions

Cut 24 inches from the 60-inch board for the sliding lid and bottom. Cut this into two pieces: one exactly 5½ inches wide × 11³⁄₁₆ inches long for the lid,

and another 5½ inches wide × 11⅝ inches long for the bottom. Label the parts and set aside. Then cut the remaining 36 inches to exactly 5 inches wide × 36 inches long. Rabbet the entire length of one edge ³⁄₁₆ inch deep × ⅜ inch wide, per the drawing. Next notch (dado) the entire length of the opposite edge as shown, ³⁄₁₆ inches wide, and ⅜ inch down from the top edge. Cut the board into four pieces as illustrated: 12 inches long, 5½ inches long, 12 inches long, and 5½ inches long. Label them, "right side," "left side," and "ends." Cutting the sides and ends in this order will make the grain pattern "flow" around the box.

On one of the 5½-inch pieces, cut off ⅜ inch from the top surface (to bottom of notch), as shown. On the two 12-inch-long pieces, rabbet both ends as shown. It is important to rabbet through lip on the front end but *do not* rabbet through the lip at the back end. Be sure to make a left- and right-hand pair.

Glue the four sides together along with the bottom piece. Nail together with two square-cut nails per joint and along the bottom. Set the nails slightly and putty along all joints for a tight fit.

Feather the top of the lid by using either a table saw set at 10 degrees or a hand plane, and bevel all four sides of the lid per the drawing. Set the blade of the saw at a height of ¼ inch and, starting in exactly ⁵⁄₃₂ inch from the saw

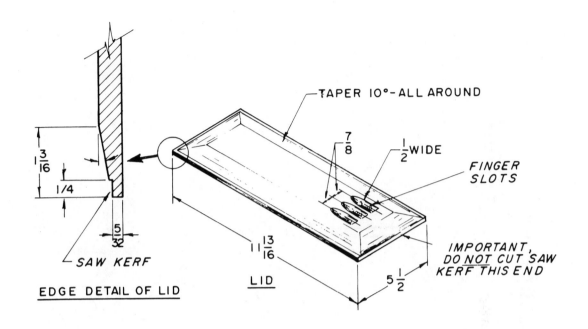

TAPER 10°- ALL AROUND

$\frac{7}{8}$

$\frac{1}{2}$ WIDE

FINGER SLOTS

$1\frac{3}{16}$

1/4

$\frac{5}{32}$

SAW KERF

EDGE DETAIL OF LID

$11\frac{13}{16}$

LID

$5\frac{1}{2}$

IMPORTANT,
DO NOT CUT SAW
KERF THIS END

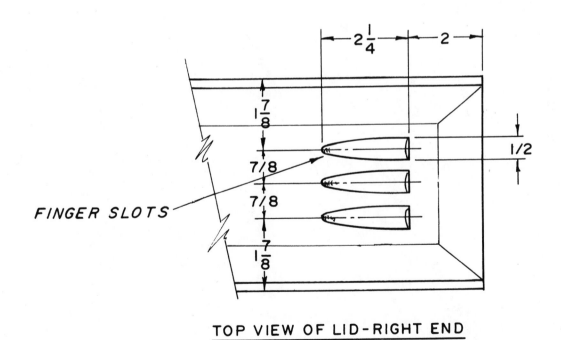

$2\frac{1}{4}$

2

$1\frac{7}{8}$

7/8

7/8

$1\frac{7}{8}$

1/2

FINGER SLOTS

TOP VIEW OF LID-RIGHT END

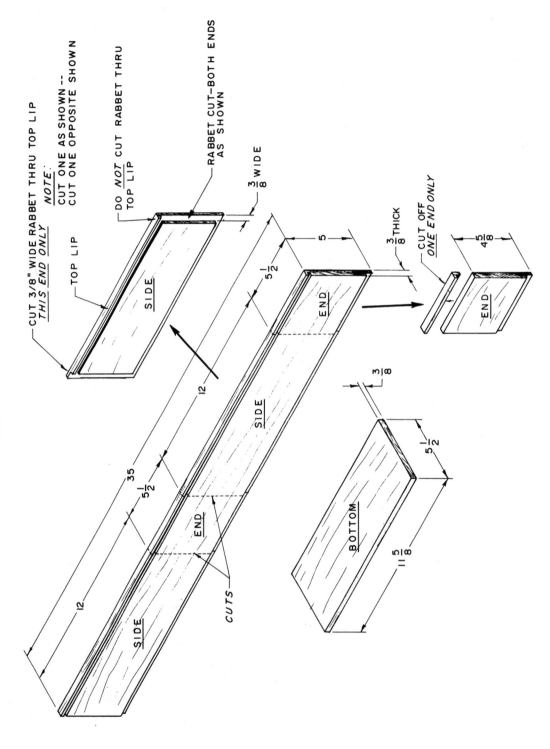

EDGE DETAIL OF LID

CUT 3/8" WIDE RABBET THRU TOP LIP
*THIS END ONLY*

TOP LIP

*NOTE:*
CUT ONE AS SHOWN --
CUT ONE OPPOSITE SHOWN

DO *NOT* CUT RABBET THRU
TOP LIP

RABBET CUT—BOTH ENDS
AS SHOWN

$\frac{3}{8}$ WIDE

SIDE

5

$5\frac{1}{2}$

$\frac{3}{8}$ THICK

CUT OFF
*ONE END ONLY*

$4\frac{5}{8}$

END

12

SIDE

35

$5\frac{1}{2}$

$5\frac{1}{2}$

END

END

12

SIDE

CUTS

$\frac{3}{8}$

BOTTOM

$5\frac{1}{2}$

$11\frac{5}{8}$

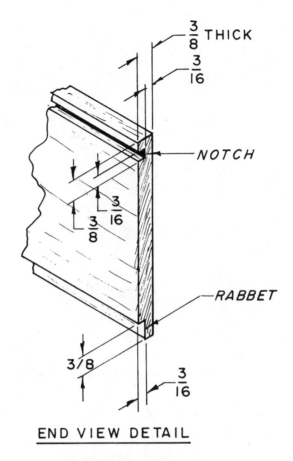

$\frac{3}{8}$ THICK

$\frac{3}{16}$

NOTCH

$\frac{3}{16}$

$\frac{3}{8}$

RABBET

3/8

$\frac{3}{16}$

END VIEW DETAIL

fence, cut the flat area in the lid. Be sure to cut along the two sides and only *one* end. Check to see that the lid slides freely within the box without binding. Sand or recut the 5/32-inch lip to suit, if necessary.

Finally, locate and cut the three finger slots by either carving in by hand with a chisel or by drilling in place with a ½-inch Forstner bit on a drill press set at approximately 5 degrees.

# Finishing

First, sand all over to suit, taking care to keep sharp edges at all corners. Next, apply either a stain of your choice or apply paint, using an old-fashioned color. The finish was applied to the outer surface only on the original box. Finally, if the box has been painted, sand all edges slightly to give it that worn look.

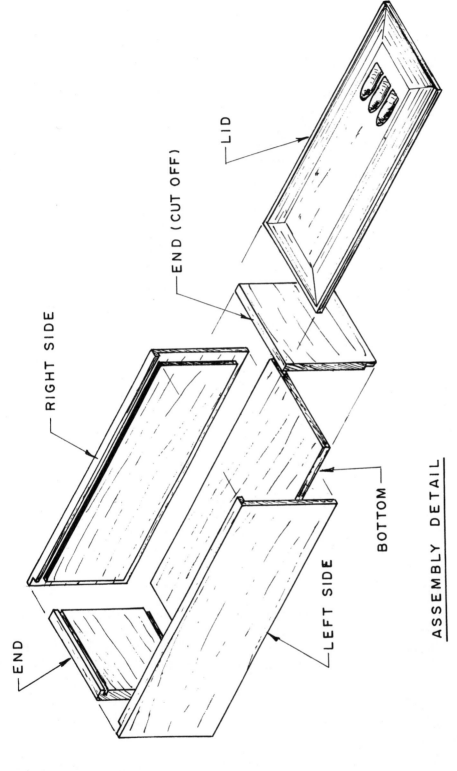

RIGHT SIDE

END (CUT OFF)

LID

END

LEFT SIDE

BOTTOM

ASSEMBLY DETAIL

# Towel Rack

THIS IS A COPY OF AN OLD TOWEL RACK FOUND IN A MILK HOUSE IN ST. JOHNS-bury, Vermont. It is an interesting very functional design that blends in well with Early American decor. Because milk houses were always white-washed, the original towel rack had been whitewashed many times throughout the years and could still be seen today.

## Instructions

On a piece of 6-×-19-inch paper, draw out a ½-inch grid. On this grid locate the various swing points, and from each, swing the given arcs to form the shape of the sides (part 1).

Temporarily tack together two pieces of wood about 6 × 19 inches, using thin finishing nails. Transfer this shape of the rack side to the top piece of 9/16-inch-thick board. If a 9/16-inch thickness is not available, a ¾-inch thick board could be used. Locate and drill the three 7/8-inch-diameter holes. Cut out the shape of the side.

While the parts are still attached together, sand all edges to make an exact pair. Separate the two parts and sand the surfaces, keeping all edges sharp. Locate and drill the two ⅛-inch-diameter holes as shown. Countersink to accept the screws that will attach it to the wall.

Cut the three 7/8-inch-diameter bars to a length of 30½ inches. This length can be adjusted to suit available space or a particular need.

Drill pilot holes through the sides and *into* the dowels for three finishing nails. Before nailing together, check that the rack sits flat on a flat surface. If there is any racking, adjust the dowels accordingly before driving the nails in.

# Finishing

This towel rack can be either stained or painted to blend into the room in which it will be placed.

## MATERIALS LIST

| Part No. | Name | Size | Req'd. |
|---|---|---|---|
| 1 | Side | $^{11}/_{16} \times 6 - 18^{1}/_{16}$ Long | 2 |
| 2 | Bar | $^{7}/_{8}$ Dia. $- 30^{1}/_{2}$ Long | 3 |

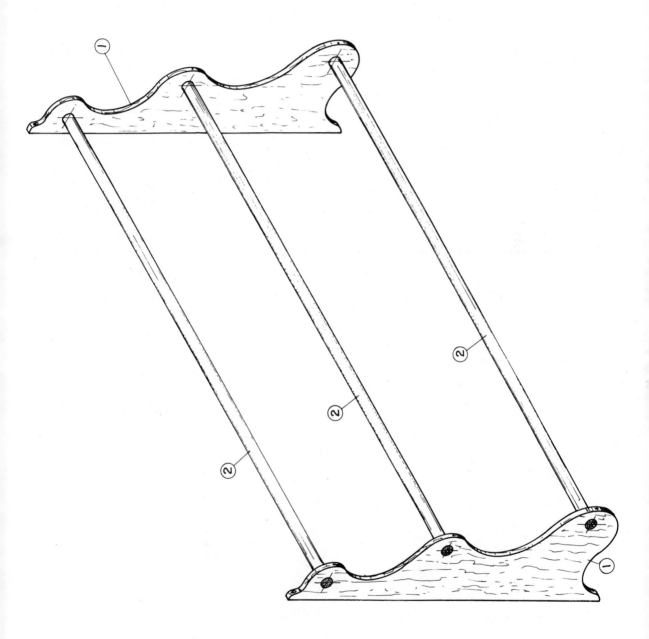

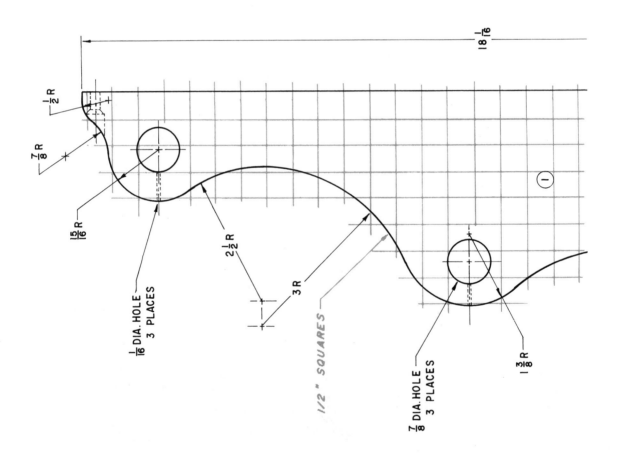

$18\frac{1}{16}$

$\frac{1}{2}R$

$\frac{7}{8}R$

$\frac{15}{16}R$

$\frac{1}{16}$ DIA. HOLE
3 PLACES

$2\frac{1}{2}R$

3 R

1/2" SQUARES

$\frac{7}{8}$ DIA. HOLE
3 PLACES

$1\frac{3}{8}R$

—①—

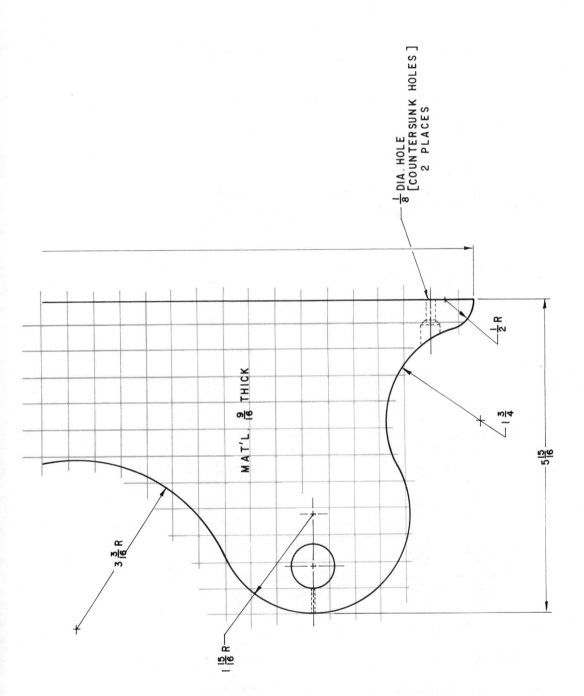

MAT'L. $\frac{9}{16}$ THICK

$\frac{1}{8}$ DIA. HOLE
[COUNTERSUNK HOLES]
2 PLACES

$\frac{1}{2}$ R

$1\frac{3}{4}$

$5\frac{15}{16}$

$3\frac{3}{16}$ R

$1\frac{15}{16}$ R

# Bonnet Chest

T HIS INTERESTING ANTIQUE, SOMETIMES REFERRED TO AS A CHIMNEY CUPBOARD, is very tall for its width and has an almost awkward proportion. In years past they were used, as their name implies, to store the many bonnets that the lady of the house owned, probably one bonnet per shelf. This is a takeoff of an original bonnet chest I found in New Hampshire a few years ago. It was sold at a local auction for a rather high price.

As early homes were not always well designed, it was not uncommon to have a chimney run right through the middle of a bedroom or some other room on the second floor. They can still be found today in older homes throughout New England. These bonnet chests or chimney cupboards were built tall and thin so they could be placed up against a chimney and form a divider that was not as unsightly as the sole chimney in the middle of the room.

Today, these tall, narrow cupboards are great for all kinds of storage. The nice thing about them, is the fact that they do not take up very much floor space, yet provide a lot of shelf space. This bonnet chest, as illustrated, contains almost 10 full feet of 8-inch-deep shelf space.

## Instructions

The original was made of maple, but I have made a lot of these bonnet chests out of pine. When painted, it looks as good as the original did.

Carefully study the drawings in order that you fully understand how it is put together before starting.

Cut all parts to size per the Materials List. Locate and cut the dadoes in the two side boards (part 1). Glue up material for the backboard (part 2).

# Assembly/Case

Assemble the sides, shelves and the back, taking care to keep the unit square. The original had square-cut nails which were exposed. Today, square-cut nails can still be purchased from Tremont Nail Company (see Appendix A). Notice the backboard is simply added to the back of the case and *not* mortised into the sides, as is usually done in better furniture. This is the way the original was made and is a lot easier to make.

Next, add the shelf front (part 10) to the third shelf from the bottom with glue and nails as shown. Attach the two false shelf ends (part 11) with nail and glue, making sure it is attached squarely to the side boards. This part should be glued and nailed securely because this is where the cupboard will be held each time it is moved. Fit and add the top stile (part 4) and the bottom stile (part 5). Add the top rail (part 6), and the top and bottom dust stops (parts 9 and 12).

Fit and add the top boards (part 7) to the top of the cupboard. Purchase, rout, or shape the molding approximately as shown, and fit to the case assembly with 45-degree joints. Be sure to fit it tightly against the top board.

On a piece of cardboard, lay out the foot shape and cut out for a pattern. Trace the foot shape to the front and sides and cut them out as shown. Sand all edges. Cut legs into the backboard, also. They can be the same shape as the front or cut simply as straight legs.

This completes the assembly of the case. Sand all over and fit the doors to the door openings.

# Assembly/Doors

Make the doors as you would any raised-panel door. Note the different sizes of the rails (parts 15 and 16); take care to keep track of the different sizes and where they are assembled. Carefully fit the doors to the respective door openings in the case. Leave about $1/16$ inch all around to allow for expansion.

Fit the door panels to the stiles and rails. Do not glue the door panels inside the door stiles and rails—let them float. If you paint or stain the doors, be sure to paint or stain the door panels *before* assembling the doors. If you don't, the first time the panel shrinks slightly, the unpainted or unstained areas will be seen.

Attach the doors to the case, mortising for the hinges (part 21). These cupboards were usually very plain and the hinges were not exposed any more than necessary.

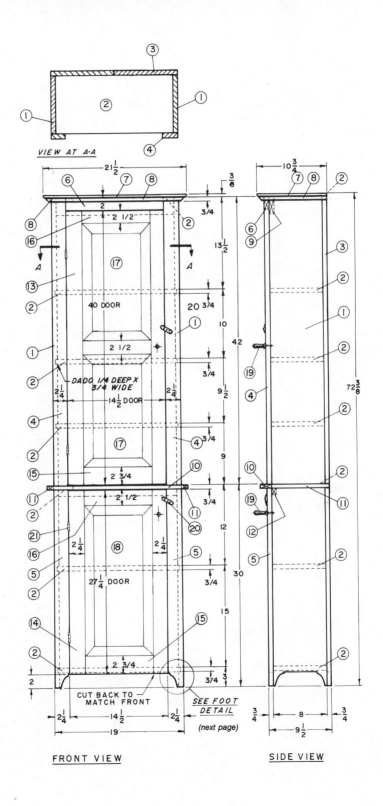

VIEW AT A-A

DADO 1/4 DEEP X 3/4 WIDE

40 DOOR

14½ DOOR

27¼ DOOR

CUT BACK TO MATCH FRONT

SEE FOOT DETAIL

(next page)

FRONT VIEW

SIDE VIEW

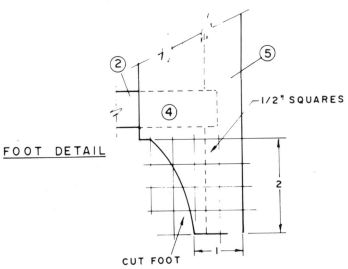

FOOT DETAIL

—1/2" SQUARES

CUT FOOT
AFTER ASSEMBLY

## MATERIALS LIST

| Part No. | Name | Size | Req'd. |
|---|---|---|---|
| 1 | Side | ¾ × 8 – 72 Long | 2 |
| 2 | Shelf | ¾ × 8 – 18 Long | 7 |
| 3 | Backboard | ¾ × 19 – 72 Long | 1 |
| 4 | Stile – Top | ¾ × 2¼ – 42 Long | 2 |
| 5 | Stile – Bottom | ¾ × 2¼ – 30 Long | 2 |
| 6 | Top Rail | ¾ × 2 – 14½ Long | 1 |
| 7 | Top | ⅜ × 10¾ – 21½ Long | 1 |
| 8 | Molding – Cut to Size | ¾ × ¾ – 60 Long | 1 |
| 9 | Top Dust Stop | ¾ × 2½ – 17½ Long | 1 |
| 10 | Shelf – Front | ¾ × 1¾ – 21 Long | 1 |
| 11 | Shelf – End | ¾ × 1 – 8¾ Long | 2 |
| 12 | Dust Stop Bottom | ¾ × ⅞ – 17½ Long | 1 |
| 13 | Door Stile – Top | ¾ × 2¼ – 40 Long | 2 |
| 14 | Door Stile – Bottom | ¾ × 2¼ – 27¼ Long | 2 |
| 15 | Door Rail – Bottom | ¾ × 2¾ – 11½ Long | 2 |
| 16 | Door Rail – Ctr/Top | ¾ × 2½ – 11½ Long | 3 |
| 17 | Panel – Top | ½ × 10¾ – 16¾ Long | 2 |
| 18 | Panel – Bottom | ½ × 10¾ – 22¾ Long | 1 |
| 19 | Door Pull | ¾ Dia. – 3 Long | 2 |
| 20 | Door Latch | ½ × ¾ – 3 Long | 2 |
| 21 | Hinge | 1½ × 1½ | 4 |

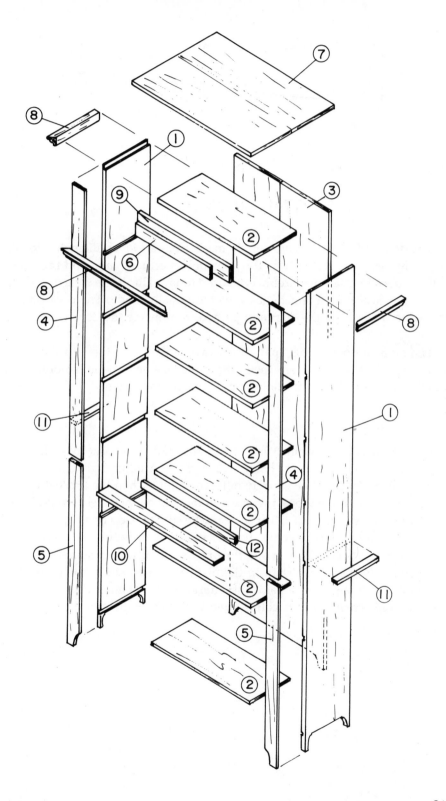

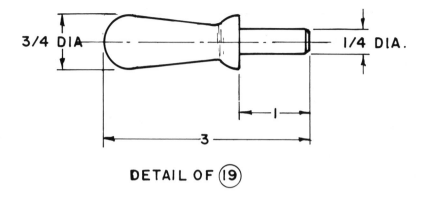

The door pulls (part 19) are simply made from a ¾-inch-diameter dowel about 3 inches long. Notice how the door pull is actually long and thin, not at all like the short, fat, mushroom type used today. This is the style door pull used in the days these bonnet chests were originally made. The door pull is inserted into a hole on the door and pinned from inside the door with a pin or nail.

The original door latches (part 20) always looked as if they were carved from scrap. They were never exactly the same size and shape, so don't try to make yours exact. Attach them approximately as shown.

# Finishing

This bonnet chest can be stained or painted. To obtain an antique look, distress your bonnet chest. Then paint a basecoat of an Early American color, and when it dries, add a topcoat of an entirely different color. When the topcoat dries, sand down through the topcoat where you feel the bonnet chest would have naturally worn over the past 150 or so years. Be sure to use a fine paper. Don't be afraid of sanding down too far. If you sand down through the basecoat to the bare wood, it will look even older! Apply a coat of walnut stain and wipe off immediately. Leave the stain in the distress marks and in the corners.

Another nice effect is to paint the interior of the bonnet chest an Early American red, green, or blue color—even if you stain the case and doors.

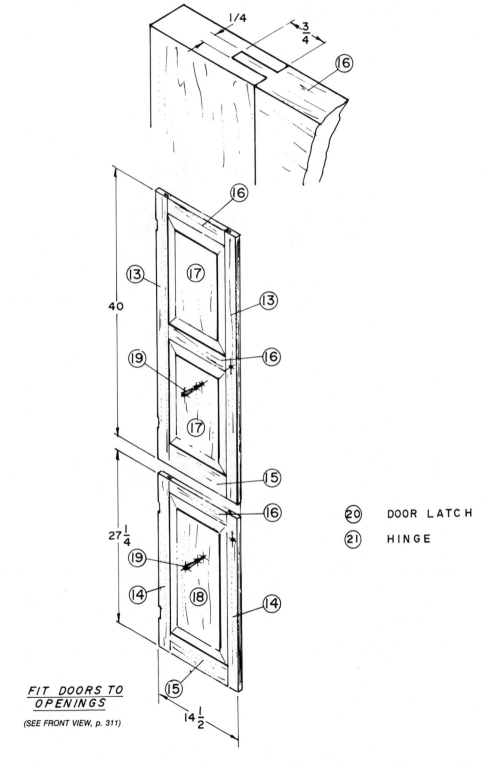

1/4

3/4

16

16

13

13

40

17

19

16

17

15

20  DOOR LATCH

21  HINGE

16

19

27 1/4

14

18

14

*FIT DOORS TO*
*OPENINGS*

*(SEE FRONT VIEW, p. 311)*

15

14 1/2

315

# Stepback Cupboard

MOST EARLY STEPBACK CUPBOARDS HAD TWO OR THREE OPEN SHELVES AT THE top to display their owner's pewter and a closed area at the bottom to hold less attractive kitchen supplies. As years passed and glass became lower in price, this type of open cupboard was replaced by the more formal glass door china cabinets of the late 1800s.

The original of this stepback cupboard, was found in New Hampshire, made around 1815. All measurements were taken directly from the original hutch, but were altered slightly to coincide with today's lumber sizes. This cupboard was made of pine, distressed slightly, and painted, in order to make it look exactly as the original did. Large, square-cut nails (available from Tremont Nail Company, see Appendix A) were also used with no attempt to hide them. If you want a "country" look for your home, this project will surely provide that.

## Instructions

Pine was used on the original cupboard and probably should be used for the copy. As most early country-style cupboards were usually made of pine, any other kind of wood would not look authentic. As always, carefully study the drawings in order that you fully understand how the cupboard is put together before starting.

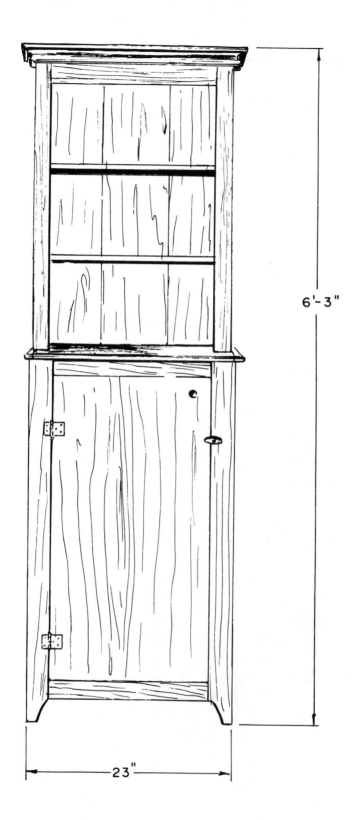

6'-3"

23"

This project can be made with only three 1-×-12-inch boards, 12 feet long, and one 1-×-12-inch board, 8 feet long. With pine selling for around $1.25 a board foot, this project should cost about $60. Try to choose lumber that does not have too many knots, or at least only small knots.

Study the Materials List and note how the lumber should be cut up, so that you will have the least amount of waste. Cut all pieces to size as indicated and label each part as you cut, in order to keep track of the pieces. Take care to cut a matching right-hand and left-hand pair of sides.

If you do not have the equipment or ability to cut the dadoes or grooves in the two side boards, simply cut the shelves (parts 3 and 4) ½ inch shorter than the required 21-inch length, and abut the shelves to the sides with nails. The assembly will be just about as strong after it is all put together and will not show anyway. Glue and nail the shelves (parts 3, 4 and 6) to the sides (part 2), using square-cut nails, keeping everything square as you go. Glue and nail the three backboards (part 1) and the side trim pieces (parts 8 and 9) in place, again using square-cut nails. Let these pieces overlap the sides slightly, so that you can sand the edges square after assembly. Sand both sides at this time, keeping all corners square and sharp.

## MATERIALS LIST

| Part No. | Name | Size | Req'd. |
|---|---|---|---|
| 1 | Backboard | ⅝ × 7³⁄₁₆ – 71⅞ | 3 |
| 2 | Sides | ¾ × 14¾ – 74⅜ | 2 |
| 3 | Top Shelf | ¾ × 7⅞ – 22¹⁄₁₆ | 3 |
| 4 | Center Shelf | ¾ × 15⅞ – 23¹⁄₁₆ | 1 |
| 5 | Door Stop | ¾ × 1 – 21⁹⁄₁₆ | 1 |
| 6 | Bottom Shelf | ¾ × 14⅛ – 22¹⁄₁₆ | 3 |
| 7 | Shelf End | ¾ × 1 – 16½ | 2 |
| 8 | Shelf Dowel | ¼ Dia. – 3 Long | 8 |
| 9 | Side Trim Top | ¾ × 1½ – 33⅜ | 2 |
| 10 | Top Trim | ¾ × 3¾ – 20¹⁄₁₆ | 1 |
| 11 | Dowel | ¼ Dia. × 2 Long | 4 |
| 12 | Side Trim | ¾ × 2¼ – 40½ | 2 |
| 13 | Top Board | ⅜ × 11¼ – 27½ | 1 |
| 14 | Molding | 1¾ × 1¾ – 60 | 1 |
| 15 | Door | ¾ × 18½ – 34¾ | 1 |
| 16 | Spline | ¾ × 1¾ – 18½ | 2 |
| 17 | Knob | 1 Dia. × 2⅞ | 1 |
| 18 | Hinge | 2½ × 2½ | 2 |
| 19 | Latch | To Suit | 1 |

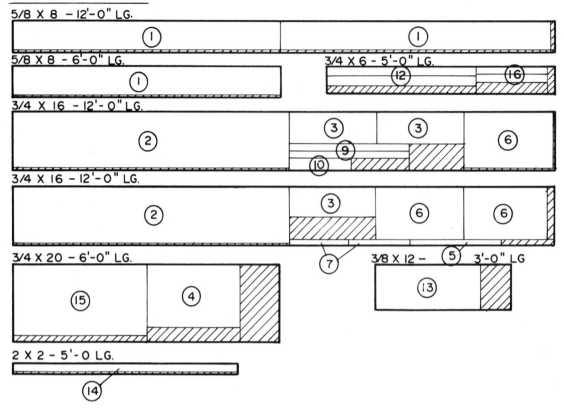

Cut to size and add the two side trim pieces (part 7). Drill three ¼-inch-diameter holes in each side as indicated and add the six dowels (part 8). Today, these dowels are more for appearance than function. Glue and attach the shelf front (part 5) using the square-cut nails. Add the top trim, taking care to cut exact 45-degree angles so you will have a tight fit at the two seams. The top molding is now cut and added. In the event you do not have the equipment to make the molding yourself, a very close facsimile can be found at most lumberyards and will be all right to use.

The door (parts 15 and 16), should be cut and glued together as illustrated. Make the door slightly oversize and plane it down so it has about ¹⁄₁₆ inch all around to allow for expansion throughout the changing seasons to come.

The knob (part 17) will have to be turned to size with a lathe, if you want a knob similar to the original, but any purchased knob close in size and shape can be used. However, it should be longer in length than its overall diameter. Add the knob to the door using only a small slightly tapered ¹⁄₁₆-inch-diameter hardwood pin through the shank of the knob.

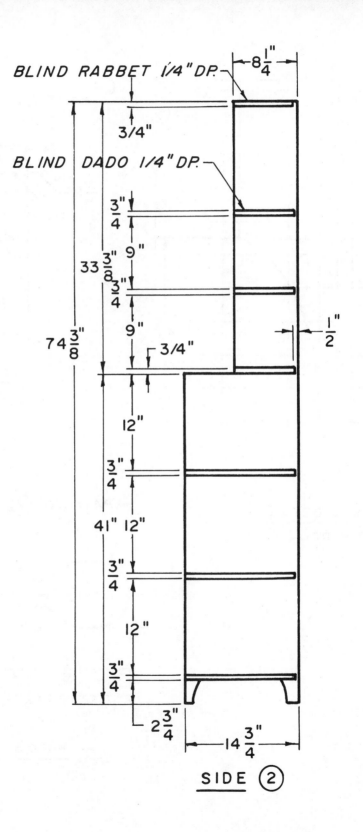

BLIND RABBET 1/4" DP.

$8\frac{1}{4}$"

3/4"

BLIND DADO 1/4" DP.

$\frac{3"}{4}$

$33\frac{3}{8}$" $\quad$ 9"

$\frac{3"}{4}$

9"

$74\frac{3}{8}$"

$\frac{1"}{2}$

3/4"

12"

$\frac{3"}{4}$

41" 12"

$\frac{3"}{4}$

12"

$\frac{3"}{4}$

$2\frac{3}{4}$"

$14\frac{3}{4}$"

SIDE ②

321

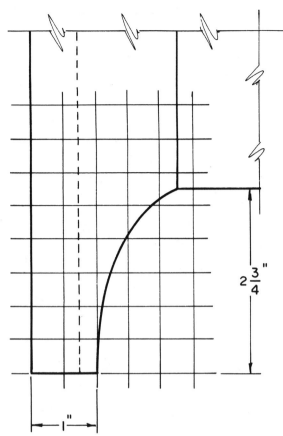

## LEG DETAIL
### ( 6 REQ'D )

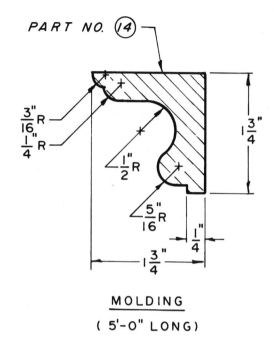

PART NO. ⑭

$\frac{3"}{16}$R

$\frac{1"}{4}$R

$\frac{1"}{2}$R

$\frac{5"}{16}$R

$1\frac{3}{4}"$

$\frac{1"}{4}$

$1\frac{3}{4}"$

## MOLDING
### ( 5'-0" LONG )

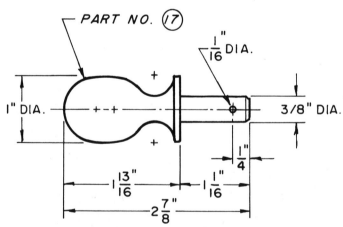

PART NO. ⑰

$\frac{1"}{16}$DIA.

1" DIA.

3/8" DIA.

$\frac{1"}{4}$

$1\frac{13}{16}"$

$1\frac{1}{16}"$

$2\frac{7}{8}"$

## KNOB

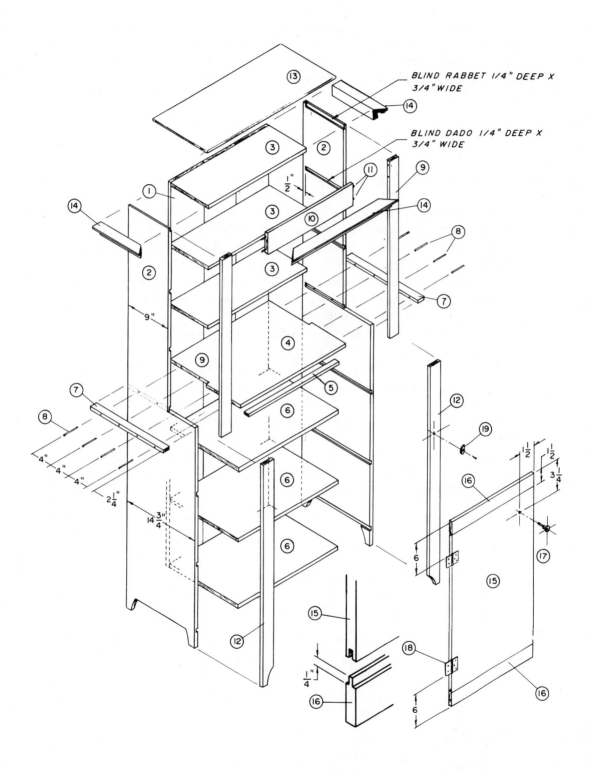

BLIND RABBET 1/4" DEEP X 3/4" WIDE

BLIND DADO 1/4" DEEP X 3/4" WIDE

Cut the latch (part 19) from scrap to the approximate size and shape illustrated. Do not be too fussy with this as early latches were somewhat crude and were used only to hold the door shut. Attach using a roundhead screw.

Add the butt hinge (part 18) as shown, keeping an even 1/16-inch space all around the door.

# Finishing

The original cupboard had a brownish painted finish, which, of course, was very worn. I distressed this copy by rolling a rough rock across the surfaces, and then resanded all over using fine sandpaper.

Paint all interior surfaces with an off-white color. I used "Meetinghouse white" for this copy. A basecoat of "cabinetmakers' blue" paint was put in and allowed to dry for 24 hours or more. A topcoat of "British red" was then added and allowed to dry for 48 hours. (These colors are available from Stulb Paint and Chemical Company; see Appendix A.) Sand the entire cupboard all over, sanding right through the red paint to allow the blue to show here and there, just as it would have worn through from everyday use for the past 150 years. Sand all front-top edges of the shelves and all edges to simulate wear. Don't be afraid to sand some edges right down to the bare wood.

Wipe the cupboard down with a cloth dampened with paint thinner to remove all dust. Allow to dry thoroughly. Add a little burnt sienna to clear, low luster latex urethane acrylic paint and paint the entire cupboard inside and out to give it an aged look. (Clean latex urethane acrylic, #416-00, is available from Benjamin Moore and Company; see Appendix A.)

This cupboard will add a lot of warmth to any room it is placed in and well might become a family heirloom for years to come.

# Ladderback
# Chair

THE LADDERBACK CHAIR, WITH ITS NAME QUITE OBVIOUSLY TAKEN FROM THE LAD-
derback appearance of the chair back, is still in production today. A giant
of a chair stands on the common in Gardner, Massachusetts, advertising
continued production of colonial-style chairs. One might find these popular
and sturdy chairs in Sturbridge Village, Massachusetts; Strawberry Bank,
Portsmouth, New Hampshire; and most all Early American museums.

Ladderbacks were made with a straight back, sloped back, or bent back.
The straight-back chair was the simplest, most prevalent, and surely most
uncomfortable of the ladderbacks, with the back of the chair at right angles
to the seat and floor. The more comfortable slope-backed chairs had straight
rear posts that were slanted backwards from the ground up. The best chairs
were bent back, with curved rear posts, either steamed or green-bent, that kept
the rear legs back for stability.

The project that I have chosen for this book is a ladderback chair that can
be made on a standard 36-inch lathe. The chair is straight backed for simplicity,
and on rockers for comfort. The chair is a reproduction of an antique made
in early New England, passed down through the generations, and in use today.
It is a small rocker, lower than a standard chair, comfortable and suitable as
a nursing chair.

# Instructions

Start by choosing hardwood stock for the chair parts. I chose cherry wood for its beauty, representing a popular wood choice of the colonial and American craftsman. Oak, maple, beech, birch, and ash would do as well. The top rungs of the rocker supporting the seat are made of oak for strength. Turned hardwood dowels are available from Woodworker's Supply of New Mexico (see Appendix A) for those who wish to minimize turning time.

Once the stock is selected, turn the back posts to size, cut the finial, and sand per Fig. 2. On the long back turnings, it may be necessary to use a lathe mid-rest, or support the back of the turning with a hand to prevent chatter.

Next, lay out the slat mortices and rung locations and mark with a pencil while turning on the lathe. The slat locations and rung holes of the posts must be located on a straight line down the length of the post. This may be done sliding the tool rest down the length of the piece with the head stock secured with an indexing pin, or simply with a straight edge.

As the locations of these holes are marked, be sure to orient the straight grain of the post toward the front of the chair, so the post will be strongest when leaning back in the chair. If a lathe indexing pin is used, the side rung locations may be marked at 94 degrees in the back posts and 86 degrees in the front posts, for the obtuse and acute angles. Study the diagram (VIEW AT A-A), and do not overlook that there is a *left* and *right* layout of the rung locations, both front and back.

## MATERIALS LIST

| Part No. | Name | Size | Req'd. |
|----------|------|------|--------|
| 1 | Back Post | $1^1/_2$ Dia. − 36 Long | 2 |
| 2 | Front Post | $1^1/_2$ Dia. − $13^1/_2$ Long | 2 |
| 3 | Rocker | $^3/_8 \times 5$ − 27 Long | 2 |
| 4 | Rung "A" | $^5/_8$ Dia. − $13^3/_8$ Long | 2 |
|   | Rung "B" | $^5/_8$ Dia. − $15^1/_4$ Long | 1 |
|   | Rung "C" | $^5/_8$ Dia. − $13^1/_4$ Long | 6 |
|   | Rung "D" | 1 Dia. − $15^1/_4$ Long | 2 |
| 5 | Slats | $2^1/_2 \times 3$ − 13 Long | 1 |
| 6 | Pin | $^1/_4$ Dia. − $1^1/_2$ Long | 4 |
| 7 | Fiber Twisted Paper | 400 feet | 1 |

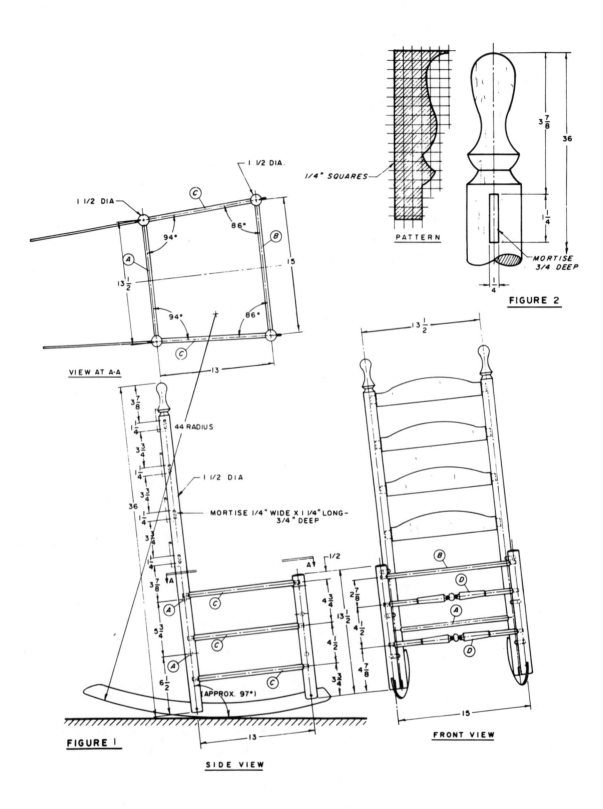

1 1/2 DIA.

1/4" SQUARES

1 1/2 DIA

C

B

94°

86°

A

15

13 1/2

94°

86°

C

VIEW AT A-A

13

PATTERN

3 7/8

36

1 1/4

MORTISE
3/4 DEEP

1
4

FIGURE 2

3 7/8
1 1/4
3 3/4
1 1/4
3 3/4

44 RADIUS

1 1/2 DIA

36

MORTISE 1/4" WIDE X 1 1/4" LONG—
3/4" DEEP

1 1/4
3 3/4
1 1/4
3 7/8

A

A

1/2

A

A

C

4 3/4

2 7/8

13 1/2

4 1/2

5 3/4

C

4 1/2

A

C

4 7/8

6 1/2

(APPROX. 97°)

3 3/4

13 1/2

B

D

A

D

FIGURE 1

13

15

SIDE VIEW

FRONT VIEW

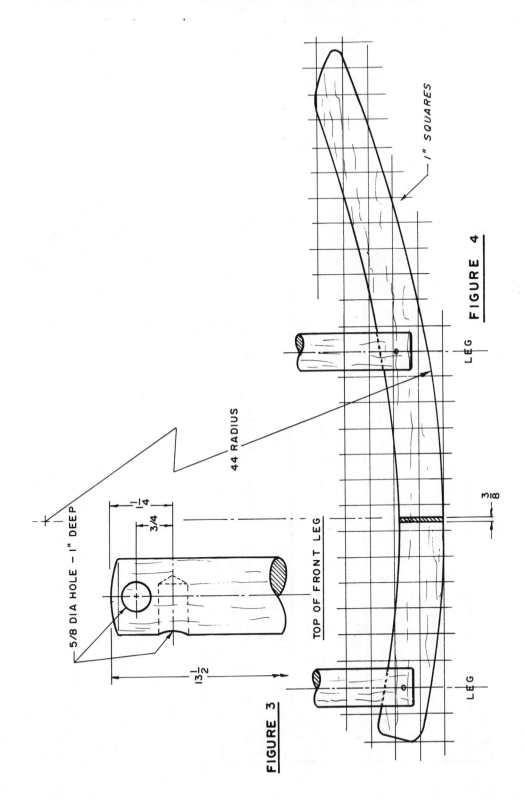

5/8 DIA HOLE – 1" DEEP

$13\frac{1}{2}$

$\frac{1}{4}$

3/4

44 RADIUS

TOP OF FRONT LEG

FIGURE 3

1" SQUARES

LEG

$\frac{3}{8}$

LEG

FIGURE 4

329

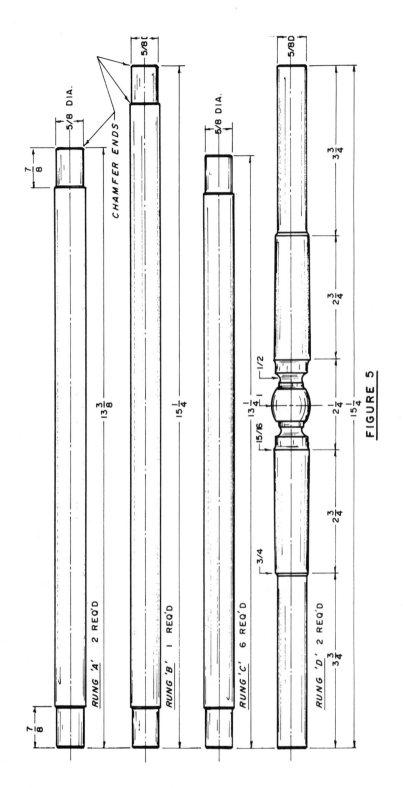

CHAMFER ENDS

5/8 DIA.

7/8

13 3/8

RUNG 'A' 2 REQ'D

7/8

5/8[

15 1/4

RUNG 'B' 1 REQ'D

5/8 DIA.

RUNG 'C' 6 REQ'D

5/8D

3 3/4

2 3/4

1/2

13 1/4

2 1/4

15/16

3/4

2 3/4

15 1/4

3 3/4

RUNG 'D' 2 REQ'D

FIGURE 5

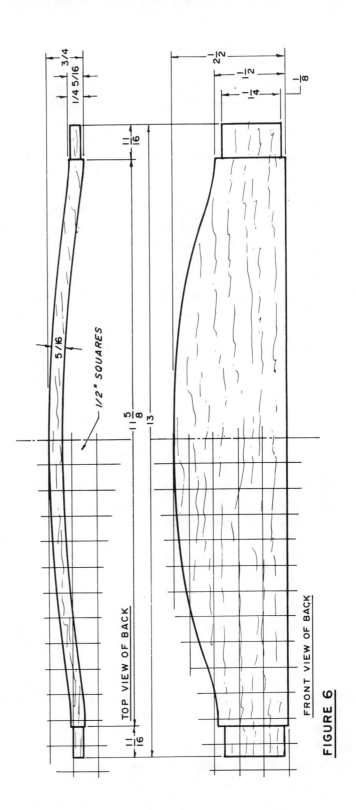

TOP VIEW OF BACK

FRONT VIEW OF BACK

FIGURE 6

3/4

1/4 5/16

5/16

1/2" SQUARES

11/16

11/16

11 5/8

13

2 1/2

1 1/2

1 1/4

1/8

331

A simple way to estimate the 94 and 86-degree angles is to mark the side rung locations ⅛ inch off (along the circumference) of the 90-degree mark from the front rungs, respectively. If you don't have a lathe, you can mark & drill the side rung locations, after the front and back sections of the chair have been dry-fit, with a sliding T bevel and a careful eye. At this time do not cut the spindle ends off the post. Later, after the mortices have been cut and the holes for the rungs drilled, the post can be remounted and any marks and scratches removed before assembly. Turn and mark the front posts in similar fashion (Fig. 3).

Turn the rungs (parts A,B,C, and D) to the dimensions shown, sizing the length and the end diameter accurately (Fig. 5). Then cut the mortices in the back posts of the chair. A morticing attachment on the drill press used with a V-Block on the table works well. That not available, drill straight holes and chop the mortices with a chisel. (A handy attachment is the drill guide sold for hand-held electric drills.) Next, drill holes for the rung locations laid out.

The slats are band sawed out of a single block of wood (Fig. 6). Cut the block to size and lay out the tenons. Notch the tenons with the table saw before the band saw operation to ensure they will be the same size when cut out. Mark the curves of the slats on the top of the block and the side. Cut the top curve of the block (with the block on its side) first, then tape or rubber cement the marked waste pieces back on their respective locations, so that the layout lines may be seen to cut the individual curved slats from the block. The band saw marks on the slats may be cleaned with either a drum sander or hand tools. Be careful to size the thickness of the tenons to fit the mortises in the posts (Fig. 7).

Trial-fit the slats and rungs between the back posts. Dry-fit the rungs and front posts. If the locations of the side rungs have not been marked earlier, separate the front and back of the chair, and mark them using a sliding T-bevel and a careful eye. Drill the side rung locations before the front and back of the chairs are assembled. Remount the posts on the lathe for final sanding and cut to finished length.

Glue and assemble the front posts and their rungs, checking for squareness between the rung and post. A ³⁄₁₆-inch dowel drilled and inserted into the post through the rung will increase strength. Follow suit for the back posts of the chair. Clamp the assemblies flat on a table to ensure the posts stay parallel, avoiding possible rack in the finished chair.

When the front and back halves of the chair have dried, glue and assemble the subassemblies into a chair (without the rockers), again check for squareness and set aside to dry.

Lay out the rockers (Fig. 4), stack the stock, and cut them out together, sanding them so that they will be the same size. The bottom of each rocker must be a smooth curve without flat spots that might interrupt the rocking

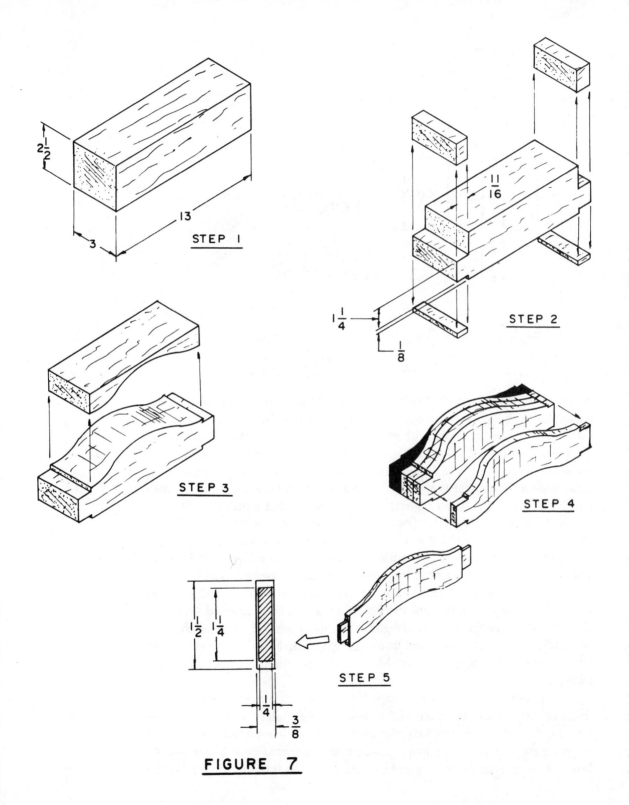

STEP 1

STEP 2

STEP 3

STEP 4

STEP 5

FIGURE 7

333

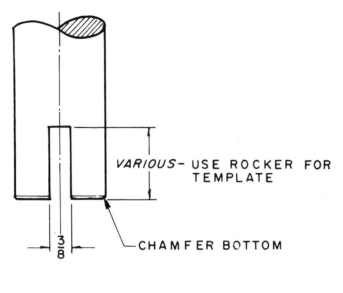

VARIOUS- USE ROCKER FOR
TEMPLATE

CHAMFER BOTTOM

$\frac{3}{8}$

LEG BOTTOM

## FIGURE 8

action of the chair. Lay the rockers on the bottom of the chair to mark the locations for the slots in the bottom of the posts (Fig. 8). Cut the slots, and install the rockers, securing with glue and ¼-inch dowels through the posts.

Sand the finished woodwork and apply your favorite finish. The time has come to make a seat. To rush the seat, buy at least 400 feet of fiber or machine-twisted paper. The fiber is easiest to work with. Natural plant stems are also used, but must be twisted together, and are somewhat more difficult.

Next, study the diagram (Fig. 9). The chair is not square and STEPS 1 through 12, repeated, show how to weave and nail in a square area. While the chair can be rushed single-handedly, it is a lot more efficient (and fun) to call a friend over to help hold the cord tight during the process.

When the area to be finished is square, move to STEP 13 and start the weave that will continue until the center of the chair is reached (Fig. 10). Concentrate on keeping the cord tight at all times, passing a bundle that can be handled around the rungs and through the pattern. More cord can be added later by tying underneath the chair. Move clockwise around the seat going over each rung.

After some cord has been wrapped, you will notice that the rungs seem to fill up faster than the space in the center of the chair. This is because the cord tends to flatten from its circular cross section when pulled tight around the rung and takes up more space. Consequently the cord must be continually brought toward the nearest leg to keep the area to be finished square. As the

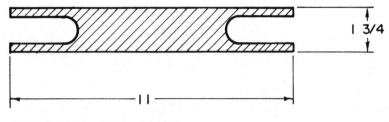

SHUTTLE FOR LINE

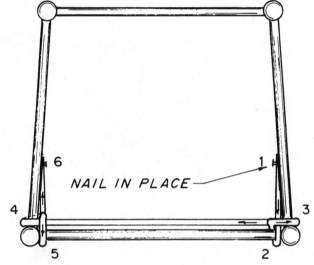

NAIL IN PLACE

APPROX. 400' OF CORD ON SHUTTLE

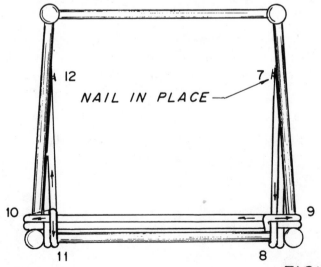

NAIL IN PLACE

FIGURE 9

335

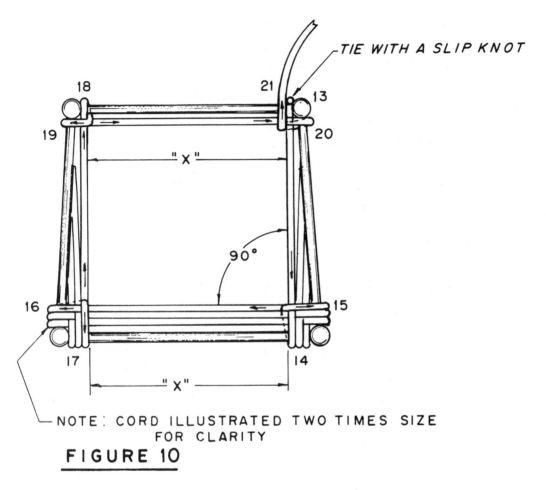

*TIE WITH A SLIP KNOT*

NOTE: CORD ILLUSTRATED TWO TIMES SIZE
FOR CLARITY

## FIGURE 10

weave continues toward the center of the chair, the space between the rungs is stuffed with scraps of the fiber to fill and strengthen the seat. When the center of the chair is reached check for tightness and then tie off.

## Finishing

The chair seat should be finished with several coats of elastic varnish to seal and hold the cords.

# Platform
# Rocker

AS ROCKING CHAIRS BECAME MORE AND MORE ACCEPTED AS PARLOR FURNITURE, the platform rocker came into its own. Its invention is credited to Samuel H. Bean from Philadelphia. As noted in his patent of 1840: ''[Bean's] stationary-base rocker would do away with the long and cumbersome rockers on the common chair, which occupy a great deal of room and are very destructive to carpets.'' The platform rocker idea really got moving after 1850 or so. These rockers were very expensive for their time and ranged in price from $26 for a plain chair to $45 or more for a fancy model. By 1891, the platform rocker was considered an essential piece of furniture.

The platform rocker was mass-produced by somewhat crude automatic lathes. As I was measuring the original chair, I found none of the supposedly identical turnings matched each other very closely. Nevertheless, these chairs were built to last.

I found this particular chair in northern Vermont way back in 1953. It originally had a coarse, stiff, leathery seat and back which was in very poor condition. For over 30 years, this chair has traveled back and forth across the country with me and, with the exception of the seat and back cloth material, it is as solid today as it was the day I found it.

As far as I can tell, most platform rockers were made of oak and stained with a dark stain. For this project, maple, cherry, or walnut could be used for a very beautiful chair. To save material and the time of turning squares into

diameters, use large, round dowels, in diameters of 2 inches or more. But if you like lathe work, you will enjoy making the 15 different turnings (31 turnings total). All of the turnings are relatively simple to make.

# Instructions

As with any project, carefully study the two-view drawing of the chair, illustrating the FRONT VIEW and the RIGHT-SIDE VIEW. Note the various turnings (parts A through O) and the three different, 1¾-inch-thick flat parts (parts P, Q, and R). Be sure you fully understand how all parts are assembled before beginning.

Make each of the turnings per the dimensioned illustrations. Take care to make tight-fitting end diameters where the turnings are glued into mating holes. You may want to drill a hole into a piece of scrap wood, using the same drill as the one you will be using for the holes on the chair. Then make a test-turning to determine the exact size needed for a good tight fit.

Short turnings, such as the 1½-inch-diameter part G and the two part J's, could be turned as one unit and cut into individual parts when completed. The four identical part I's could also be turned as one unit and parted when completed. Part H can be simply cut from a ½-inch-diameter dowel. Take care in drilling part A. There must be a mating pair—that is, a right-hand and left-hand pair.

Draw the shape of parts P, Q, and R on a sheet of heavy paper using a full-size ½-inch-square grid and copying the shapes per the given illustrations. Transfer these shapes to the pieces of wood and cut the parts out. Carefully locate and drill all holes in the parts, but be sure to make a matching pair of all three parts (one right-hand and one left-hand). Sand all surfaces until smooth. The arc of part P must be a perfect 14½-inch radius with no irregular waves. The chair will not rock smoothly unless this arc is very smooth. Do not round the edges too much, as they should be somewhat sharp. Using a router, and a V-groove bit, cut the simple designs as illustrated into the outer surfaces of parts P and Q. Using an ⅛-inch-radius bit, cut the edge of part R, 12⅝ inches long, as illustrated.

# Assembly

After all parts have been carefully made, the chair is actually very easy to put together. Think of the chair simply as four subassemblies: the back subassembly, the arm subasssembly, the rocker subassembly, and the base subassembly.

Glue the back subassembly together on a flat surface, using parts A, B, C, D, E, F, G, H, and O. Keep all joints square and the subassembly flat. Glue the two arm subassemblies together on a flat surface using parts J, K, L, and M. Keep all parts flat.

Next, glue the rocker subassembly together using parts I, N, P, and R. Keep this subassembly square, also. Drill for and set the 8 finishing nails from underneath, through part P and into part I, then through part R and into part I.

Glue the base subassembly together, using parts Q and N as shown, keeping everything square. Be sure the feet all set square so the base will not rock. Drill for and set the 4 finishing nails from underneath through part Q and into part N. This completes the four subassemblies.

Assemble the back subassembly to the rocker subassembly using glue and the two roundhead screws (part V). Attach the *lower* part of the arm subassemblies to the rocker and back subassemblies using two 4-inch-long, ¼-inch-diameter carriage bolts, washer, and square nut (part U). Locate the arm subassemblies into position and using the *upper* hole in part L as a template, drill a ¼-inch-diameter hole through both part A's, as shown. Attach the two arm subassemblies using the other two 4-inch-long, ¼-inch-diameter carriage bolts. Refer to the right SIDE VIEW illustration.

Add the two swivel wheels to the front feet of part Q. Attach all three top subassemblies to the base subassembly with two springs (part S). Center the springs on the center lines, as illustrated on the drawings for parts P and Q. Adjust tension on the springs by spacing the upper and lower parts of the spring, either closer together or further apart. The seat should lean backwards slightly more than shown on the drawing. Test the seat and adjust the springs to suit.

# Finishing

If you used oak or any open-pored hardwood you must fill it before staining and finishing. Stain using a stain of your choice and finish using any good finishing process. Follow recommended instructions on the containers.

# Adding Headrest, Back, and Seat

All that remains is to add the cloth portions of the chair. Use a heavy material that will not rip. Velour-type corduroy works well for this.

## Headrest

Using two pieces, measure the material 10½ inches wide and 9 inches long. This measurement allows for a ½-inch seam all the way around. Measure a piece of batting material 10 inches wide and 8½ inches long, to fit between

## MATERIALS LIST

| Part Letter | Size | Req'd. |
|---|---|---|
| A | 1 ¾ Dia. – 30 ¾ Long | 2* |
| B | 1¾ Dia. – 16¾ Long | 1 |
| C | 1¼ Dia. – 16¾ Long | 1 |
| D | 1¼ Dia. – 16¾ Long | 1 |
| E | 1¼ Dia. – 16¾ Long | 1 |
| F | 1 Dia. – 18 Long | 2 |
| G | 1½ Dia. – 3¼ Long | 2 |
| H | ½ Dia. – 3⅞ Long | 2 |
| I | 1½ Dia. – 3¼ Long | 4 |
| J | 1½ Dia. – 3½ Long | 2 |
| K | 1½ Dia. – 8⅛ Long | 2 |
| L | 1 ¾ Dia. – 22⅛ Long | 2 |
| M | 1 ¾ Dia. – 14½ Long | 2 |
| N | 1¼ Dia. – 17 Long | 6 |
| O | ⅞ Dia. – 12¾ Long | 1 |
| P | 1 ¾ × 4¼ – 17½ Long | 2* |
| Q | 1¾ × 5½ – 30 Long | 2* |
| R | 1¾ × 1¾ – 18½ Long | 2* |
| S | Spring Assembly | 2 |
| T | Swivel Caster (¾ Dia.) | 2 |
| U | Carriage Bolt w/Washer and Square Nut | 4 |
| V | Screw – Round head | 2 |
| W | Brass Tacks ½"Long | As Req'd |
| X | Finish Nail 10d | 12 |

\* Make one R.H. and one L.H.

the two pieces of material. Sew the two pieces of material together inside out, allowing ½-inch seams and leaving one end opened. When the three sides are sewn together, fit the batting material in and turn the material right-side-out with the batting material in it. Turn the last seam in and handstitch it together. Put this on the headrest of the rocker and pin it together at the seams; handstitch together. (One end will overlap the other where you have to pin and handstitch.)

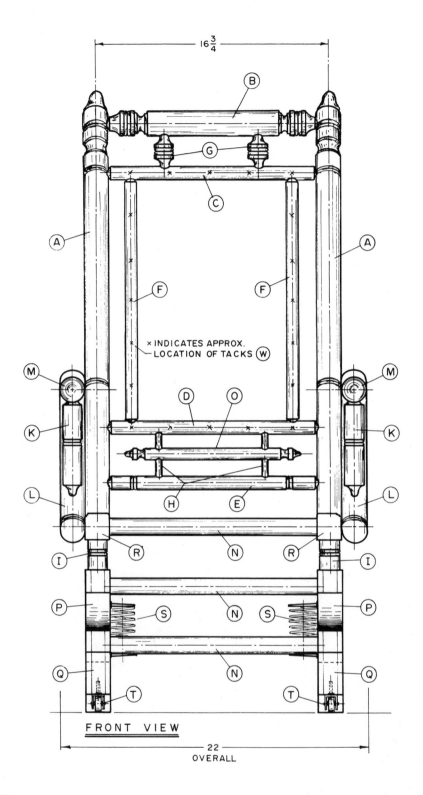

$16\frac{3}{4}$

× INDICATES APPROX.
LOCATION OF TACKS Ⓦ

FRONT VIEW

22
OVERALL

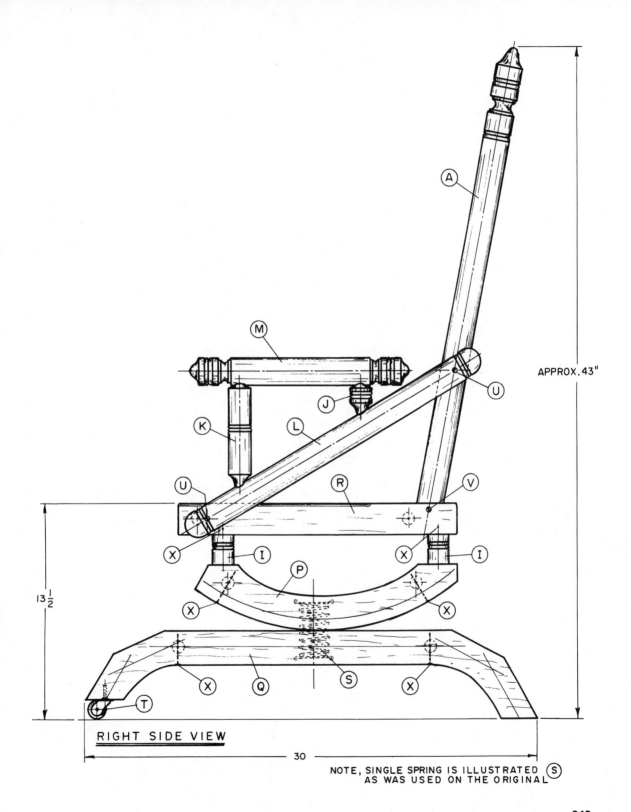

APPROX. 43"

13 $\frac{1}{2}$

RIGHT SIDE VIEW

30

NOTE, SINGLE SPRING IS ILLUSTRATED (S)
AS WAS USED ON THE ORIGINAL

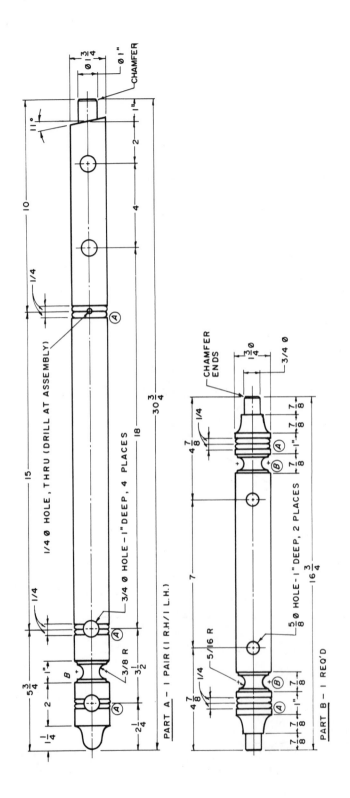

PART A – 1 PAIR (1 R.H./1 L.H.)

1/4 Ø HOLE, THRU (DRILL AT ASSEMBLY)

3/4 Ø HOLE – 1" DEEP, 4 PLACES

Ø 1"

CHAMFER

3/4 Ø

11°

PART B – 1 REQ'D

5/8 Ø HOLE – 1" DEEP, 2 PLACES

5/16 R

CHAMFER ENDS

3/4 Ø

3/4 Ø

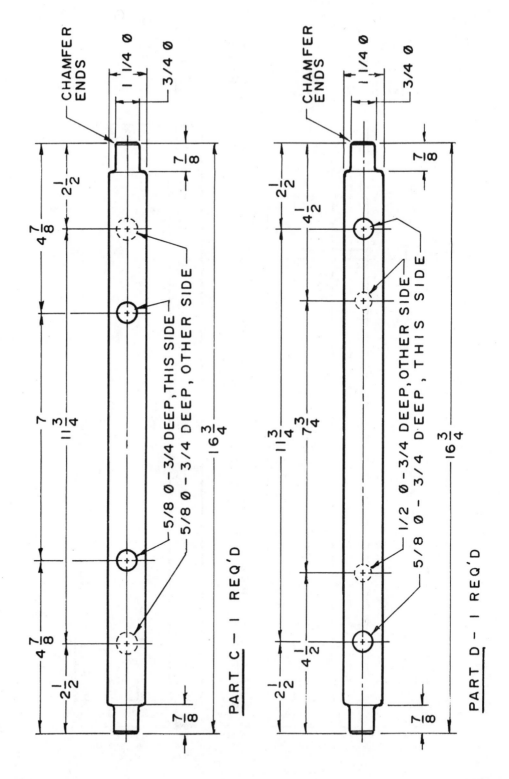

CHAMFER ENDS

$1\frac{1}{4}$ Ø

$\frac{3}{4}$ Ø

$2\frac{1}{2}$

$4\frac{7}{8}$

$7\frac{3}{4}$

$11\frac{3}{4}$

$16\frac{3}{4}$

$4\frac{7}{8}$

$2\frac{1}{2}$

$\frac{7}{8}$

5/8 Ø - 3/4 DEEP, THIS SIDE
5/8 Ø - 3/4 DEEP, OTHER SIDE

PART C - 1 REQ'D

CHAMFER ENDS

$1\frac{1}{4}$ Ø

$\frac{3}{4}$ Ø

$2\frac{1}{2}$

$4\frac{1}{2}$

$7\frac{3}{4}$

$11\frac{3}{4}$

$16\frac{3}{4}$

$4\frac{1}{2}$

$2\frac{1}{2}$

$\frac{7}{8}$

$\frac{7}{8}$

1/2 Ø - 3/4 DEEP, OTHER SIDE
5/8 Ø - 3/4 DEEP, THIS SIDE

PART D - 1 REQ'D

345

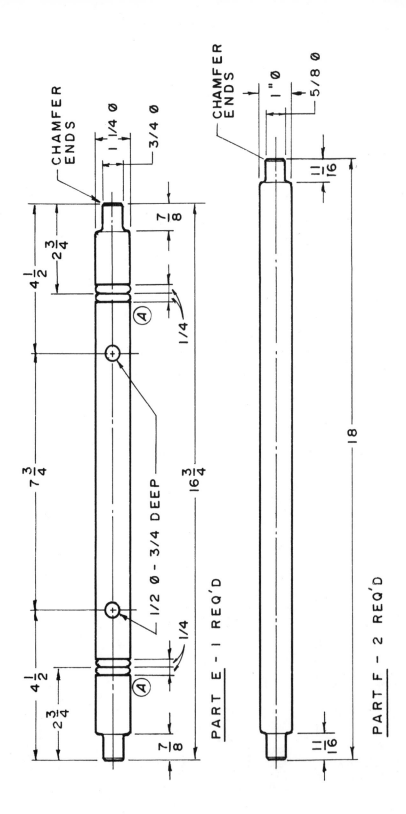

CHAMFER ENDS

$\frac{1}{4}$ Ø

1

$\frac{3}{4}$ Ø

$2\frac{3}{4}$

$4\frac{1}{2}$

$\frac{7}{8}$

Ⓐ

$\frac{1}{4}$

$7\frac{3}{4}$

$16\frac{3}{4}$

$\frac{1}{2}$ Ø - 3/4 DEEP

$\frac{1}{4}$

Ⓐ

$4\frac{1}{2}$

$2\frac{3}{4}$

$\frac{7}{8}$

PART E - 1 REQ'D

CHAMFER ENDS

1" Ø

5/8 Ø

$\frac{11}{16}$

18

$\frac{11}{16}$

PART F - 2 REQ'D

346

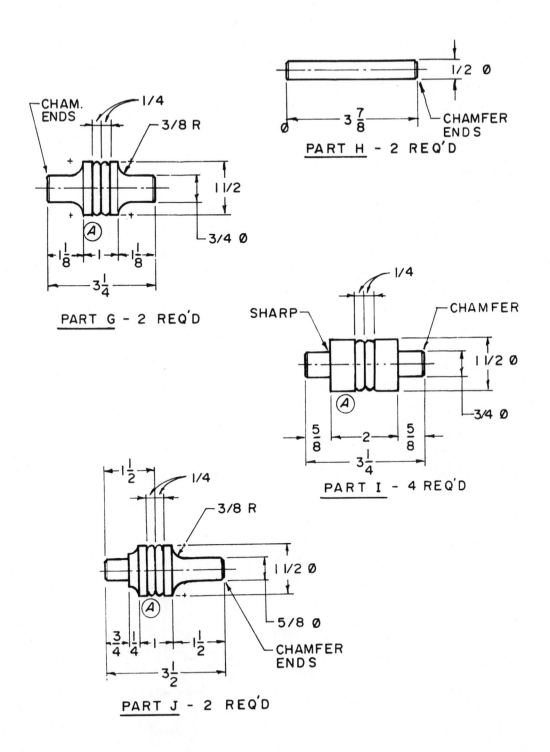

CHAM. ENDS

1/4

3/8 R

1 1/2

3/4 Ø

A

1 1/8  1  1 1/8

3 1/4

PART G - 2 REQ'D

1/2 Ø

Ø

3 7/8

CHAMFER ENDS

PART H - 2 REQ'D

1/4

SHARP

CHAMFER

1 1/2 Ø

3/4 Ø

A

5/8  2  5/8

3 1/4

PART I - 4 REQ'D

1 1/2

1/4

3/8 R

1 1/2 Ø

A

5/8 Ø

3/4  1/4  1  1 1/2

3 1/2

CHAMFER ENDS

PART J - 2 REQ'D

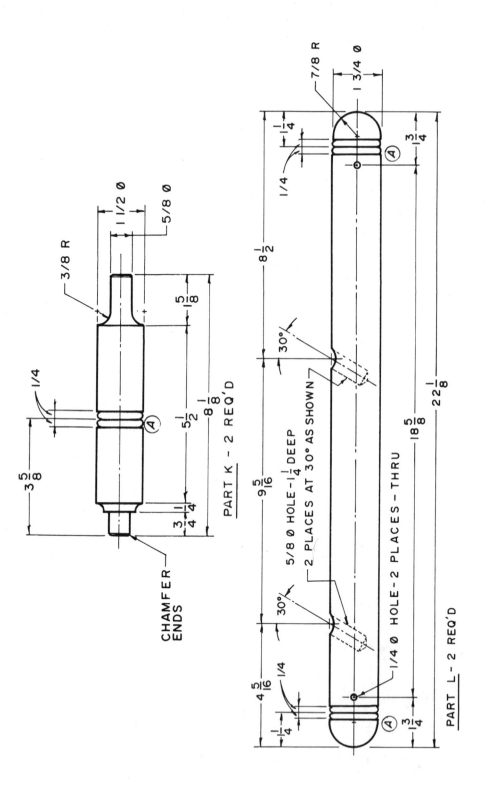

PART K - 2 REQ'D

PART L - 2 REQ'D

CHAMFER ENDS

3/8 R

1 1/2 Ø

5/8 Ø

1/4

3 5/8

3 1/4

5 1/2

8 1/8

5 1/8

7/8 R

1 3/4 Ø

1 1/4

1/4

3/4

8 1/2

30°

5/8 Ø HOLE - 1 1/4 DEEP
2 PLACES AT 30° AS SHOWN

1/4 Ø HOLE - 2 PLACES - THRU

9 5/16

18 5/8

22 1/8

30°

4 5/16

1/4

1 1/4

3/4

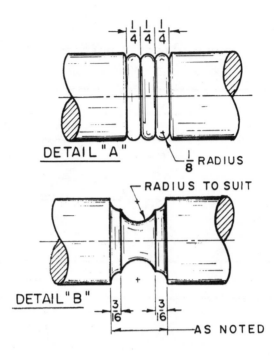

DETAIL "A"

$\frac{1}{8}$ RADIUS

RADIUS TO SUIT

DETAIL "B"

AS NOTED

## Back

Using two pieces of material 21 inches long and 15 inches wide, make the piece for the back of the chair. This measurement will also allow for a ½-inch seam all the way around the material. Follow the instructions above given for the headrest. Remember to measure the batting material ½-inch smaller all the way around, 20½ inches × 14½ inches. When you are finished sewing this together, tack the back to the back of the chair with upholstery tacks, as shown in the photograph.

## Seat

Using two pieces of material 26 inches long and 17 inches wide, make the piece for the seat of the chair. This measurement also allows for a ½-inch seam all the way around. The batting material is measured ½ inch smaller all the way around: 25½ inches × 16½ inches wide. Put the seat together and sew as above for the back and headrest. When you are finished sewing it together, tack it underneath to the round turnings at the front and back of the chair.

Before you put the material on the seat portion, you should make up a support for the seat. I used a canvas-type material, one piece 38 inches long and 17 inches wide, and added two to three layers of batting in between, slightly

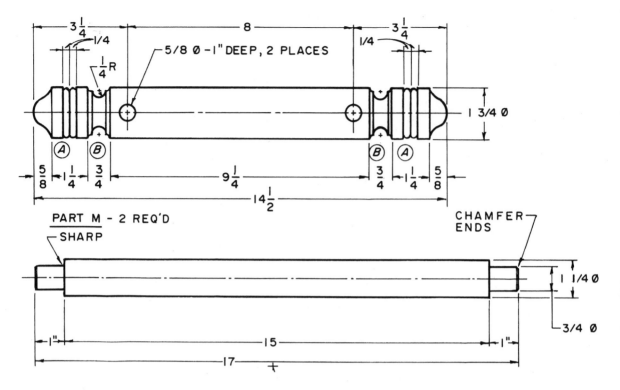

PART M - 2 REQ'D

narrower than the canvas-type material. Take the canvas, with the batting material in between, and sew it together. Wrap all this around the back and front wood turnings, folding under a 1-inch seam allowance where both ends meet. Staple or tack to the two round turnings at the back and front of the chair.

This is the way my wife, Joyce, made the pieces for the headrest, back, and seat. It is only one possibility. Perhaps you can come up with a better way. Sit back and enjoy. This rocker will be around for a long time.

# Suppliers

Springs (H-5520, Cotton batting (H-9654), Upholstery nails (H-9680), and turning squares can be purchased from:

> *Craftsman Wood Service*
> 1735 West Cortland Court
> Adderson, IL 60101

Swivel casters, C-1 can be purchased from:

> *Anglo-American Brass Company*
> 4146 Mitzi Road
> P.O. Box 9792
> San Jose, CA 95157-0792

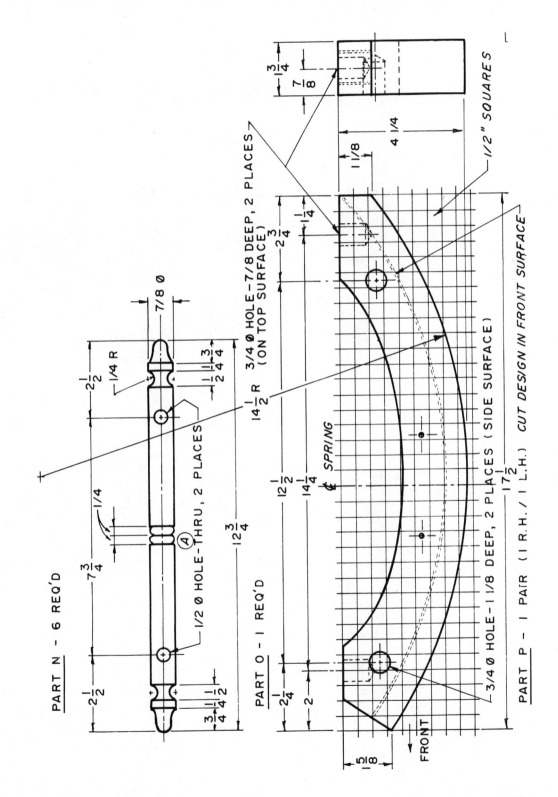

PART N - 6 REQ'D

$2\frac{1}{2}$  $7\frac{3}{4}$  $12\frac{3}{4}$  $2\frac{1}{2}$

$\frac{7}{8}$ Ø

$\frac{1}{4}$ R

$\frac{1}{2}\frac{3}{4}\frac{1}{4}$

$\frac{1}{4}$

1/2 Ø HOLE-THRU, 2 PLACES

$\frac{1}{2}\frac{1}{4}$

$\frac{3}{4}\frac{1}{4}\frac{1}{2}$

Ⓐ

PART O - 1 REQ'D

3/4 Ø HOLE-7/8 DEEP, 2 PLACES
(ON TOP SURFACE)

$14\frac{1}{2}$ R

$12\frac{1}{2}$  $14\frac{1}{4}$

SPRING

$2\frac{3}{4}$  $1\frac{1}{4}$

$1\frac{1}{8}$  4 1/4

$1\frac{3}{4}$  $\frac{7}{8}$

1/2" SQUARES

CUT DESIGN IN FRONT SURFACE

3/4 Ø HOLE-1 1/8 DEEP, 2 PLACES (SIDE SURFACE)

$17\frac{1}{2}$

$2\frac{1}{4}$  2

$\frac{5}{8}$

FRONT

PART P - 1 PAIR  (I R.H. / I L.H.)

351

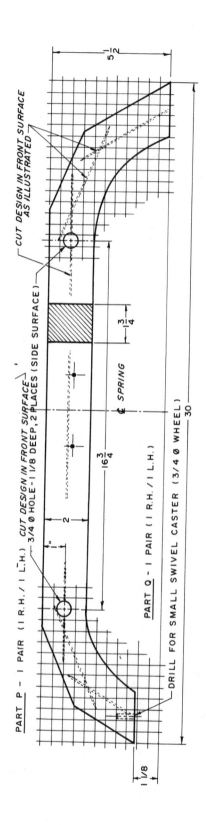

CUT DESIGN IN FRONT SURFACE AS ILLUSTRATED

CUT DESIGN IN FRONT SURFACE

CUT DESIGN IN FRONT SURFACE

3/4 Ø HOLE - 1 I/8 DEEP, 2 PLACES (SIDE SURFACE)

PART P - I PAIR ( I R.H. / I L.H.)

PART Q - I PAIR ( I R.H. / I L.H.)

DRILL FOR SMALL SWIVEL CASTER (3/4 Ø WHEEL)

℄ SPRING

$5\frac{1}{2}$

$16\frac{3}{4}$

$\frac{3}{4}$

2

30

1 I/8

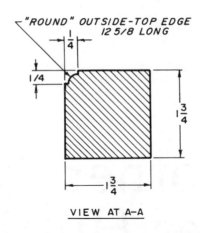

"ROUND" OUTSIDE-TOP EDGE
12 5/8 LONG

$\frac{1}{4}$

1/4

1$\frac{3}{4}$

1$\frac{3}{4}$

VIEW AT A-A

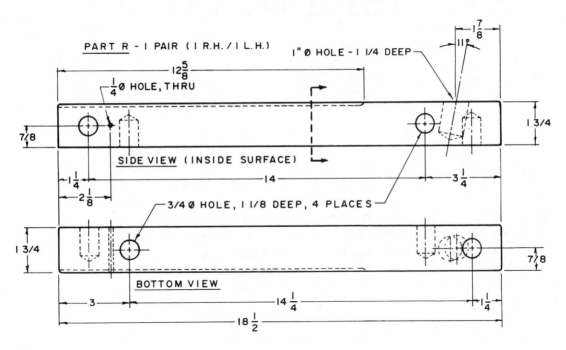

PART R - 1 PAIR ( 1 R.H. / 1 L.H. )

1" Ø HOLE - 1 1/4 DEEP

1$\frac{7}{8}$

11°

12$\frac{5}{8}$

$\frac{1}{4}$ Ø HOLE, THRU

7/8

1 3/4

SIDE VIEW (INSIDE SURFACE)

1$\frac{1}{4}$

2$\frac{1}{8}$

14

3$\frac{1}{4}$

3/4 Ø HOLE, 1 1/8 DEEP, 4 PLACES

1 3/4

BOTTOM VIEW

7/8

3

14$\frac{1}{4}$

1$\frac{1}{4}$

18$\frac{1}{2}$

# Corner
# Pewter Hutch

As PEWTER AND POTTERY PLATES BEGAN TO REPLACE THE CRUDE WOODEN plates used by early Americans, the pewter hutch became very popular. At first, rails were used along the front to support the plates vertically. As time went by, the rail was replaced by grooves cut into the shelves, and the plates were stored or displayed vertically, supported by these grooves.

Most early pewter hutches had two or three open shelves at the top to display the owner's best pewter, and a closed area at the bottom to hold other kitchen supplies. When low-priced glass plates began replacing the old original pewter and pottery plates, this open hutch was replaced by the more formal glass-fronted china cabinet of the late 1800s.

The original of this pewter hutch was made around 1835 and was found in Francestown, New Hampshire. All measurements and imprints of the fine cyma curves were taken directly from the original hutch. The copy, shown here, was made of used pine wood and was distressed further to make it look exactly like the original. Large square-cut nails were also used with no attempt to hide them. The original had a pumpkin pine finish that had mellowed just beautifully.

## Instructions

Pine was used on the original and probably should be used for the copy, as most early country-style hutches were usually made of pine. Carefully study

the drawings in order that you fully understand how the hutch is put together before starting anything.

The six shelves (parts 1 and 2) and the two backboards (part 3) should be glued-up, in order to obtain the wide widths. Cut all other pieces to size per the Materials List given. Take care to keep all parts square and all duplicate parts exactly the same size.

While allowing the glue to set, draw out a 1-inch-square grid on a sheet of paper and transfer the shape of the front trim (part 5), per the drawing. Cut the 45-degree angle on the two front trim boards (part 5) and tack them together-keeping the two sharp edges of the cut angle together. Transfer the shape from the paper to the boards and cut out with the two boards tacked together so the pattern will be exactly the same size and shape. Don't forget, they must be the same size and shape but there must be a right and left-hand pair. Do the same for the top trim (part 6) and cut out.

It is important that all six shelves be the exact same size and shape. Lay out and rough-cut all six shelves a little oversized and tack them all together. Carefully re-lay out the exact size on the shelf on top and recut them all to exact size while they are still tacked together. Before untacking them, number them 1,2,3,4,5, and 6, and indicate the top surface of each in the order that they will be assembled.

Untack all the shelves then retack shelves numbered as 2 and 3 only (on the Materials List, part 2). Lay out and cut the two shelves per the drawing.

*Note*: these two shelves on the original were cut on a 20-degree angle as shown.

On shelves numbered 2, 3, and 4, cut the dish groove as shown. I found the original 2-inch dimension for the dish groove a little too narrow for the dishes of today and would recommend changing this dimension to 3 inches.

Locate and cut the dado grooves in the two glued-up backboards (part 3). (You might want to refer to the August/September 1986 issue of *Popular Woodworking*, page 45, for William Bigelow's router fence jig.) Take care to keep all dadoes absolutely square and with the exact same spacing.

*Important*: Before actually cutting the dadoes, check that they are located exactly in the center of each outer curve of the front trim (part 5). Adjust if necessary.

## Assembly/Case

Assemble the six shelves in the order listed, with the two backboards. Add the corner board (part 4), add the two side boards (part 7). Assemble the two front trim boards with the top trim (part 6), as shown. Nail these three pieces to the main assembly and, using a hand plane, plane all corners so they have smooth 45-degree angle edges. I used square-cut nails from Tremont Nail Company to match the original hutch as closely as possible.

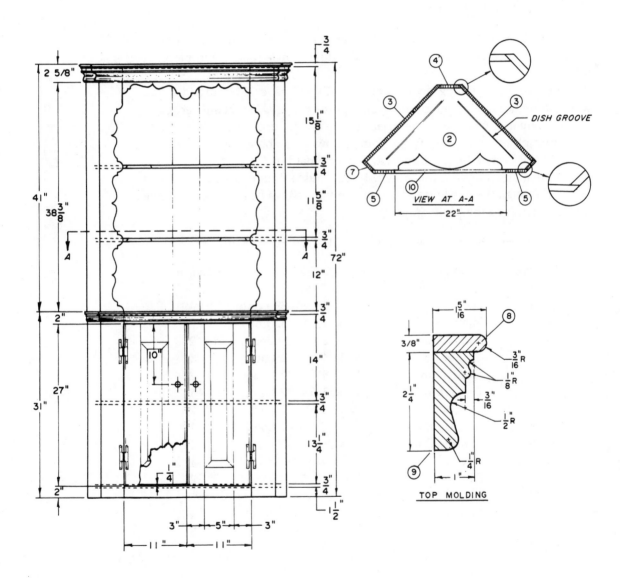

VIEW AT A-A

DISH GROOVE

TOP MOLDING

Add molding to the assembly per the drawings. I was unable to match the original exactly with the cutters I had, but I came very close. The drawing illustrates the original size and shape of the molding. This completes the case assembly.

# Assembly/Door

Make the door per the drawing, taking care to keep it square and properly fitted to the door opening. Do *not* glue the door panels (part 16) in place, at this time.

The two unusual long door pulls (part 17) will have to be turned if you want authenticity, although commercial copies are available that are very close to the original. If you use commercially made knobs, drill a ⅜-inch-diameter hole through the knob and add a ⅜-inch dowel, as shown.

Add the H-style hinge as shown. The original hutch had 4-inch hinges, which are a little large for this hutch. I had trouble finding a 4-inch H hinge in Peterborough the day I was assembling my hutch, so I used a 3-inch hinge instead. (Refer to the photograph.)

## ——————— MATERIALS LIST ———————

| Part No. | Name | Size | Req'd. |
|---|---|---|---|
| 1 | Shelf | ¾ × 15⅝ – 33 Long | 4 |
| 2 | Shelf | ¾ × 15⅝ – 33 Long | 2 |
| 3 | Backboard | ¾ × 21 – 72 Long | 2 |
| 4 | Corner Board | ¾ × 4½ – 72 Long | 1 |
| 5 | Front Trim | ¾ × 5⅛ – 72 Long | 2 |
| 6 | Top Trim | ¾ × 5½ – 22 Long | 1 |
| 7 | Side Board | ¾ × 2⅞ – 72 Long | 2 |
| 8 | Top Moulding | ⅜ × 1½ – 48 Long | 1 |
| 9 | Top Moulding | 1 × 2¼ – 48 Long | 1 |
| 10 | Filler | ¾ × ¾ – 22 Long | 1 |
| 11 | Divider | ¾ × 2 – 22 Long | 2 |
| 12 | Waist Molding | ½ × 1½ – 48 Long | 1 |
| 13 | Dowel | ¼ Dia. – 1½ Long | 8 |
| 14 | Door Side | ¾ × 3 – 28½ Long | 4 |
| 15 | Door T/B | ¾ × 3 – 7 Long | 4 |
| 16 | Door Panel | ¾ × 6 – 23½ Long | 2 |
| 17 | Knob | 1¼ Dia. – 23½ Long | 2 |
| 18 | Hinge "H" | 4" Size | 4 |

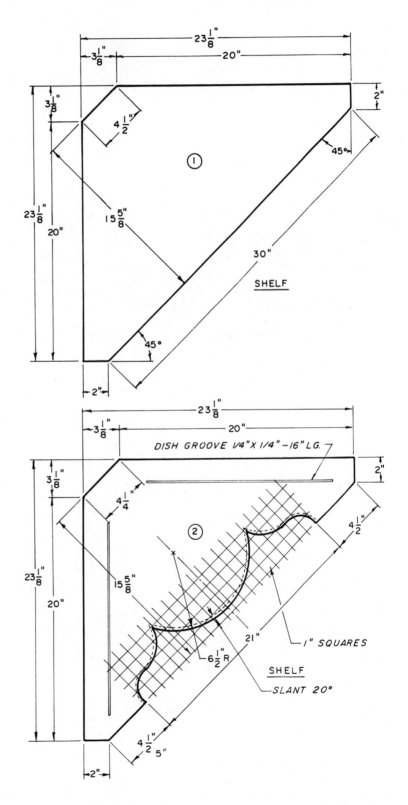

$23\frac{1}{8}$"

$3\frac{1}{8}$" 20"

$3\frac{1}{8}$"

$4\frac{1}{2}$"

2"

45°

1

$23\frac{1}{8}$" 20"

$15\frac{5}{8}$"

30"

SHELF

45°

2"

$23\frac{1}{8}$"

$3\frac{1}{8}$" 20"

DISH GROOVE 1/4"X 1/4" – 16" LG.

2"

$3\frac{1}{8}$"

$4\frac{1}{4}$"

2

$4\frac{1}{2}$"

$23\frac{1}{8}$" 20"

$15\frac{5}{8}$"

21"

1" SQUARES

$6\frac{1}{2}$"R

SHELF

SLANT 20°

$4\frac{1}{2}$" 5"

2"

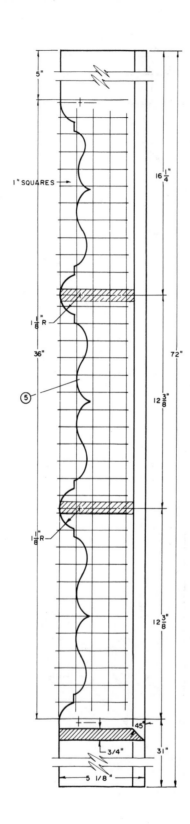

1" SQUARES

16 1/4"

1 1/8" R

36"

72"

12 3/8"

5

1 1/8" R

12 3/8"

45°

3/4"

31"

5 1/8"

5"

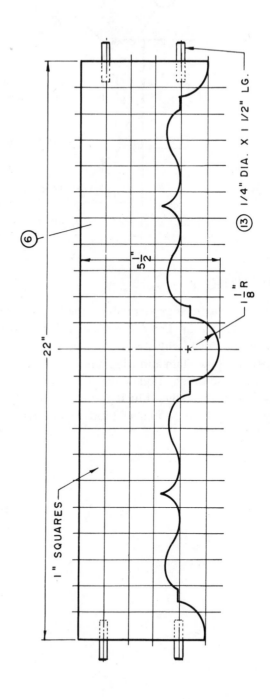

6

22"

5 1/2"

1/8" R

1" SQUARES

13 1/4" DIA. X 1 1/2" LG.

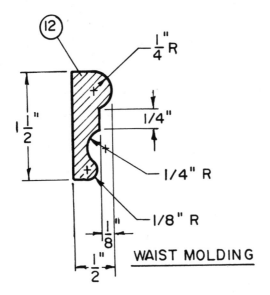

WAIST MOLDING

# Finishing

Early pewter hutches were usually stained; however, you could paint yours, provided you use an Early American color. The original had a beautiful pumpkin pine finish with the usual aged patina. I stained my copy with an early Ipswitch pine stain and tried a new product: Deft semigloss clear wood finish. The wood finish dried in only half an hour and turned out beautifully. Usually I do not have good luck getting a good finish on pine, but the Deft gave me one of the best finishes I have ever had—and without a lot of work!

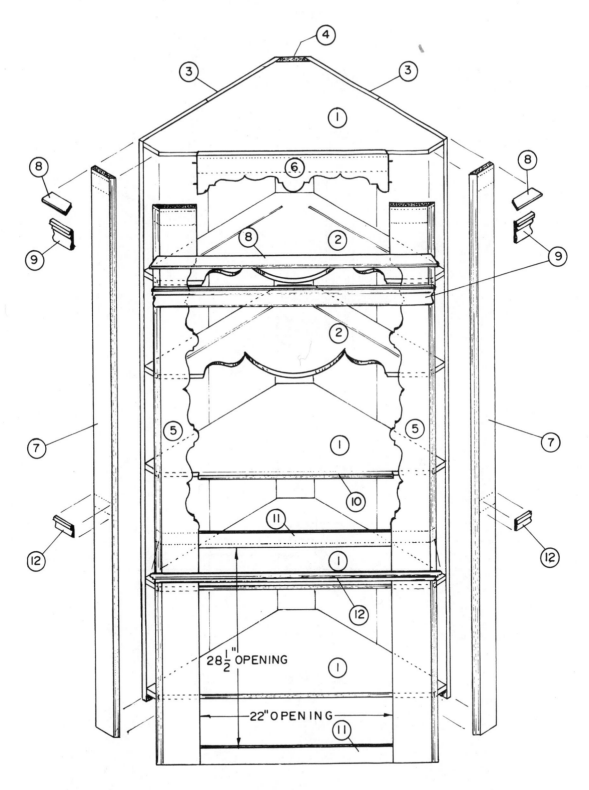

$28\frac{1}{2}$" OPENING

22" OPENING

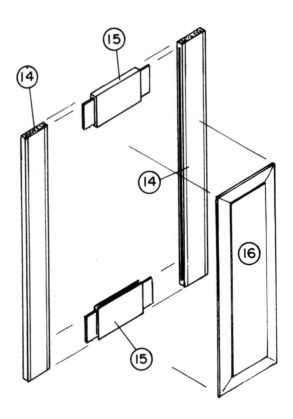

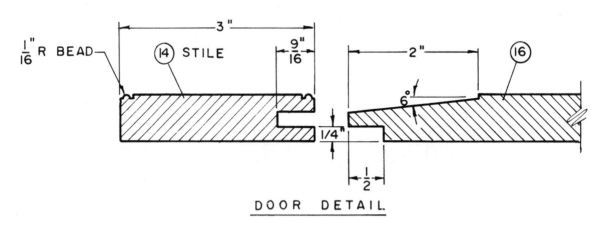

$\frac{1}{16}$" R BEAD

⑭ STILE

3 "

$\frac{9}{16}$"

1/4"

$\frac{1}{2}$

2 "

6°

⑯

DOOR DETAIL

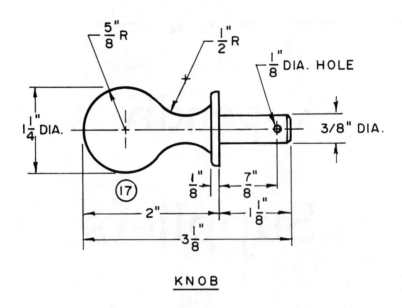

$\frac{5}{8}"$R  $\frac{1}{2}"$R  $\frac{1}{8}"$DIA. HOLE

$1\frac{1}{4}"$ DIA.

3/8" DIA.

17

$\frac{1}{8}"$  $\frac{7}{8}"$

2"  $1\frac{1}{8}"$

$3\frac{1}{8}"$

KNOB

365

# Appendix A

# Suppliers

THE EXTRA MONEY SPENT ON HIGH-QUALITY HARDWARE VERSES LOW-COST hardware is very little in the overall cost of your project. This is the part of the project that stands out, so the extra spent in cost will be well worth the difference, for many years to come.

Listed below are quality vendors that sell authentic, high-quality hardware. It is best to use the same kind of hardware as was used on the original piece, if possible. Another good place to purchase old hardware is a flea market. An old authentic hinge or door lock, although rusty and worn, will add a lot to your project and will really make it look original.

## Beveled Glass

*Beveled Glass Works*
11721 S.E. Talor
Portland, OR 97216

## Measured Drawings (of Antiques)

*Caryle Lynch*
196 Holly Hill
Broadway, VA 22815

*John A. Nelson*
220 General Miller Rd.
Peterborough, NH 03458

# Paint

*Cohassett Colonials*
Cohassett, MA 02025

*Stulb Paint and Chemical Co.*
P.O. Box 297
Norristown, PA 19404

# Stains/Tung Oil

*Cohassett Colonials*
Cohassett, MA 02025

*Deft Inc.*
17451 Von Darman Ave.
Irvine, CA 92713-9507

*Formby's Inc.*
825 Crossover Lane, Suite 240
Memphis, TN 38117

*Stulb Paint and Chemical Co.*
P.O. Box 297
Norristown, PA 19404

*Watco-Dennis Corp.*
Michigan Ave. & 22nd St.
Santa Monica, CA 90404

# Old-Fashioned Nails/ Brass Screws

*Equality Screw Co.*
P.O. Box 1296
El Cajon, CA 92002

*Horton Brasses*
P.O. Box 95 Nooks Hill Rd.
Cromwell, CT 06416

*Tremont Nail Co.*
21 Elm St.
P.O. Box 111
Wareham, MA 02571

# Brasses

*Anglo-American Brass Co.*
4146 Mitzi Drive
P.O. Box 9792
San Jose, CA 95157-0792

*Ball and Ball*
463 W. Lincoln Hwy.
Exton, PA 19341

*The Brass Tree*
308 N. Main St.
Charles, MO 63301

*Garrett Wade Co.*
161 Avenue of the Americas
New York, NY 10013

*Heirloom Antiques Brass Co.*
P.O. Box 146
Dundass, MN 55019

*Horton Brasses*
P.O. Box 95
Nooks Hill Rd.
Cromwell, CT 06416

*Imported European Hardware*
4295 S. Arville St.
Las Vegas, NV 89103

*19th Century Hardware Supply Co.*
P.O. Box 599
Rough and Ready, CA 95975

*The Renovators' Supply*
Millers Falls, MA 01349

*The Shop, Inc.*
P.O. Box 3711, R.D. 3
Reading, PA 19606

*Ritter and Son Hardware*
Dept. WJ
Gualala, CA 95445

# Veneering

*Bob Morgan Woodworking Supplies*
1123 Bardstown Rd.
Louisville, KY 40204

# General Catalogs

*Brookstone Co.*
Vose Farm Rd.
Peterborough, NH 03458

*Constantine*
2050 Eastchester Rd.
Bronx, NY 10461

*Cryder Creek Wood Shoppe, Inc.*
P.O. Box 19
Whitesville, NY 14897

*The Fine Tool Shops*
20 Backus Ave.
P.O. Box 1262
Danbury, CT 06810

*Leichtung Inc.*
4944 Commerce Pkwy
Cleveland, OH 44128

*Silvo Hardware Co.*
2205 Richmond St.
Philadelphia, PA 19125

*Trendlines*
375 Beacham St.
Chelsea, MA 02150

*Woodcraft*
41 Atlantic Ave.
P.O. Box 4000
Woburn, MA 01888

*The Woodworkers Store*
21801 Industrial Blvd.
Rogers, MN 55374

*Woodworkers Supply of New Mexico*
5604 Alameda N.E.
Albuquerque, NM 87113

# Appendix B

# Publications

THE FOLLOWING IS A LIST OF NATIONAL WOODWORKING MAGAZINES:

*The American Woodworker*
33 East Minor Street
Emmaus, PA 18098

*Early American Life*
P.O. Box 8200
Harrisburg, PA 17105

*Fine Woodworking*
The Taunton Press
52 Church Hill Road
P.O. Box 355
Newton, CT 06470

*Hands On*
6640 Poe Ave.
Dayton, OH 45414-2591

*International Woodworking Magazine*
Plymouth, NH 03264

*Popular Woodworking*
EGW Publishing Co.
1300 Galaxy Way
Concord, CA 94520

*Wood*
P.O. Box 10625
Des Moines, IA 50380-0625

*Woodsmith*
2200 Grand Ave.
Des Moines, IA 50312

*The Woodworkers Journal*
517 Litchfield Rd.
P.O. Box 1629
New Milford, CT 06776

*Workbench Magazine*
P.O. Box 5965
Kansas City, MO 64110

# Index